WHERE KINGS AND GODS MEET

The Royal Centre at Vijayanagara, India

John M. Fritz, George Michell, and M. S. Nagaraja Rao

Preface by Burton Stein

THE UNIVERSITY OF ARIZONA PRESS

Tucson, Arizona

Endpapers. Sculptural frieze, enclosure wall of Ramachandra Temple (photograph, John Gollings).

CONTENTS

PREFACE

Several years ago when I first came to know of the Fritz-Michell project on the Vijayanagara site at Hampi, I had doubts about what the project could add to our admittedly slim and inadequate understanding of this capital of the last imperial polity in peninsular India before the British. My reservations about their approach were based on my perhaps false notion of the competence of conventional approaches to the further study of Vijayanagara — that is, the usual epigraphical-historical method based upon texts, along with limited assistance from art history. The present monograph is proof to me that the Fritz-Michell approach is valid and independent for Vijayanagara, and for similar sites in South Asia. It is not a substitute for conventional methods, but an additional means of deepening our knowledge, a way of opening new questions. This work is also an impressive demonstration of international co-operation between Indian scholar-officials and foreign scholars, and a tribute to the intellectual dedication of all participants, of which Dr. M.S. Nagaraja Rao's co-authorship of this volume is but one manifestation.

It was only subsequently, after twice visiting the Vijayanagara site and discussing the work that was being done there, that I began to understand better my intuition that the approach of these scholars might be valid and ultimately valuable. Scattered over the twenty-five square kilometres of the site are an enormous number of structures — buildings, walls, surfaced roads, broad built-up areas — whose identifications, dating from nearly a century before in some cases, had been based upon little evidence and, often, less sense. Structures had been named "Lotus Mahal", "queen's bath", etc., and complexes had been labelled as "mint" or "zenana", with only the slightest evidence. In fact, many of these identifications were based upon nothing more substantial than the supposition that this great Hindu capital must have had mints, quarters for royal women, and pleasure parks. Such assumptions are not implausible, but the identifications of specific functions as these often have little reference to extant ruins or inscriptions. Few historians who have written on Vijayanagara have spent much time on the site; of those who made their way to this somewhat remote corner of Karnataka, none were trained to read the site with the eyes of the archaeologist or architectural historian.

What the project in operation also revealed to me was that the methods of the archaeologist and historical architect attracted the interests and labours of many students, Indian and others. What will always be a memorable moment in my career as a student of South Indian history was the experience of discussing the site under the night sky in the tented area of the Vijayanagara camp with Dr. Nagaraja Rao and his staff, Sri L.K. Srinivasan and his team, Drs. Fritz and Michell and their students, and several other visitors, including Dr. K.V. Ramesh, Chief Epigraphist of the Government of India. Our views then and those discussed in the present monograph must be regarded as tentative: as much an effort to deconstruct the earlier, uninformed, and hasty judgements about the site, as an effort to frame new propositions based not only upon the information that all who were working on the site were bringing forward daily, but upon the recent research of other archaeologists, epigraphists, historians and art historians.

These views — more refined and better reasoned — are now presented to a larger audience, first in the publication of Dr. Nagaraja Rao, *Vijayanagara: Progress of Research 1979-1983,* and now in this volume itself. The great virtue of both these works is that they set out the emerging inventory of material remains on the vast site in a more complete and accurate way than ever before; they also frame conceptions about the site with more appropriate tentativeness than scholars have done in the past. Thus, they invite a prospectively large body of scholarly engagement with the project at Vijayanagara that may be as important for clarifying India's cultural evolution for this generation as the Harappan sites were for previous generations.

Burton Stein,
London, September, 1984

ACKNOWLEDGEMENTS

The documentation project at Vijayanagara — the preliminary results of which are published here — would not have been possible without the generous support of several institutions, and the encouragement and enthusiasm of a great number of individuals.

To carry out field work in India we have applied to the Archaeological Survey of India, the Directors General of which have graciously granted us permission each year since 1980. At the site, L.K. Srinivasan (Superintending Archaeologist, Mid-Southern Circle), C. Prakash and K. Rangappa (Conservation Assistants), and their staff have taken great interest in our work. The Directorate of Archaeology and Museums (Government of Karnataka), under the energetic leadership of Dr M.S. Nagaraja Rao, has given us every possible assistance. Since early 1982 we have enjoyed the amenities of the Karnataka Government archaeological camp which made our stay at the site comfortable and productive. Dr Nagaraja Rao (now Director General, Archaeological Survey of India) encouraged us to participate in the ambitious "Resurrection of Hampi" project initiated by the Government of Karnataka (see Nagaraja Rao 1983, preface). All the staff of the camp, especially C.S. Patil and Balasubrahmanyam (Technical Assistants), have been of enormous help. We have also been aided by A. Satyanarayan (Assistant Superintending Archaeologist) and K.M. Suresh (Curator) of the Archaeological Museum at Kamalapuram.

Though the Vijayanagara project began as an unfinanced and somewhat improvized exercise, we have been fortunate in raising funds to cover expenses of travel and field work, and also to permit essential analytical work in London, New York and Melbourne. At the end of 1981, the British Academy made a grant. From 1982 onwards, The Smithsonian Institution (Special Foreign Currency Program) has supported our travel and living costs in India, as well as the expenses of our team. Gretchen Ellsworth (Director of the Office of Fellowships and Grants) and Francine Berkowitz (Program Manager) have been exceptionally supportive; without their encouragement we could not have accomplished our field work.

Since 1982 The National Science Foundation and The National Endowment for the Humanities have provided funds to support research costs outside India. The staff of both foundations have provided invaluable assistance, not only in the administration of funds, but also in the formation of a viable intellectual context for the project. Dr Charles Redman with Dr John Yellen (Director, Program in Anthropology) at The National Science Foundation, and Drs Katherine Abramowitz and Eugene Sterud (Program Officers, Division of Research Grants) at The National Endowment for the Humanities, deserve particular thanks. American grants for this project are administered by the University of New Mexico (Albuquerque). Under Drs Jeremy Sabloff and Linda Cordell (Chairpersons), the faculty and students of the Department of Anthropology have provided a friendly institutional base for the project. The staff of the Department has been painstaking and expeditious in preparing various proposals, reports, and articles. June-el Piper has introduced us to the wonders of the microprocessor, and has expertly prepared successive drafts of the manuscript for this publication.

During the 1983 and 1984 seasons, Fritz has worked in India as a Fellow of the American Institute of Indian Studies. We are most grateful to Dr Pradip Mehendiratta (Director), L.S. Suri (Associate Director), and the staff of the Institute for their kind interest in the project.

In the first two years of work at Vijayanagara (1980 and 1981), we benefitted enormously from our association with Prof. Pierre Filliozat and Dr Vasundhara Filliozat who shared with us their detailed knowledge of the site, gained over more than a decade of research. Other scholars, too, have been generous with their information and experience. Among the historians, epigraphists, archaeologists, and art historians who visited us at the site are: Dr Carol Appadurai-Breckenridge, Dr Catherine Asher, Prof. Frederick Asher, Prof. R. Champakalakshmi, Dr Yolande Crowe, Prof. Anna Dallapiccola, Antony Hutt, Prof. K.S. Kannan, Dr John Marr, Prof. S. Nagaraju, Hugh O'Neill, Dr K.V. Ramesh, Dr S. Rajasekhara, Prof. Burton Stein, Prof. Barbara Stoler-Miller, Dr Allan Shapiro, Dr A. Sundara, and Dr Phil Wagoner. Even an archaeo-astronomer, Dr Scott Smith, spent one month at Vijayanagara. Of all these visits, that of Dr Kapila Vatsyayan was particularly inspiring.

Documentation of the archaeological and architectural features of the royal centre at Vijayanagara has been largely undertaken by a vol-

ACKNOWLEDGEMENTS

unteer group of students and professionals. Since 1980, schools and university departments of architecture at New Delhi, Ahmedabad, Bombay, Bangalore, Hassan, Deakin, Melbourne, Sydney, London, and Cambridge have all permitted students to join us at the site. Professional architects have also contributed their valuable services: these include David Chanter, Ross Feller, Bakul Jani, Peter Lovell, Yamini Patel, Alison Rowe, Pru Sanderson, Suchitra Sholapurkar, Michael Sutherill, Nalini Thakur, and Ada Wilson. Archaeology students from Pune (Deccan College) and Ann Arbor (University of Michigan) have also participated in the project. Among the graduate students who were with us at the site are Richard Blurton, Laura Junker, Wolfgang Maschek, Sugandha Purandare, and Carla Sinopoli. In addition, we have utilized the services of a professional team of surveyors from Bangalore under the expert leadership of R.S. Ramamoorthy.

Photographers, too, have made substantial contributions to the recording of Vijayanagara's architecture and sculpture. Together with their assistants, John and Kate Gollings have spent several seasons at the site. Snehal Shah and Raimonda Buitoni have also photographed extensively.

The rapid publication of this report would not have been possible without the support of the Department of Architecture and Building, University of Melbourne. As visiting research fellows in 1984 (with an honorarium from the Eleanor Edna Norris Bequest Fund), we were able to complete the manuscript, and to prepare line drawings for this volume. We are thankful to the Department for advice and logistical support. The Department also kindly agreed to subvene the printing costs of this volume, and appears here — together with the University of Arizona Press — as co-publisher. In the final checking and revisions we were helped by Burton Stein, Richard Blurton and Wolfgang Maschek. Prof. Stein also kindly agreed to provide the volume with a preface.

John M. Fritz and George Michell
Melbourne, May 1984

Fortified gateway at Vijayanagara.
James Fergusson, *History of Indian and Eastern Architecture*, London, 1910, I, Figure 168.

1. INTRODUCTION

Research Aims and Methods

Vijayanagara — the "City of Victory" — was the capital of the last great Hindu empire of south India. Founded in the middle of the fourteenth century, Vijayanagara rapidly became one of the largest and wealthiest cities of its day. The power and magnificence of its rulers were the envy of the Muslim sultans and of lesser Hindu kings. The reputation of the city even reached Europe, and there were several foreign visitors to Vijayanagara who left vivid accounts of life at the capital. In 1565 the city was sacked by Muslim armies, and abandoned.

For the archaeologist as well as the urban and architectural historian, Vijayanagara offers a unique opportunity to investigate medieval Hindu urbanism. Spread over an area of more than 25 sq.km., the ruins of the city consist of many standing and ruined structures, both sacred and secular. In addition to these plainly visible remains, there are large expanses of uncleared rubble piles and numerous overgrown mounds. Such architectural and archaeological evidence provides a remarkable record of what was probably the greatest of all medieval Hindu capitals in India. Furthermore, the extraordinary circumstances surrounding the establishment of the city and its sudden destruction means that most of these features are dated to a limited period of just over two hundred years.

The historical record of Vijayanagara is also rich and varied. Epigraphic and literary sources inform on particular events that took place at the capital. A knowledge of these sources is essential for any functional interpretation of the different parts of the city. As for the overall. meaning of the capital, this can only be investigated by integrating both the archaeological and historical material.

PREVIOUS WORK AT THE SITE

The city of Vijayanagara has been uninhabited now for more than four hundred years, the action of men and weather hastening its decay. But the ruined capital was never entirely overlooked, as implied by Robert Sewell in his famous book, *A Forgotten Empire* (1900). At the beginning of the nineteenth century, maps of the site and sketches of the monuments were prepared by Colonel Mackenzie; by the 1830s, the first inscriptions had been translated (Ravenshaw 1836); in 1856,

the site was extensively photographed (on waxed-paper negatives) by Alexander Greenlaw. The first publication of illustrations and a map of the site appeared in 1866 (Fergusson and Meadows Taylor). Efforts to protect and conserve the various monuments began at the end of the last century, and have continued, though with several interruptions, up to the present day. At least two guidebooks on Vijayanagara have been widely available (Longhurst 1917; Devakunjari 1970); short notices of conservation and epigraphical research at the site have appeared regularly in the appropriate annual reports. (For a survey of scholarship at Vijayanagara, including a bibliography of relevant publications, see Michell 1985a.).

In the 1970s, Vijayanagara became one of three medieval sites designated by the Indian Government as a "national project". Archaeological investigation was cooperatively undertaken by the Archaeological Survey (Government of India) and the Directorate of Archaeology and Museums (Government of Karnataka). As a result, a number of stone foundations of palaces and ceremonial buildings were revealed, as well as the stone pavements of roads (Thapar 1982; Mitra 1983; Nagaraja Rao 1983 and 1984); this work is still in progress. Though about sixty monuments at Vijayanagara are now protected by both the central and state authorities, a large proportion of the site, with the greatest number of features, is still unlisted. Recently, the Government of Karnataka has notified residents in the region of a planned protection order.

OVERALL AIMS OF THE PROJECT

Our work at Vijayanagara began in 1980, and, from the beginning, was conceived as a complement to the excavation programmes of the central and state governments. The virtual absence of documentation at the site led us to initiate a project of surface archaeology. But the vast area covered by the ruins made it impossible for us to survey in detail the whole site; nor was such a complete coverage essential for our research.

The central theme of our investigation — the meeting of king and god — is mostly clearly manifested, we believe, in one part of the city, the royal centre. It was here that the public and private activities of the kings were mainly focused. Our documentation project concentrates on this

1. INTRODUCTION

zone, and aims at recording the form and spatial organization of all visible features. We interpret these urban elements — walls, gateways, palaces, pavilions, towers, stables, baths, fountains, aqueducts, tanks, temples, sculptures, inscriptions, ceramics, etc. — as critical components in a system that established and maintained the authority of the imperial rulers. Urban form and monumental architecture and art at Vijayanagara, we propose, helped to define specific concepts of state and kingship. Furthermore, we consider that the city itself was instrumental in asserting a particular relationship between king and god. Here the temporal power of the ruler was seen to be a manifestation of a divinely inspired order.

The documentary and interpretive skills required to address this theme are not possessed by any single scholar. We believe that an interdisciplinary approach is the most effective way to investigate a topic as complex as Vijayanagara —where were focused many of the political, economic, religious, and artistic forces of the period. As co-authors, we bring together the perspectives and techniques of two distinct disciplines — archaeology in an anthropological framework, and architectural history. Archaeology seeks to record the forms and spatial relationships of ruined buildings, pottery, and other material residues of life in the city; it poses questions about the evolution of systems of social and political control, and their relation to changing systems of meaning expressed in a variety of symbolic media. Architectural history aims at documenting the forms and carved details of standing structures; it explores questions about the evolution of artistic styles, and attempts to relate these to changing social, economic, and religious conditions.

Epigraphists and social and cultural historians are also contributing to the study of Vijayanagara. Their efforts are essential for the uncovering of historical information contained in the relevant inscribed and written records about the city. We are fortunate that a robust historical literature exists on the nature of the Vijayanagara state, and its relation to local politics, agrarian systems, and temple institutions. This literature is attended with spirited controversy. More broadly, the nature of kingship has been an important problem of long standing for Indian historiography; the discussions of this topic have stimulated and informed our explanations of the imperial capital.

At this stage in the study of Vijayanagara, more research has been focused on the material record of the site than on the relevant historical sources. Inscriptions at the site are only now being systematically recorded and translated; literary references to the city, especially in Kannada and Telegu, have still to be compiled and thoroughly examined. We also note that archaeological work is very much in progress, and each year the overall "picture" of the site changes as more and more remains are brought to light. Most sculptures and artefacts discovered at the site await detailed attention.

The material presented in this volume does not claim any final or definitive status; rather, it is in the nature of an expanded progress report. Our verbal and graphic descriptions of the architectural and archaeological features of the royal centre are intended as a basis for interpreting this part of the site and, indeed, the complete city. (Our preliminary conclusions are presented in Chapter 8).

DOCUMENTATION METHODS

Two sets of archaeological techniques are employed in the study of the material record of Vijayanagara — excavation and surface archaeology. In general, excavation is a destructive process since it involves the removal of buried structures from their contexts, and their exposure to the elements. By its nature it is slow work and is limited to a fairly restricted area. All artefacts that are discovered have to be collected, classified, and stored; revealed structures and other features require careful conservation. Excavation permits the discovery of buried structures; the accompanying stratigraphic analysis supports chronological interpretation. In contrast, surface archaeology concentrates only on the visible features of the site; since it does not involve destructive techniques or intensive labour, it is more rapid and can cover extensive areas with a wide variety of characteristics. While all observable structures may be documented, only a selective collection of kinds and numbers of portable artefacts need be made.

By applying these techniques of surface archaeology to the investigation of various areas of the site, we hope to obtain a variety of data that informs on different aspects of past life at Vijayanagara. For instance, the soil in many areas contains quantities of pottery that may have been locally used and produced. By charting the distribution of this material we may be able to perceive occupation patterns of different population groups. Around collapsed buildings the soil contains brick, plaster, and roof tiles that inform on fallen architectural elements (like brick superstructures). Artefacts found here suggest the function of these buildings. Even the difference in the density of artefacts on the ground is an important factor as it probably indicates variation in the intensity of past use. The limitations of surface archaeology are obvious: since vertical superimposition of evidence cannot be observed, no stratigraphic — and thus chronological — interpretation is possible.

In our archaeological investigation of Vijaya-nagara, we aim at recording all visible structures of the site. We are, therefore, mainly involved with techniques of mapping, surveying, measuring, and photographing. In order to cover the whole site — an area of no less than 25 sq. km. — we have developed a sketch map series (1:4,000) based on published Survey of India maps and an enlarged aerial photograph (displayed in the Archaeological Museum). By employing a specially developed three-letter code, we have designated almost two thousand separate features, varying from standing structures in different states of preservation to barely noticeable alignments of buried walls. We have photographed most of these features, and provided each with a map reference.

Most of our surveying and measuring work, however, has been concentrated in and around the royal centre. Here we are preparing detailed maps (1:400) of different zones, documenting the spatial distribution of individual features and, wherever possible, relating these to physical topography. All structures, even if not surviving beyond their stone basements, are measured so as to prepare accurate plans, elevations, and sections (1:100). Architectural details, such as masonry jointing, basement mouldings, balustrades, columns, plasterwork, etc., are also being drawn (1:20, 1:10). Photography is an important part of this documentation, and here we attempt to capture the architecture in its physical and urban setting, as well as to record all sculptural reliefs on sacred and secular monuments.

We have also initiated a study of ceramics found on the surface of the site, particularly pottery sherds associated with the newly revealed palace structures (Sinopoli 1983). (The Chinese ceramics occasionally found across the site, though, have yet to attract the attention of a specialist).

HISTORICAL SOURCES

Unlike prehistoric and even early historic sites, medieval cities such as Vijayanagara are provided with a large variety of epigraphical and literary sources. These inform on various activities that took place at the capital — from dynastic successions, royal ceremonies and battles, to details of everyday life. Despite the fact that an abundance of such sources are available for Vijayanagara — both capital and empire — much of this material has yet to be systematically examined.

To begin with, more than two hundred epigraphs exist at Vijayanagara, mostly inscribed on the stone walls of temples, but also on granite boulders; almost all these epigraphs are in Sanskrit, Kannada, or Telugu languages. While the texts of a few of these have been published in various reports — South Indian Inscriptions, Epigraphia Indica, South Indian Epigraphy, etc., — only now are these inscriptions being edited and translated. Many of these inscriptions record royal donations, and much information is included on political, religious, and economic issues, as well as on the history of the building and its sponsor (see Filliozat n.d.; Rajasekhara 1984). Recently, a number of inscriptions have been discovered that name parts of the site and several of the monuments (see Nagaraja Rao 1983 and 1984). We should add that inscriptions found elsewhere in South India during this period occasionally refer to events at the capital.

By far the most popular historical sources for Vijayanagara are the widely quoted accounts of the foreign visitors. From the fifteenth century we have the descriptions of the Italian traveller, Nicolo di Conti (c.1420), and of the Persian ambassador, Abd ar-Razzaq (c.1442) (both translated by Major in 1857). Sixteenth-century accounts include the Italian, Ludovico di Varthema (c.1504), and the Portuguese travellers, Duarte Barbosa (c.1518), Domingo Paes (c.1520), and Fernao Nuniz (c.1535) (translated by Sewell in 1900 and Dames in 1918). Even after the abandonment of the city, we have a brief notice of the ruins by Ceasaro Federici (1567).

A perusal of these accounts (many of which are assembled in Sewell 1900) yields a vivid picture of life at Vijayanagara; in particular, of the king, court and army. Abd ar-Razzaq, Domingo Paes, and Fernao Nuniz were at the capital during the spectacular mahanavami festival, and noted with awe the display of royal magnificence. They also attempted to describe the layout of the city and some of its principal monuments. Unfortunately, we encounter considerable difficulties in matching these contemporary urban "portraits" with the material record of the site. Unfamiliar as they were with the cultural context of Vijayanagara, the European visitors could hardly be expected to understand everything they observed, or evaluate all they were told. Furthermore, many of their chronicles seem to have been composed only after they had left India.

Less well known are the literary sources of the Vijayanagara period, some of which are of direct relevance for understanding life at the capital. As yet, few of these Sanskrit, Kannada, and Telugu texts have been translated into English, and no critical study exists for the literature of this period (see, however, Sherwani 1974); here we merely note the range of sources in Sanskrit there are historical works, including royal biographies with direct or indirect reference to the Vijayanagara kings and the city — for instance, the fourteenth-century Madhuravijayam by Gangadevi, and the sixteenth-century Achyutarayabhyudaya by Rajanatha (see Sridhara Babu 1975). Certain historical

1. INTRODUCTION

romances — like the *Virupaksha Vasantotsava Champu* by Ahobala (Panchamukhi 1953) — incidentally describe the capital and its inhabitants. Dramas, too, sometimes ascribed to royal authors, exist for the period, and contain information on the life of the king.

For other literary sources we have to turn to Kannada and Telugu works. The *Amuktamalyada* is supposed to be by Krishna Raya himself (Rangasvami Sarasvati 1926); recently a version of this ruler's diary has been published (Sitaramiah and Acharya 1983). Other than such literary works, we note contemporary texts on philosophy and religion, also poetical and dramatic compositions, all of which are important for studying developments that took place at the capital. Tamil sources, too, occasionally shed light on activities at Vijayanagara.

Historical works in Kannada and Telugu also exist, including several accounts of the great battle of 1565 (collected by Colonel Mackenzie). Among the Persian works of Muslim historians, we note the celebrated account of Vijayanagara by Ferishta (Briggs 1829). Though only composed in 1612, Ferishta's history contains interesting information about the capital.

URBAN TRADITIONS

Our investigation of Vijayanagara forms part of a much larger study — the process of urbanization in India. Though we are especially concerned with a medieval imperial city, we understand little about the possible connection between Vijayanagara and earlier dynastic centres in this part of India. Archaeological investigation has not yet revealed the urban plans of Early Chalukya, Hoysala, Late Chalukya, or Kakatiya capitals — as, for instance, at Badami, Halebid, Kalyani, and Warangal. Though we have temple architecture in abundance at these and related sites, information about fortification systems, street layouts, palaces and other civic buildings, etc., is still very limited. In general, studies of South Indian urbanization (Champakalakshmi 1979, for instance) have been hampered by the lack of visible evidence. As for the field of medieval archaeology, this has been recognized only recently (Mehta 1979).

Also relevant to our study is the process of urbanization at contemporary Islamic sites. In the Deccan, as elsewhere in India, this resulted in a number of strongly defended capitals, such as at Daulatabad, Gulbarga, Firuzabad, Bidar, Bijapur, Golconda, etc. (see Schotten-Merklinger 1981). Intensive archaeological projects at Fatehpur Sikri (still mostly unpublished), Champaner (Mehta 1981), and Daulatabad (Mate 1983), however, are making substantial contributions to our knowledge about Indian Islamic town planning. The possible influence of Muslim practice on contemporary Hindu cities — in terms of stone fortifications, elaborate palace designs, waterworks, etc. — has yet to be investigated.

NOTE ON TERMINOLOGY

To designate the different zones of Vijayanagara, we employ terms that facilitate the description of the site — sacred centre, urban core, royal centre, etc. While these terms suggest functional attributes and symbolic meanings, we do not take these to be definitive; rather these have proved useful in this stage of our work. Within the royal centre we have avoided labels by which certain enclosures are generally known — mint, zenana, etc; likewise, we have not adopted the accepted identifications of several monuments in this part of the site — Lotus Mahal, queens' bath, guards' quarters, etc. Our research indicates that such labels and identifications lack historical and archaeological evidence; in some cases they appear to be misleading. For this reason we propose a completely new numbering system for enclosures, structures and other features within the royal centre (see p. 16).

As for the descriptive treatment of the site, our work is by no means complete. In some areas (e.g., enclosures X-XII) descriptions have been written where sketch mapping has not yet been carried out. In some peripheral areas (enclosures XX-XXVIII) detailed descriptions are still to be written. The enclosure maps reproduced here have all been sketched; detailed surveying of the part of the royal centre only began in 1983, and topographic maps will be presented in subsequent reports. We note that a few minor features with map numbers are not referred to in our text; other features found in the text are not indicated on the maps.

The archictectural drawings reproduced here represent only a selection of the work completed. We hope to publish a complete series of these plans, sections, elevations and details in a number of monographs on the site.

2. ELEMENTS OF URBANISM

Zones of the City

Before examining the architectural and archaeological features of the royal centre at Vijayanagara, we first have to consider the environs of the capital. Here we observe a transition from wild and rocky gorges to flat and open plains. This transition coincides with the different zones of the city, separated one from another by both natural and man-made features. We distinguish three urban zones: (1) the sacred centre beside the Tungabhadra River; (2) the urban core containing the royal centre in the limited level areas; and, (3) the sub-urban centres in the plains beyond (see Figures 2.1 and 2.2).

THE PHYSICAL SETTING

No one visiting the ruins of Vijayanagara can be unaffected by the strangely wild landscape in which the capital is situated. Though the rocky outcrops of granite boulders that surround the city, and intrude into the various zones, certainly provide effective protection, this environment also embodies potent sacred associations. (The mythical geography of the Tungabhadra River and the surrounding hills is discussed in Chapter 8.)

Perhaps the most important feature of Vijayanagara's setting is the natural basin in which the city is located. Through this basin flows the Tungabhadra River in a northeasterly direction. To the north, rocky outcrops partly contain the river in a narrow gorge; elsewhere, these hills open up to define a wide valley through which the river and its branches flow. The rocks are of granite weathered to every shade of grey, brown, and pink, and are split into the most astonishing shapes. Piled high one upon the other, these boulders form steep hills with deep fissures. North of the river, this inhospitable landscape is intensified, and there are fewer flat areas.

Overlooking the south bank of the river is a high rocky ridge with several elevated outcrops (such as Hemakuta and Matanga hills). This ridge, together with another that runs parallel to it further south, defines a richly irrigated valley. This valley was once an earlier course of the river; now, only a tributary is found here. At either end, the valley is open. To the south are valleys bounded by lower ridges and isolated outcrops (like Malyavanta hill). Gradually, these hills disappear altogether and the landscape becomes increasingly flat and open. This plain extends for several kilometres to the east, south, and west, limited by further ridges (east and south) and the river (west).

SACRED CENTRE

Dominated by the granite wilderness through which the Tungabhadra River flows, the sacred centre of Vijayanagara has a longer history than the capital itself (Kotraiah 1983). On the sloping shelf of Hemakuta hill, as well as at other sites along the south bank of the river, small temples are found, some of which date back to the tenth and eleventh centuries. During the Vijayanagara period this zone witnessed an intense religious activity, and many new temples were erected beside the water, on rocks and limited portions of level ground.

The principal focus of this sacred centre is the Virupaksha Temple. Around the enclosure walls and chariot street of this complex cluster the houses of the village of Hampi. This temple is currently in worship, and is an important place of pilgrimage in the region. To the south rises Hemakuta hill, ringed by a circuit of fortification walls, broken only by gateways and isolated boulders. Within these walls are several small (mostly pre-Vijayanagara period) temples, monolithic columns, and tanks.

Most of the great sixteenth-century temple projects at Vijayanagara — such as the Virupaksha, Krishna, Tiruvengalanatha, and Vitthala complexes —are located in the sacred centre of the capital. These temples are distinguished by their vast rectangular enclosures created by high stone walls; the enclosures are entered through towered gateways, and approached by long chariot streets flanked by colonnades. Within the enclosures are shrines, altars, halls, porches, columns, kitchens, stores, wells, tanks, and other features, all set in paved courtyards. This is religious architecture on a truly urban scale. (The colonnaded street of the Virupaksha Temple is almost 750m. long; that of the Krishna Temple is nearly 50m. wide.) Stretching eastwards into the landscape — except for the Tiruvengalanatha Temple which is oriented to the north — these streets are dominant elements in the organization of the sacred centre. In fact, each temple complex is in itself the nucleus of an urban quarter, and is often referred to as a city ("pura") — thus Krishnapura, Vitthalapura,

2. ELEMENTS OF URBANISM

etc. Accompanied by a series of subsidiary structures — such as tanks, aqueducts, walls, gateways, and even possibly residences (now ruined) — each temple complex was also linked with substantial areas of land, including parts (or even all) of the irrigated valley to the south.

Some of these projects were built over a long period. The Virupaksha Temple complex even incorporates a ninth-tenth century shrine — now concealed within later additions — testifying to the longevity of Shaiva worship at the site. The Vitthala Temple complex was constructed in a number of phases throughout the sixteenth century.

The sacred centre also has many smaller structures, some of which are temples with halls and porches, while others are simple shrines, indicated by only a few columns, a carved doorway, or a pedestal. Columned halls are also found here. Most of these structures are clustered along the south bank of the river between the Virupaksha and Vitthala Temple complexes (a distance of about 2km.). Along this route are traces of a road, onto which many of the shrines face; here too are found gateways and segments of protective walls. Other shrines are elevated on rocky ledges, or are built on nearby hills reached by flights of steps. Probably the most dramatically sited temple is the Virabhadra shrine on the summit of Matanga hill. From here the layout of the sacred centre and the irrigated valley to the south are displayed with remarkable clarity.

Associated with these numerous temples are sacred icons — the emanations and incarnations of Vishnu; Shiva linga; Nandi; Hanuman, etc. — carved on boulders and in rocky clefts. Beside the river, some of these icons are found unattached to any temple. During flooding many of these sculptures are submerged. Elsewhere in the sacred centre, colossal monolithic images are carved out of huge granite boulders. The most spectacular example is a gigantic Narasimha (6.7m. high) south of the Krishna Temple.

Temples and sculptures are also found on the north bank of the river where there is spacious level ground. These may also have formed part of the sacred centre of the capital, reached by a bridge (now ruined) or, as today, by coracles.

INTERMEDIATE IRRIGATED VALLEY

South of the sacred centre is a long valley running southwest-northeast between parallel rocky ridges. The rich cultivation, facilitated by canalization, appears to be original. As a confirmation of the non-residential character of the valley floor, no pottery concentrations are found here (in contrast with the urban core where these are common). Despite the fact that parts of the Krishna and Tiruvengalanatha Temple complexes

intrude into the valley, few structures seem to have been built here, with the exception of an Islamic-styled structure (see Chapter 7). A few small shrines are located beside the canal; others are found on the elevated sides of the valley. On the south there is also evidence of roads, tanks, mortars, and even some pottery, suggesting habitation; however, no structural remains are seen.

Of interest in this valley is the system of waterworks. Canals are raised up above the level of the valley at either side, the water channels being cut into the rocks or supported on stone walls. (The Turuttu canal running along the south periphery of the valley preserves its original name.) Through the middle of the valley a natural stream flows northeastwards towards the river. The wall extending across the valley at its narrowest point (south of Matanga hill) appears to have been a dam associated with spillways, canals, channels, etc. At its northeast end the valley is cut off by a fortification wall with gateways.

URBAN CORE
(Figure 2.3)

South of the irrigated valley is the urban core, clearly defined by a complete ring of massive fortifications, broken only by strongly defended gateways. These walls enclose an area approximately elliptical in shape (the southwest-northeast axis is more than 4km. long). The fortifications ingeniously utilize the natural terrain wherever possible: Walls run along the tops of rocky ridges, or traverse flat land at the shortest possible distance between granite outcrops. This partly explains the angular configuration of the walls, particularly on the north, but also partly on the east and west. To the south the land is mostly flat; here the walls are more linear, though rarely straight.

Within the urban core, on granite shelves and between boulders — sometimes even perched on rocky summits — are numerous temples and shrines. These are especially clustered along the north ridge, or line the roads. The largest sacred complex is located on Malyavanta hill, rising within the urban core at its east end. Many of the lower valleys are now deeply filled with accumulated soil. Here can be seen parts of buried temples and gateways, also roads, tanks, wells, and abundant pottery sherds, indicating habitation. On the surrounding hillsides, evidence of residential areas is marked. Here are found columned halls, temples, shrines, tanks, roads, pottery, and, significantly, rubble remains of habitations. It may be possible to identify several residential areas associated with different social groups. Certain shrines (east and northeast valleys) suggest the existence of a Jaina community;

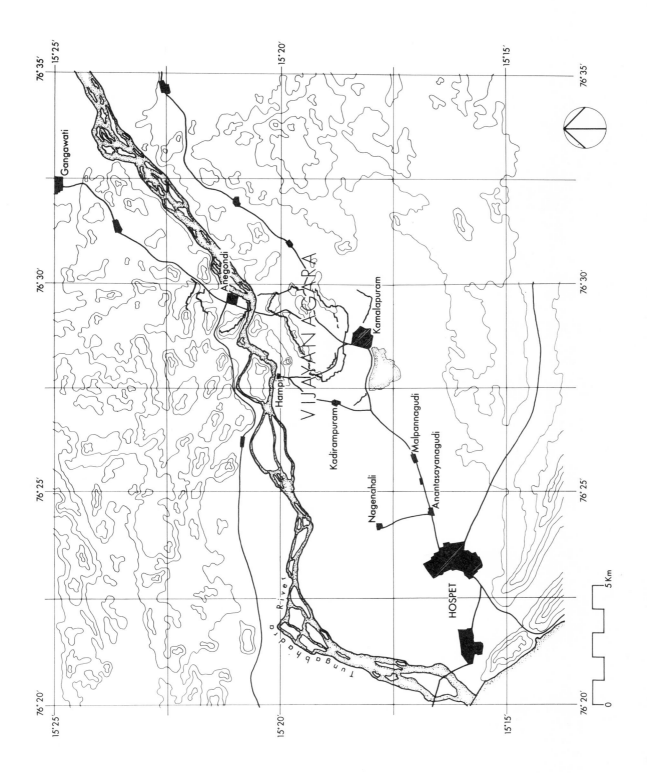

Figure 2.1 Regional context of Vijayanagara.

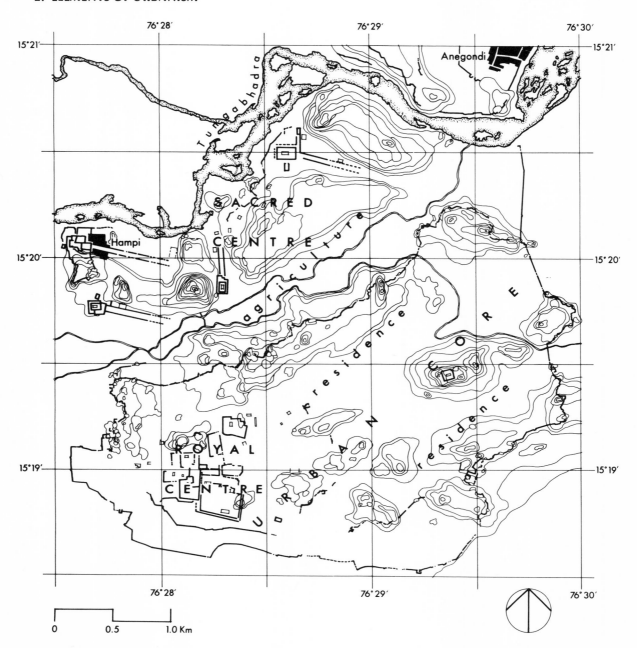

Figure 2.2   Zonal arrangement of Vijayanagara.

numerous Islamic tombs, a cemetery, and two mosques (northeast valley), indicate a Muslim quarter (Michell 1984b).

In the southeast of the urban core are segments of an internal wall, part of which dammed a large tank. (The area demarcated by these walls is now partly occupied by a modern irrigation basin.) Elsewhere, tanks, wells, aqueducts, and drains testify to an elaborate hydraulic system.

The southwest end of the urban core is domi-

nated by the royal centre, contained by its own (incomplete) ring of fortifications. Within these walls is a concentration of many different features; these are set within irregular enclosures defined by high walls (see Chapter 3). At the heart of the royal centre is the Ramachandra Temple, the focus for many of the roads of the urban core. Between the royal centre and the periphery of the urban core, particularly on the south and west, modern cultivation obliterates many features.

SUB-URBAN CENTRES
(Figure 2.1)

Surrounding the urban core, especially on the west and south, is an expansive area of level ground; this is limited on the west by the river and on the south by the Sandur hills (about 10 km. away). Here are preserved fragmentary arcs of fortification walls, all that have survived of the concentric protective zones around the urban core. Some of these walls — together with their gateways, and connecting roads — are described by Domingo Paes (Sewell 1900, pp. 253-254); however, the "seven fortresses" noted by Abd ar-Razzaq (Major 1857, p. 23) are not easily traced

The modern villages located in this plain — Kamalapuram, Kadirampuram, Malpannagudi, Anantasayanagudi, etc., and even the town of Hospet — all incorporate the original sub-urban centres (pattana) of the capital. We know that Hospet was laid out as a royal residence by Krishna Raya, and even named after one of his queens (Filliozat 1978b, p. 55). Today, evidence of these Vijayanagara period nuclei is seen in the various temples, walls, and gateways (but mostly obliterated by modern development in Hospet). Several elaborate sacred complexes are also found outside the urban core, including the Pattabhirama Temple to the southeast.

This zone incorporates extensive waterworks. Great tanks were built — including the impressive tank preserved southwest of Kamalapuram — and a major dam was constructed in the hills to the south (observed by the Portuguese visitors; Sewell 1900, p. 162). An extensive network of channels and canals, much renovated, is still in use today. The open land between the suburban centres served by these waterworks was used for agriculture, probably providing much of the city's food. Here, too, may have been located the large military encampments; perhaps here took place the various festivities and martial exercises associated with the urban festivals.

ANEGONDI

Northeast of the sacred centre, on the north bank of the Tungabhadra River, is the town of Anegondi. Well established before the foundation of the capital, Anegondi is still the residence of a local royal family claiming direct descent from the rulers of Vijayanagara. The town is contained within its own circuit of walls, entered through gateways. Nearby, on the banks of the river, a series of temples and sculptures — some of which are as early as the tenth and eleventh centuries — proclaims the holiness of the site. West of the town is the fortified citadel, elevated on rocky hills. Here are seen fortifications and defensive gateways, as well as the remains of other civic

structures (palace, barracks?, stores). North of Anegondi are several lines of walls with protected entrances; in effect, these constitute the extreme north boundary of the capital. Today, as in the past, Anegondi is reached by coracles from Talarighat.

ROADS
(Figures 2.4 and 4.12)

All these different zones of the city are linked by a network of roads, along which occurred commercial, military, and ceremonial movement. The major roads tend to run through the middle of valleys and around rocky ridges. We identify these routes by gateways in the fortification walls or by isolated entrances, and also by fragments of stone pavements, ramps, steps, or worn rocks. The alignments of temples, colonnades, monolithic columns, and other structures, and even the location of carvings on rocks, often indicate roads (now vanished). Finally, literary evidence, especially inscriptions, helps to identify and name some of the roads (Filliozat 1978b; Nagaraja Rao 1983, pp. 57-59).

Three types of roads are observed in the city: radial, ring, and linear (Fritz 1983). Significantly, the radial road system of Vijayanagara is focused on the royal centre. The roads here pass through two or more gateways in the rings of walls — which define both the urban core and the royal centre — and converge on the enclosure in front of the Ramachandra Temple. The north road (N1) leads from the royal centre to the foot of Matanga hill, and there branches off, both to the east and west, towards the Virupaksha and Tiruvengalanatha Temple complexes respectively. A third branch ascends the staircase to the Virabhadra shrine at the summit of the hill. Another north road (N2) may lead towards the street running eastward from the Krishna Temple complex. One of the most important roads running through the urban core, and certainly the longest, is the northeast route (NE). This passes through the northeast valley, and eventually divides into two branches; one (NE1) leading to Talarighat, the river crossing to Anegondi, the other (NE2) to an unidentified destination to the east. Within the royal centre, an east road (E) branches off this northeast route and travels south of Malyavanta hill to one of the east gateways of the urban core. A southeast road (SE1) also connects with this east road. Other southeast roads (SE2, 3) probably connect with routes passing through gateways in the walls outside the urban core.

There is also evidence of a south road system. S1 leads directly towards Kamalapuram, possibly passing through a gateway (now vanished) in the walls south of the Shaiva Temple complex (near the modern road?), as well as a second gateway

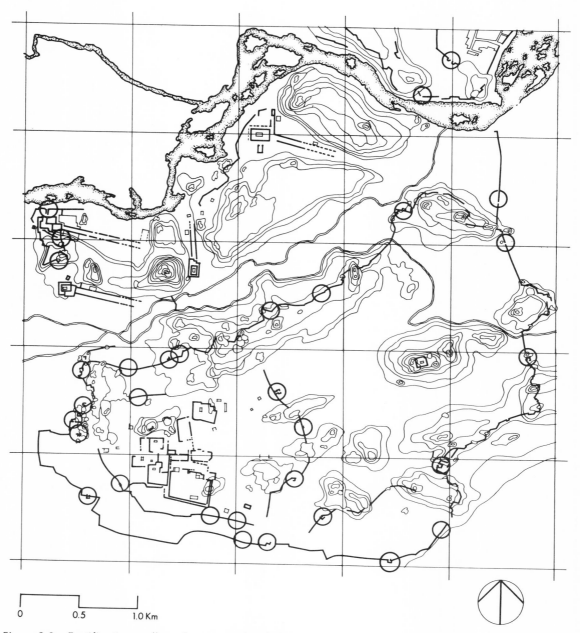

Figure 2.3   Fortification walls and gateways (circled) of Vijayanagara.

in the urban core walls. Beyond Kamalapuram, a road continued all the way to Hospet (coinciding with the modern road?). Other south roads (S2 and 3) also exist. A southwest road (SW) joins up with the linear Hospet-Hampi road (HH); the northwest routes (NW1, NW2) also appear to link with the road leading to Hampi. Fragmentary evidence of other radial roads is provided by gateways found elsewhere in the walls of the urban core.

A second, or ring, series of roads encircles the royal centre. The south and east ring roads (SR, ER) and one of the two north ring roads (NR2), pass outside the walls of the royal centre. The south ring road continues northwards towards Hampi. Here is encountered part of a third, or linear, system. This includes a major Hospet-Hampi route (HH), also a road that follows the Turuttu canal (TC), running along the south periphery of the intermediate irrigated valley. Linear roads (VR, K,

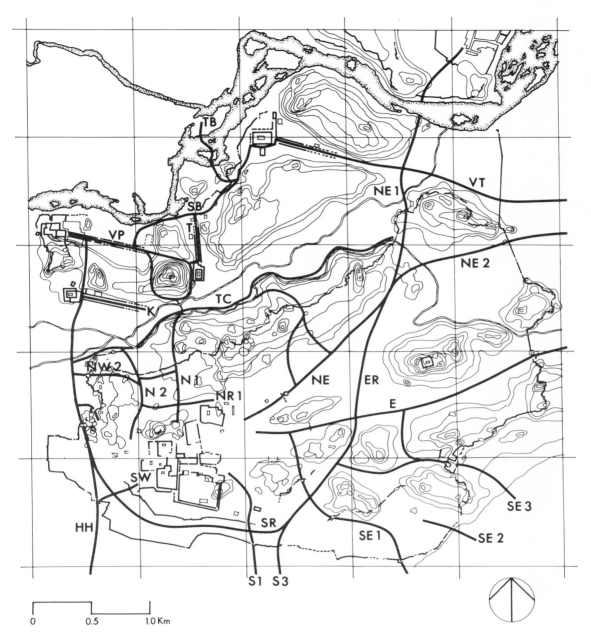

Figure 2.4   Road system of Vijayanagara.

VT) proceed along the streets extending eastwards
from the Virupaksha, Krishna, and Vitthala Temple
complexes, and also northwards (T) from the
Tiruvengalanatha Temple complex. Several of
these routes link up to become the road (SB)
flanking the south bank of the river. Stone pylons
standing in the river provide evidence of a bridge
that once linked the north and south banks (bridge
road TB).

3. THE ROYAL ENCLOSURES

Layout of Features

We come now to a detailed description of the royal centre at Vijayanagara; in particular, the architectural and archaeological features contained within the high walls of the various enclosures. The forms of standing buildings are, of course, plainly visible and can be easily described. Many other structures, however, are represented only by collapsed and partly buried remains; these are more difficult to describe completely. Though the excavators have revealed the plans of several collapsed buildings, in most cases we determine the building form by a detailed examination of the elements exposed on the surface.

BOUNDARIES OF THE ROYAL CENTRE
(Figure 3.1)

Located at the southwest end of the urban core, the royal centre is partly bounded by ridges on the north and rocky outcrops on the east. We can be fairly confident that the royal centre was originally encircled by fortification walls, substantial portions of which are still visible (see Chapter 4). To the south the land is flat; here, the royal centre is clearly limited by walls, with gateways. To the east are valleys with many partly buried features; even so, gateways and walls can still be made out. On the west, the walls disappear beneath the modern road (which possibly follows the line of the walls northwards). A gateway and fragmentary traces of walls are discovered on the north.

Connecting these walls and associated gateways, we perceive that the royal centre is approximately elliptical (1km. north-south, more than 1.5km. east-west). Just as in the urban core within which it is contained, the fortification walls of the royal centre utilize natural ridges wherever possible, choosing the shortest distance between rocks for connecting walls. The focus of the royal centre is a group of enclosures clustered around the Ramachandra Temple complex. Those enclosures nearest to this temple — that is, at the heart of the royal centre — have their boundaries better preserved than those on the periphery where the zones are not always clearly distinguished.

East of the principal group of enclosures are a number of features that line the northeast (NE), east (E), and southeast (SE1) roads; these include

temples and shrines of different cults, and colonnades. Here, too, are the remains of palace structures, as well as the only example of a completely rock-cut temple; nearby is an octagonal bath. In the southeast corner are the Shaiva temple complex and the Tiruvengalanatha Temple and also an Islamic-styled bath. Throughout, there are indications of aqueducts and other waterworks. South and west of the enclosures, many original features are obliterated by modern cultivation. The west boundary of the royal centre is indistinct; the Virupaksha Temple complex — dedicated to the same deity as the sanctuary at Hampi — was located near to the walls where, possibly, a gateway (now vanished) was also positioned. In the lower areas immediately to the west and south, the walls have been levelled. Further north, remnants of stone walls occur on the outcrops. The north limit of the royal centre is also obscure. Here, partly levelled and buried walls appear to have linked ridges and outcrops. Buildings on these ridges may have formed part of the defensive arrangements. In the valley to the south, small shrines are oriented in different directions (to face onto vanished roads?).

CONFIGURATION OF ENCLOSURES
(Figure 3.2)

Perhaps the most outstanding characteristics of the enclosures of the royal centre are the irregular shapes, the tightly juxtaposed and interlocking spaces, and the defining high walls. Not all enclosures, however, open into each other. In order to designate these enclosures we number each (Roman numerals) in a spiralling clockwise sequence, beginning with the enclosure (I) north and east of the Ramachandra Temple complex (thereafter II, III, IV, etc.). Where subdivisions are encountered within enclosures, these are noted (with letters, IIIa, b, c, etc.). Features within each enclosure — temples, shrines, platforms, colonnades, palaces, bath-houses, stables, tanks, aqueducts, drains, etc., or any fragmentary indications of these — are all numbered consecutively (II/1, 2, 3, etc.). As for those features described in greater detail elsewhere in this report, only a brief notice is given here (together with the appropriate chapter reference).

Before separately describing the characteristics of each enclosure, the various features it contains,

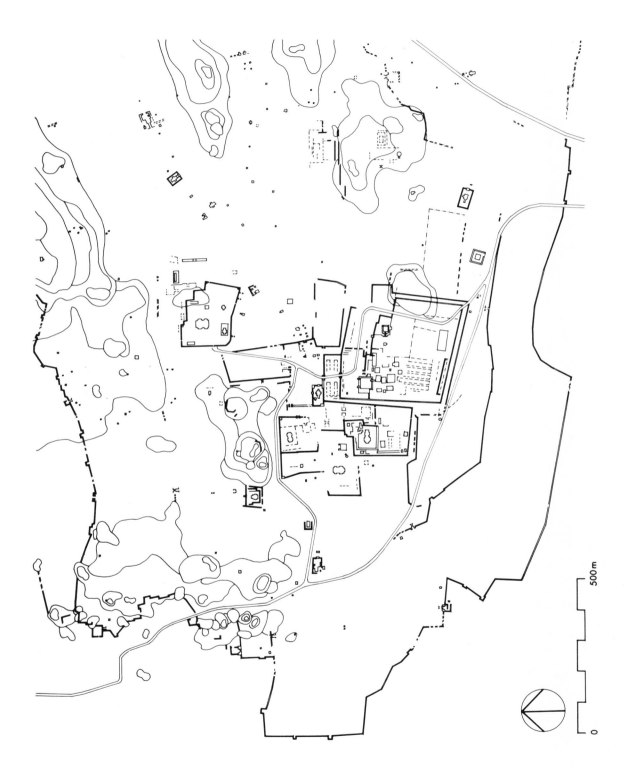

500 m

0

Figure 3.1   West end of the urban core containing the royal centre.

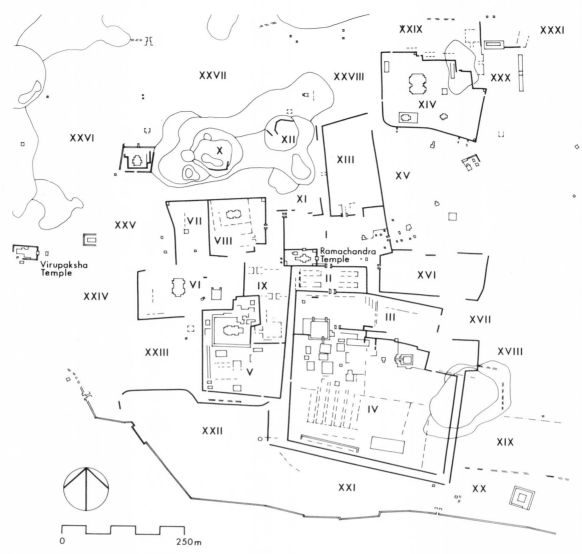

Figure 3.2   Royal centre, numbering of enclosures.

and its relationship to adjacent zones, we note some overall organizing patterns. To begin with, it is possible to perceive certain groupings of enclosures. South of the Ramachandra Temple, a north-south alley, defined by parallel walls, separates a number of zones on the east (II-IV) from those on the west (V and IX). To the northeast is another group of enclosures (XIII-XV, XXVIII-XXX), bounded on the south by a road (NE). Northwest of the Ramachandra Temple is a high granite outcrop (comprising X-XII), west and north of which are two zones (XXVI-XXVII). Running around the periphery of the enclosures already noted are several other zones, not always defined by walls. (For convenience we designate all these zones as enclosures.)

ENCLOSURE I
(Figure 3.3)

Approximately rectangular, enclosure I is not bounded by a coherent series of walls; rather, it consists of a large open space defined by wall segments and a number of gateways. Some of these multiple gateways are indicators of the principal routes that meet in this open space; other gateways provide access into the numerous enclosures that surround I on all sides.

The Ramachandra Temple complex, set within its own rectangular courtyard, is located in the southwest corner of I (see Chapter 5). Two gateways in the walls of the temple complex lead into I. On the south periphery of I, high walls

18

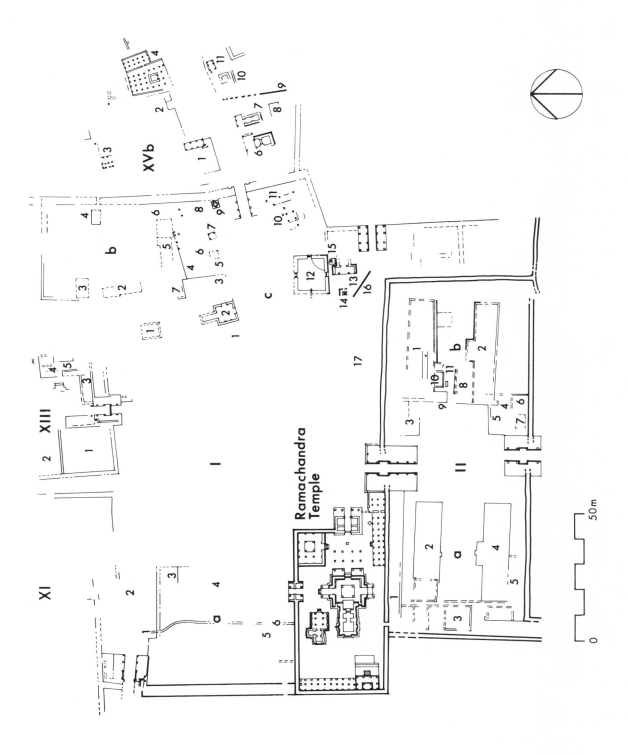

Figure 3.3   Ramachandra Temple complex and enclosures I, II and XVb.

(common with II) are broken in the middle by a large gateway (I-II), across which portions of the wall continue. At its east and west ends, the enclosure is limited by substantial walls with stepped profiles on the inner faces.

To facilitate our description of I, we divide the enclosure into three parts (a-c). Ia comprises the west portion. On the south of Ia are the walls of the temple (with processional friezes). On the west is a massive wall running northwards from the northwest corner of the temple complex until it meets a gateway (Ia-IXa). Remains of walls (1) define a court east of this gateway. On the north of Ia are short segments of walls (once connected?) in which evidence of a doorway is found. (This doorway appears to be on axis with the north gateway of the temple.) Further east is the north alley defined by walls (of enclosures XI and XIII), marking the beginning of the north road (N1). East of the alley, walls demarcate the boundary between Ia and XIII; here also is a gateway (Ia-XIII). East of the gateway, the wall is broken by the modern road. Only a few features are identified with Ia: a worn rocky surface (part of a road?) (2), stone slabs (remains of structures?) (3b), and cut rocks and lamp holes in a block (5).

Ib, in the northeast of the enclosure, is bounded on the east by the buried remains of a massive wall; less substantial walls are on the north and partly on the west. Within Ib the outlines of several rectilinear structures with earth and rubble walls (1-3, 5) are seen; another similar structure (4) is located in front of a small doorway that leads into enclosure XVa to the east. Walls built of large rectilinear slabs on the south (7) partly enclose a temple immediately to the south; these walls separate Ib (higher) from Ic (lower).

Presenting a mass of stone and concrete rubble with many ruined structures, Ic consists of features lining the northeast road (NE). On its north boundary, Ic is limited by a wall (4), with slabs set on edge, partly turning southwards (3), demarcating the change in ground level. Of interest here is the panel carved on the wall depicting a courtly devotee and attendant standing before a linga with a Nandi. To the east is the massive enclosure wall, in the middle of which is a gateway (Ic-XVb), through which the northeast road passes. The gateway is characterized by a partly preserved Islamic-style arch (see Chapter 4). North of the road are ruined shrines (2, 5, 7) (see Chapter 5), fallen colonnades (6, 8), and a well (9). The well has a rotated square opening at the top, and abuts the wall. South of the road are the remains of another small shrine (10) and colonnade (11); here also is a square tank (12) with seating (curved backs) on all sides. Three flights of steps enter the tank, and on the west is a water conduit. On the north, the tank walls are carved with fish emblems; in the southeast corner, the tank is partly blocked. To the south is a dilapidated shrine (13), with the stump of a monolithic column (14) set into a broken platform in front (west). The shattered remains of the column lie scattered around. Both shrine and column are on axis with the east gateway of the Ramachandra Temple complex (see Chapter 5). Between the shrine and the tank is a finely carved square pedestal (15) with a hole in its stone top (for a column?). In the debris nearby, traces of a drain (16) and an aqueduct (17) can be made out. On its east side, Ic is bounded by a wall that turns southwards to define the southeast alley through which passes a branch of the south road (S1a). Here also is located the gateway Ic-XVI.

ENCLOSURE II
(Figure 3.3)

Laid out more or less in a regular rectangle, this zone is entered in the middle of the long (north and south) sides through large gateways (I-II, II-IIIa), not precisely aligned. These divide II into two parts (a and b). The north and east walls of II are continuous; the south wall (common with IIIa) employs differently shaped blocks (see Chapter 4). The walls do not quite meet in the southeast corner (entry into IIIa?). At its west end, II is blocked off from an alley by the remains of enclosure walls and other structures.

The most significant features of II are four large rectangular platforms (IIa/2, 4; IIb/1, 2), bounded by single stone basements, and with traces of earth and rubble walls. Entry is in the middle of the long sides (projections on the two south examples). In the west half of the enclosure (IIa) other raised areas (1) are positioned against the north wall; a structure (?) (5) is also positioned against the south wall. A complex of chambers and/or platforms (?) (3) defined in part by two parallel rubble walls occupies the west end of the enclosure. Part of this complex extends into the alley, almost meeting its west wall, leaving a narrow passage of about 1.5m. Between the two rectangular platforms of the east half of the enclosure (IIb) are a small tank with curved side slabs (10), and a stone trough (11). A long narrow room is positioned on the north platform, and the south platform has an extension to the north (8). Poorly preserved earth and rubble walls indicate additional chambers (4, 6, 7) between the south platform and the enclosure wall.

ENCLOSURE III
(Figures 3.4 and 3.5)

This long (east-west) enclosure is divided into three distinct zones (a-c), each of which is examined separately.

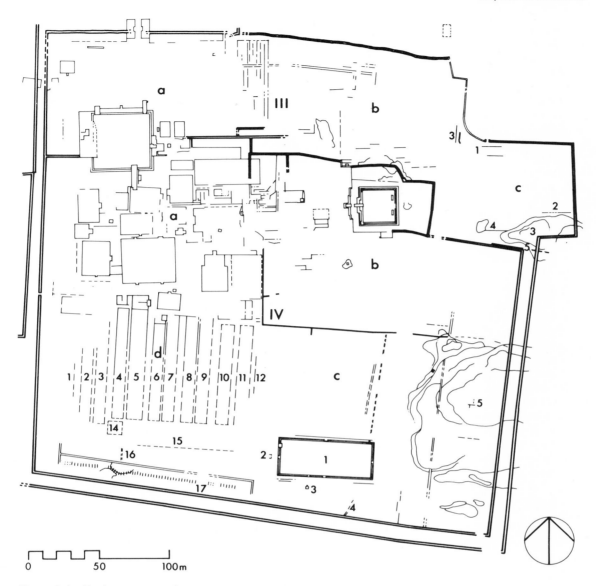

Figure 3.4   Enclosures III and IV.

IIIa is a rectangular area bounded on the north by high walls (common with II) in the middle of which is a large gateway (II-IIIa). On the west, the walls are mostly fallen but can be clearly made out; the east limit of IIIa is indicated by a series of parallel walls and cross walls (21), partly preserved above ground level. IIIa is dominated by the hundred-columned hall (IVa/1) that extends into the enclosure on the south; flights of steps and a staircase provide access to the monument (see Chapter 6). A high wall to the west of the hall separates IIIa from IVa to the south. East of the hundred-columned hall is a gateway (IIIa-IVa), also two parallel enclosure walls extending eastwards (until they collapse in IIIb).

Many features are visible in IIIa. West of the hall are the remains of a platform (1) and scattered chlorite pieces. Different sized tanks (3-5) are seen near the west wall, through which a water conduit (2) passes. Against the north wall is a long platform (6), in front of which is a monolithic trough (7), more than 12m. long. Nearby to the west, a smaller overturned trough (8) is found. East of the gateway, the long platform continues along the north wall with evidence of various walls (9-12). Traces of other walls and plaster floors (13-14) are also found. Against the south wall are the remains of a small shrine (17), wall segments (18-19), and two stone posts (20) with a mortar machine. Long parallel walls (21) (foundations of a colonnaded structure?) define the east boundary of IIIa. Two of these walls may have joined the north and south enclosure walls.

IIIb is an irregular compound, now somewhat obscured by fallen blocks and rubble fill from the excavations in IV. The enclosure is bounded on the north and east by walls partly overlain by modern construction. Most of the original east wall is no longer seen; the connection with IIIc is not apparent. The south limit of IIIb is provided by the enclosure walls (common with IVb) that pass around and over a high rocky outcrop. In the middle of these walls a staircase (later blocked up) leads down into IIIb. Within the enclosure is a wall which appears to form the south side of a long structure (1), which includes the remains of a tank and water conduit, and column footings (2). On the east, traces of the original enclosure wall (3) and a water conduit encased in brick and mortar are visible in the ground. On the south, five parallel wall segments and traces of water courses are found (5). Here, too, is displayed a monolithic door (4). A wall (6) seems to have run northwards from the staircase; to the west is a rocky outcrop cut with horizontal areas and column sockets (7).

IIIc is approximately square, the walls on four sides being incompletely preserved; the link with IIIb to the northwest is also not clear. Near to the west end of the north wall, a small gate (IIIc-XVII) has been buried in the rubble that is piled on the enclosure walls. In the middle of the south side is an entry into the alley that runs east of IV. Traces of basements (1-2, 4), possibly defining platforms, a boulder with regularly cut column sockets and steps (3), and several mortar holes are all found here. From the east, clay pipes set in brick and mortar (5) run along the south wall.

ENCLOSURE IV
(Figures 3.4 and 3.5)

Usually identified as the "king's palace" (Devakunjari 1970, p. 23), this is by far the largest enclosure in the royal centre. Here are found two of the most significant monuments in the capital: the hundred-columned hall (IVa/1), and the great platform (IVb/1). On three sides, IV is bounded by high walls, broken only by a small doorway in the middle of the west side. (Other openings in the walls are for the modern road.) The northern limit of IV is irregularly defined by segments of walls, some of which pass over and around the rocky outcrop onto which the great platform is built. The hundred-columned hall and adjacent gateway open into IIIa to the north; further east, a flight of steps descends into IIIb.

A stone aqueduct, entering the enclosure in the middle of the east side, proceeds (with breaks) into the middle of IV, and then divides into a north and west branch, the latter now mostly fallen. This aqueduct is only one element in a complex system of waterworks (see Chapter 4). It partly divides IV into four unequal quadrants, each of which displays a distinctive character according to the features preserved there. We commence with the northwest quadrant (a), and then proceed in a clockwise direction (b-d).

SUBDIVISION IVa

Only recently has this zone been cleared by the excavators to reveal a dense cluster of square and rectangular structures (see Chapter 6), gateways, aqueducts, drains, tanks, and wells. These define a complex series of narrow alleys and courts, many of which have plaster lining or stone paving. IVa is dominated by the hundred-columned hall (1) in the northwest corner, reached by steps on the east and south (see Chapter 6). Flanking this monument on the east is a gateway (IIIa-IVa) abutted by the north wall of the enclosure. Between the gateway and the hall are six columns with decorated shafts, one of which preserves a bracket with rolled ends (2). To the south are other plainer columns with beams and slabs. Lying all around are fragments of door jambs and threshold pieces. Further south is a second gateway (3), not aligned with the larger example to the north (see Chapter 4). Now mostly ruined, this gateway (3) preserves part of its north-south passageway defined by three basement mouldings. The gateway merges with the stone slabs and steps leading up to the middle of the east side of the hundred-columned hall. Adjoining the gateway are later brick walls creating a bent entrance (4). To the east is a small platform (5) bounded on two sides by a covered drain; this drain runs northwards until it disappears beneath the enclosure walls. To the north of 5 another covered drain runs westwards towards the gateway IIIa-IVa.

A long rectangular court is defined by platforms on the north and east (6), and also on the south (7-8). The high wall on the east is contiguous with the enclosure wall, and runs across the (earlier) rectangular structure to the south (8). This structure preserves most of its basement, and here are found traces of plaster floor, earth and rubble walls (south side), and several column footings. Further east is an open court (9) through which a stone drain passes, descending towards the enclosure walls under which it passes.

Southwest of the hundred-columned hall is a rectangular structure (10) with rows of column footings, earth and rubble walls, and an entrance in the middle of the east side. This structure faces onto an open court with a small well and tank. To the east is an incompletely preserved structure (11) (basement on three sides only), with a small

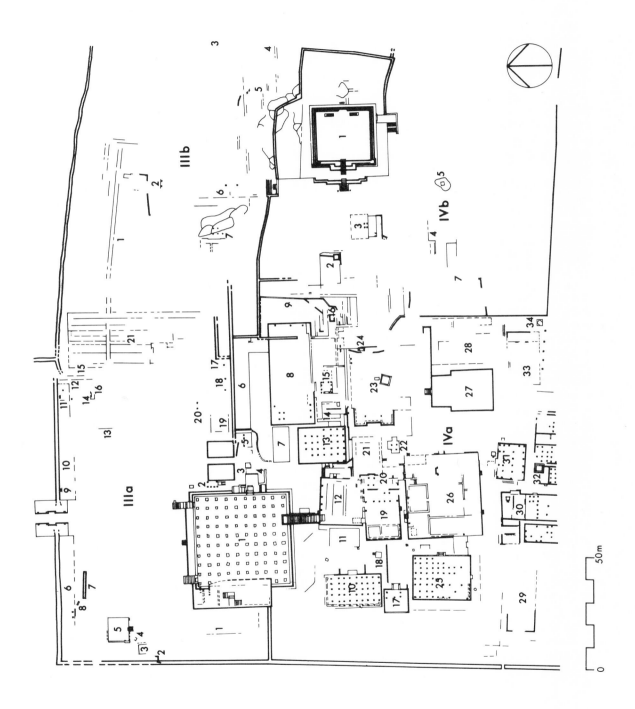

Figure 3.5   Enclosures IIIa-b and IVa-b.

plaster-lined (toilet?) pit at the southwest corner. A narrow stone-paved alley separates 11 from 12, the latter being a squarish structure, divided into two parts by an east-west earth and rubble wall. On the north side column footings suggest a verandah. At the northwest corner a steep flight of steps ascends to the (now lost) upper level of the hundred-columned hall. Cut into the lowest step is a drain. To the north of 12 is an open court with pavement slabs and traces of plaster floor on concrete. Access steps on the east lead into a narrow plaster-lined passageway; on the opposite side are the access steps of 13. This structure is rectangular, with basement mouldings and rows of column footings. A covered drain skirts 13 on the south and west.

East of 13 are the remains of several stone walls (a high north-south wall here was removed by the excavators), finely finished chlorite mouldings (engraved with Kannada numbers), and a small rectangular plaster-lined tank (14). South of these features is a complex network of drains, apparently modified and much adapted. Here, three plaster-lined stone channels at different levels meet. Nearby to the east, twelve columns, and earth and rubble walls, define a square chamber (15). To the south is a long earth and rubble wall. Considerable confusion, with much variation in level, is visible further east. Here are found two stone water channels (one linking up with that in court 9), and fragments of earth and rubble or brick walls, some with plaster adhering. Remnants of plaster floors, one of which defines a small chamber (16), can be seen.

Returning to the west of IVa: structure 17 is square and raised high on four basement mouldings with elephant balustrades on the east. It is clear that the foundation course of 17 is at a much higher level than those of the adjacent structures (10, 25). East of 17 is a courtyard with the remains of a drain, also a small plaster-lined tank with steps (18). On the east, the courtyard is bounded by another structure (19) consisting of a rectangle of basement mouldings (missing on the east), and abutting 12 to the north (at an angle, and also lower). A plaster floor associated with 19 covers the top moulding of 12, indicating the building sequence. In the west of 19 earth and rubble walls create two rooms; to the north is a plaster-lined chamber (bath?) associated with a drain, and overlying 12. Steps are seen on the south. To the east are additional chambers (20) incorporating finely finished chlorite mouldings, column footings, and large fragments of plaster floors. These features appear to face into a court (21) paved with well-dressed chlorite and lime-stone slabs, bounded by stone courses (only partly preserved); to the northeast is a large raised threshold (?). South of this court is an underground chamber (22), entered by a small flight of steps

at the northwest corner (see Chapter 6). The court is limited on the west by a basement moulding with a central projection. To the east, at a slightly lower level, is an adjacent court (23) with traces of plaster flooring. In the middle is a plastered tank. A brick-lined chamber to the north displays evidence of burning. The east edge of this court is marked by fragments of the principal aqueduct, and a small rectangular stone basin (24).

At the southwest corner of IVa is a well-defined rectangular structure (25), with the remains of many column footings, entered by steps in the middle of the east and south sides. Mouldings and carved slabs (?) appear to link 25 with another structure to the east (26). The latter is square, and is the largest structure in IVa except for the hundred-columned hall. Two flights of steps provide access to 26 on both the north and south. Internal chambers are delimited by plaster-faced rubble and earth walls. The structure faces north-wards onto a narrow plaster-lined alley (bounded by 19 and 20); at its east end the alley leads into a court defined by basement mouldings on the east. Two plastered chambers (later) intrude into this space. Some distance to the east is a rectangular structure facing north (27), defined by finely carved basement mouldings with elephant balustrades. A later continuation of two of these mouldings demarcates another rectangular structure (28) to the east, now mostly ruined, but with traces of walls and floor still visible. This structure appears to descend in several layers to the south. The east edge of 28 is flanked by the stone aqueduct.

The south boundary of IVa is not well distinguished. Here protrude the series of colonnades from IVd, interrupted by several (later?) features. These include a series of incomplete basements defining rectangular structures (29, 30), a columned hall (31) with steps on the north next to a small tank, and a plaster-lined brick tank with stepped sides (32). Further east are the stone piers that once supported the west branch of the principal aqueduct (boundary between IVa and d). This aqueduct passes south of several basement mouldings defining a rectangular structure (33). In the extreme southeast corner is a large well with a rotated square opening at the top (34).

SUBDIVISIONS IVb-d

IVb, the northeast quadrant, is dominated by the great platform (1) (see Chapter 6) elevated on a rocky outcrop, the highest point within the enclosure. Reached by flights of steps on the south and west, the platform is surrounded by enclosure walls on the north and east, partly built upon the boulders; here the ground is considerably raised. The blocked-up steps in the north wall leading into IIIb have already been noted; to the west, a segment of wall proceeds southwards (boundary of IVa). Except for several isolated hydraulic features, IVb is comparatively empty. To the northwest is a stone-lined tank and water course (2), bounded on the south by a basement moulding and on the east by a rubble wall. The water course disappears beneath the (unexcavated) ground. The large tank (3) west of the great platform is built of plaster-lined rubble and brick (see Chapter 4). A water conduit enters the tank from the southwest. Traces of basement mouldings (4) indicate the position of a structure (?). Carved into a small rock southwest of the platform is a square basin (5). Near the aqueduct on the west is a fragment of a stone pavement and a plaster floor (6). Outlines of walls are noticeable to the south (7). Towards the east end of IVb, part of a wall proceeds northwards from IVc.

Even more open is the southeast quadrant, IVc, containing the immense rectangular tank (1) and the collapsed remains of an aqueduct leading into its northeast corner (see Chapter 4). West of the tank are traces of a raised chamber (2), while to the south are a well (3) and fragments of a water conduit (4). The east part of this quadrant has a large rocky outcrop, over which passes a partly preserved north-south wall. Steps are here cut into the rock, and, further east, wall fragments define a small structure (5); nearby are several mortar holes. In the northeast corner of the quadrant the aqueduct cuts through a rocky outcrop.

IVd, the southwest quadrant, is still being cleared by the excavators. Unlike the other quadrants — which are cluttered or open — IVd incorporates a series of regularly laid out parallel structures (1-12). These are defined by basements and have numerous column footings still preserved in situ. Pairs of structures face onto long narrow alleys (see Chapter 6). Mortars and quern stones frequently occur here. At their north ends, these structures abut several features in IVa (already noted); at their south ends, however, they appear to be more or less aligned. Here can be discerned the outlines of further structures (13-16). In the south of the quadrant, three walls demarcate a long space flanking the south enclosure wall. Here a covered water course is located (17), partly following a natural crevice (see Chapter 4).

ALLEY SURROUNDING IV

High walls on the east and south define a narrow alley running around the enclosure. On the east, this alley passes over a rocky outcrop. Here, evidence of brick construction may indicate the course of an aqueduct (leading into IV). At the southwest corner the south wall extends westwards to create a wide space; here the walls are represented by only a few courses. The abundance of pottery sherds, roof tiles, and rubble found in this area indicates the original presence of structures. Bounding this zone is a collapsed wall, perhaps supporting an aqueduct. Immediately outside the walls, a sluice regulated the flow of water to the octagonal fountain (see Chapter 7).

West of IV are enclosures V and IX, each bounded on their east side by walls (not continuous, and partly collapsed in IX). Together with the west walls of IV, these define an alley, narrowing as it proceeds northwards. At its north end, the alley is partly blocked by several (later?) structures (linked with II and IXc), and is then terminated by a small doorway in the south enclosure wall of the Ramachandra Temple.

ENCLOSURE V
(Figure 3.6)

This zone is mostly referred to as the "mint" (Longhurst 1917, p. 69; Devakunjari 1970, pp. 30-31), presumably following the description of Abd ar-Razzaq (Major 1857, p. 26). However, no archaeological evidence has yet been discovered to substantiate this identification. To the contrary, the structures revealed by the recent excavations all appear to be palaces and associated features (Thapar 1982, p. 45; Nagaraja Rao 1983, pp. 11-14).

Located west of the north-south alley, V is surrounded on almost all sides by high walls. These define an irregular enclosure with several angles, particularly in the northeast corner and in the middle of the east side where two east-west wall segments occur. On the east, the enclosure is partly defined by a rubble and earth wall; here also is seen a fragment of a layered earth wall. In the middle of its east side, V adjoins IXe and f. Two small openings are found in the south wall of the enclosure, another three are positioned in the east-west wall segments. The other breaks in the walls (north side) are probably not original entrances. Carved on the stone blocks of the walls, both inside and outside, are a number of Vaishnava icons. At the south end of the east wall (north portion, inner face) is a curious elongated figure with a high hat and a dagger; nearby is a standing (royal?) figure with female attendants.

The enclosure is dominated by a large east-facing palace structure (1), complete with basement mouldings, plaster floors, and earth and rubble walls. This structure stands in its own rectangular courtyard defined by parallel (subfloor) stone walls on three sides (see Chapter 6). As the ground falls away to the northwest, these also function as retaining walls incorporating

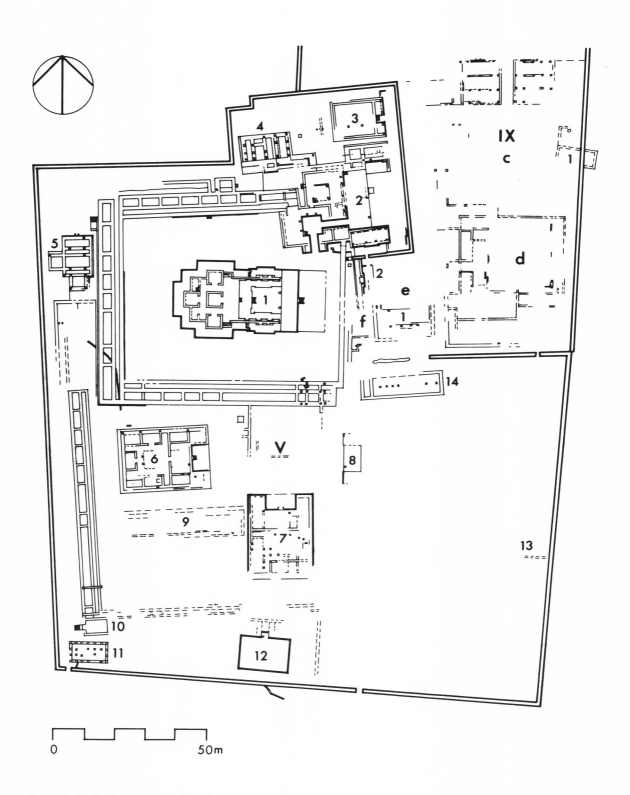

Figure 3.6   Enclosures V and IXc-f.

subfloor drains. On the east is a rubble wall. An entrance complex is found at the northeast corner of the courtyard; this leads to a sequence of chambers and courts to the north (2) (see Chapter 6). Facing east, 2 has a courtyard, bounded on the east and south by the enclosure walls. The courtyard is entered through a circuitous route from a small doorway in these walls to the south (common with IXe). North of 2 is a small palace structure (3) (see Chapter 6), positioned in the extreme northeast corner of the enclosure. West of this feature is an open space with a well; further west is a small structure (4), preserving only its subfloor walls and column footings. Between the outer walls of the courtyard surrounding 1 and the west enclosure walls is another similar north-facing structure (5), at a lower level.

South of 1 are three more or less identical palace structures (6-8), facing into a small court from the west, south and east (see Chapter 6). The east structure has now mostly disappeared. Within the court are traces of walls and a small well. South of 6 is a rectangular area (9), partly bounded by a basement. All of these buildings are contained on three sides by cellular structures consisting of parallel (subfloor) walls (discontinuous at the northwest corner; unexcavated on the south).

In the southwest corner of V, near one of the doorways in the enclosure walls, are a plaster-lined tank with steps on the west (10), and a rectangular columned structure with a plaster-lined floor (11). Entering the latter feature on the south is a small water channel. North of 10, fragments of an aqueduct pass over the parallel walls already noted. In the middle of the south side of the enclosure is a large tank (12) with steps on the north and a water chute on the south. (Parts of a conduit aligned with this spout are visible outside the walls.) The southeast part of V is devoid of any features, and the excavators in the 1970s failed to reveal any building remains here. However, traces of walls (13) are detected on the east. North of 8, and near to the southeast corner of the walls that enclose palace complex 1, is the stone basement of a long rectangular structure (14) with an extension on the west. Of interest here is the line of column footings running down the middle of the building.

ENCLOSURE VI
(Figure 3.7)

Together with the next three enclosures — VII, VIII, and IX — this part of the royal centre is usually collectively labelled as "danaik's enclosure" (Longhurst 1917, p. 87; Devakunjari 1970, pp. 31-33), again following the description of Abd ar-Razzaq (Major 1857, p. 26). Since it is not possible to identify this area with the exclusive

use of a "danaik" or governor, we here describe these enclosures separately.

Approximately rectangular (longer in the east-west direction), enclosure VI is clearly defined by walls on three sides. On the north, where only portions of walls can be made out, VI adjoins VII and VIII. We note discontinuities in the south wall (common with V and XXIII), where a jog is observed, and also the lack of any well-defined northeast corner. (The wall to the north bounding the west part of VI is a modern construction.) Only one original doorway is found (south end of west wall).

The largest feature of VI is the north-facing palace structure (1), of which only the basement survives (see Chapter 6). To the east are two well-preserved Islamic-styled buildings: a two-storeyed octagonal structure (2) and a nine-domed structure open to the north (3) (see Chapter 7). South of these two features are several column footings and stone slabs (4), possibly belonging to a colonnade. To the west, fragments of plaster floors, balustrades, column footings, concrete and basement mouldings define an east-facing palace structure, now mostly destroyed (5). Immediately south are segments of a plaster-lined water channel (6) leading into a large tank (7), the latter partly cut into a natural boulder protruding through the enclosure walls.

The southwest corner of VI now presents a vast pile of stone rubble, partly overgrown. However, here may be discerned lines of parallel walls with mounds that may indicate several cross walls (8); through these walls passes a portion of a water conduit (9). Other walls (10), column footings (11), and large fragments of concrete, plaster floor, and brickwork (12) are also found. Possibly these elements define cellular structures on two sides of an elevated court associated with 1 (compare with V/1).

Another group of buried and overgrown remains is seen north of structures 1-3. Here are found fragments of walls (13); lines of column footings and traces of plaster (14), apparently defining a rectangular structure; and a series of stone foundations, earth and rubble walls, and plaster floor (15), perhaps belonging to another palace structure (?). In this area is a high east-west wall with a deep niche on its north face (16). This wall may once have been coordinated with the nine-domed structure (3). Northeast of 3 are other segments of wall (17). The east end of VI is now buried under dirt and rubble fill from the recent excavations in V.

ENCLOSURE VII
(Figure 3.8)

This long (north-south) enclosure is bounded on three sides by high walls; on the south it is open and adjoins VI. The east wall (common with VIII) jogs slightly; at its north end is a low and narrow doorway. The north wall (abutting the east wall) has a break in the middle (originally an entrance?). The south portion of the west wall is modern.

VII is today dominated by the Islamic-styled multidomed structure (1) built upon the northwest corner of the enclosure walls (see Chapter 7). In the middle of VII is a ruined square structure (2) with finely dressed masonry (lower courses), apparently open to the west. Of interest here are the unusual engaged columns at the corners of the building, and the overturned carved threshold and jambs; the interior is now filled with collapsed masonry. At the southeast corner of VII, where the ground level abruptly rises to meet that of enclosures V and VI, is a small Islamic-styled structure (3). This may have been a gateway with a pyramidal roof (see Chapter 7).

Running along the north side of the enclosure against the walls are a row of column footings (4) and a modern raised platform. A wall containing column footings is found outside the north wall (flanking an entry?). South of this wall, columns, slabs, and part of another wall are visible (6). To the southeast is a remnant of a water course. Running parallel to the east boundary is a wall (5), preventing direct access to the entry already noted. In the middle of the north half of the enclosure many features are observed, some elevated on a rocky shelf, others partly buried in the mass of stone rubble. Here are seen the foundations of thick walls (7, 9, 11, 12), regularly aligned column footings (10, 14), fragments of concrete and plaster floor (15), long slabs of dressed stones (13), and, possibly also parts of a collapsed entryway (8). In addition, natural boulders are cut with column sockets and mortar holes.

Around the square structure (2) are many collapsed column blocks, and also traces of a wall (16, 17) (defining a passageway?). East of 2, more concrete and column footings (18), wall segments (19), and displaced basement mouldings (20) are discerned in the rubble.

ENCLOSURE VIII
(Figure 3.8)

This zone is approximately square, being limited by high walls on the north and west, and partly on the east; only a small portion of the wall on the south survives. The jog in the west wall (common with VII) and the small doorway at its north end have been noted above. A number of earth and rubble walls within the enclosure, now only incompletely preserved, divide the zone into several subdivisions. These walls create a highly complicated sequence of gateways, pas-

sageways, and courts, with many changes in direction. The ultimate destination of this circuitous route may have been the east-facing palace structure (f/1), the largest feature in the enclosure. This palace displays a series of plain and sculptured basement mouldings and ascending floor levels (see Chapter 6). A second destination may have been another similar structure to the southwest (h/1). Remains of stone foundations, column footings, and plaster floors in other parts of this enclosure indicate another palace structure (c/1).

VIII is entered in the middle of its east side through a gateway (VIIIa-IXa), connected with IXa to the east. The gateway incorporates projecting colonnades; the east-west passageway is defined by basement mouldings (see Chapter 4). The long tapering first court (a) is bounded on the north and east by the principal enclosure walls; on the west are earth and rubble walls. Abutting the walls at the northeast corner is a raised platform with projecting balconies and several extant piers (a/1). This structure is reached by a long flight of steps; though now mostly collapsed, this building appears to belong to the series of Islamic-styled buildings (see Chapter 7). To the west are the outlines of a rectangular structure (2), now mostly vanished, and fragments of a water conduit (3). At its south end, this court is bounded by a colonnade of column footings with a central north-south passageway, now mostly lacking its basement. These features comprise a gateway (a-b) leading into a small second court (b).

Court (b) is demarcated by partly collapsed earth and rubble walls on the east and south. On the west is a complex gateway (b-c) with an east-facing porch, bounded by raised colonnades. The east-west passageway is defined by basement mouldings and leads into a square third court (c). Facing into (c) from the south is a badly ruined palace structure (1), fragments of which are visible. Here, broken brick merlons (original parapet?) are scattered on the surface. Remains of a brick tower with a stepped outline lie overturned in the courtyard. Nearby occurs another brick structure, possibly part of an aqueduct. The raised area to the west (2) displays mouldings and an east-facing central projection. Remains of earth and rubble walls are seen on three sides.

An opening on the north provides access to a fourth court (d), bounded by earth and rubble walls. Here another complex entrance is seen on the west. This incorporates a porch on the front (east) with a raised colonnade and an east-west passageway lined with mouldings, and a plastered floor. This passageway leads into a small square fifth court (e), defined at least on three sides by basement mouldings with column footings. No doubt, from here it was possible to continue into the (sixth) court (f) to the north, in which the

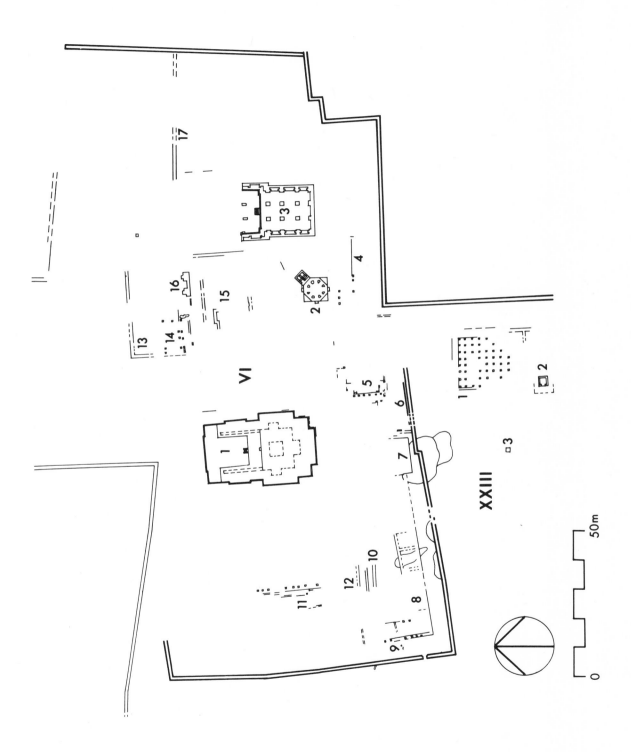

Figure 3.7   Enclosures VI and XXII.

large palace (1) stands; but nothing is now seen of any communicating route.

Structure f/1 is surrounded on four sides by earth and rubble walls, mostly collapsed on the north and unaligned with the main enclosure boundaries. North of this complex are fragments of a water channel (g/1), small rings of brickwork (2) (for plants or trees — note the proximity of 1), moulded stone slabs (3), and a small area of rubble and plaster floor (4). A wall (5) cuts off direct access to the small doorway to the west. The southwest part of VIII (h) consists of a number of mounds, partly overgrown. Buried features are indicated by stone rubble, concrete, and plaster.

ENCLOSURE IX
(Figures 3.6 and 3.8)

This zone is located between the east boundaries of V, VI, and VIII, and the west walls of I, the Ramachandra Temple complex, and the alley to the south. This long (north-south) enclosure actually comprises a series of five courts (a-e), connected by gateways, providing a transition from I (northeast) to V (southwest). This transition is accompanied by a progression from open to confined spaces, the gateways and courts becoming increasingly complex and elaborate (see Chapter 4).

The first court (a) is bounded on the east by a massive wall (common with Ia) and the west wall of the temple complex; on the west are the earth and rubble walls of VIIIa and b, now partly collapsed. To the north, this court is limited by a wall (continuing that north of Ia), now mostly buried. At the north end of the east wall is a gateway (Ia-IXa), noticeably unaligned with a gateway in the west wall (VIIIa-IXa). Abutting the south end of the temple enclosure wall are two small shrines (1, 2); one of these frames an icon carved on the outer enclosure wall (see Chapter 5). Nearby is a small well (3). The south limit of the court is represented by a segment of wall, in front (north) of which is a pile of rubble, including fragments of overturned basements, columns, and ceiling slabs, concrete, and even a pedestal (4-7); these features are all that remains of a row of small shrines (facing north?). This area in the south of IXa is also remarkable for the large quantities of iron slag lying on the surface; iron ore is also present. At the southwest of the court — which at this point turns westwards — is an elevated gateway (a-b). This consists of a rectangular structure with central chambers (only partly preserved) through which passes a north-south passageway lined with mouldings.

This gateway leads into the rectangular second court (b), limited on the east by the alley wall, and on the south and west by enclosure walls (common with V and VI). No features are observed within the court, though worked fragments and chips of chlorite are common. To the southeast is another, larger gateway (b-c), also elevated above the court. This gateway consists of a columned structure (originally 10 by 4 columns) with a central north-south passageway flanked by mouldings. The periphery of this gateway is also partly defined by mouldings; between some of the column footings are earth and rubble foundations. To either side of the gateway are rubble mounds (traces of walls?) separating this court from the next.

The third court (c) is smaller and approximately square. Like that to the north, (c) is defined on the east by the alley wall and on the west by the enclosure walls (common with V). Within the debris of the court, column footings and concrete fragments are seen on the west (2, 3). Massive basements and walls define two chambers on the east (1), raised above the level of the court. These chambers are built into the walls and protrude into the alley on the west, narrowing the passage along this route. Within these chambers are a large circular stone disc and a column capital. The south limit of this court is provided by a gateway (c-d), now mostly ruined, with a north-south passageway (mouldings missing). This gateway forms part of the colonnaded structure defining the fourth court (d).

Court (d) is now a mass of fallen stones; a close examination of this debris, however, reveals the basic plan. Here an open square area is surrounded on four sides by colonnades raised on two levels; between the column footings are traces of earth and rubble foundations. The gateway on the north has already been noted; in the middle of the west side is another gateway (d-e) consisting of a raised colonnade on three sides (with basement mouldings) and a central east-west passageway (partly defined by mouldings). South of (d) is a raised extension defined by earth and rubble walls, and by plaster on concrete floors. A water conduit runs through the middle of this structure. The south periphery wall cuts off court (d) from the enclosure walls, where there is a small doorway (common with V). Here a narrow passage (connected with e) leads towards the doorway.

West of (d) is the fifth court (e) leading into V (through an opening to the north in the enclosure walls). Court (e) is bounded on the south by a large structure (1) surrounded by walls on three sides and open to the north. Characteristic of this structure are the changes in level (stepping down to the north), marked by finely carved mouldings and column footings. Court (e) is limited on the west by an earth and rubble wall with a stone basement and a central projection in which the lower portion of a plaster-lined niche is preserved (2). (This niche appears to be axially aligned with

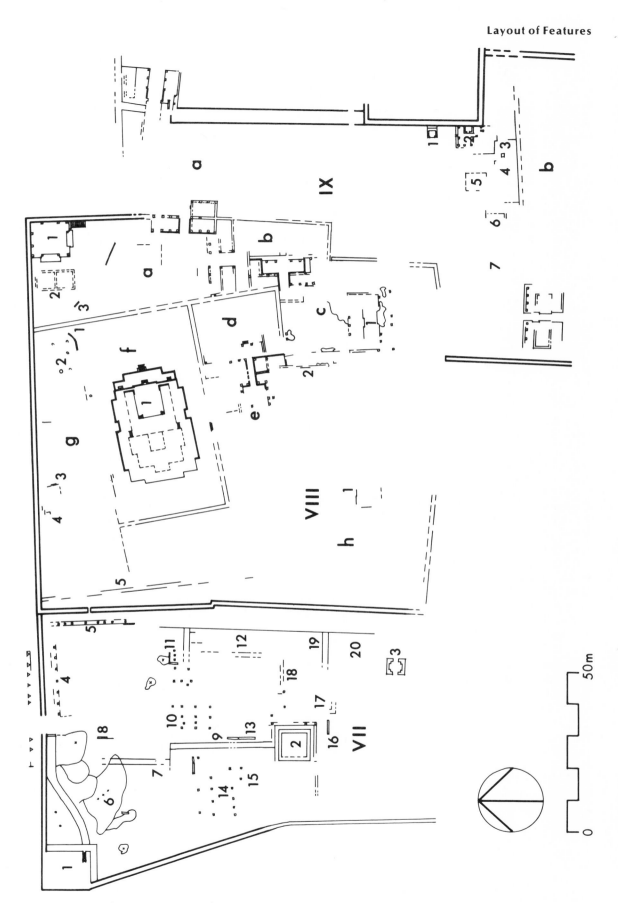

Figure 3.8   Enclosures VII, VIII and IXa.

the gateway d-e.) Outlines of another niche are found at the north end of the wall. Finely carved chlorite mouldings set into the ground seem to be coordinated with the opening (as a threshold?).

West of (e) is a long tapering chamber (f), bound on the west by another rubble wall (common with the courtyard of V/1). At the north end of this zone is a doorway (leading into V/2), in front of which is a plaster-lined pit (1). To the south, remains of an elevated plastered floor are seen (2), and there is a small chamber with a bath defined by plaster-lined brickwork (3). Further south is part of an earth wall (common with V).

North of VII, VIII, and IXa, and south of the rocky hill (X), is the west alley linking XI (east) and XXV (west); here passes a modern dirt road. From this alley, passages lead through natural rocky breaks in the hill up to Xa and c. Evidence of several features, including a well, a shrine, and a two-storeyed structure built against the hillside, is found on the north side of the alley. On the south side, another well and also a wall with column footings (in front of the probable entry into VII) are seen.

ENCLOSURES X-XII

These three zones are located, in part, on the high rocky hill and associated ridges that occur north of the middle of the royal centre. Enclosure X includes the top of the hill and the various natural terraces that descend to the east, north, and west. The east part of X comprises a lower levelled terrace (a) connected with XI to the south by a ramp. A gap between large boulders leads to a second upper terrace (b) bounded on three sides by rocks. In the middle is a declivity (tank?), limited on the south and north by boulders and earth infill. A path between high boulders leads to a small terrace (c) on the south which overlooks the west alley.

A ramp from (b) ascends to a convex expanse of sheet rock (d) (to the north) on which sits a large boulder. A complex of walls creates terraces (for structures?) on the southeast; here the presence of a building is indicated by 2 by 4 square column sockets cut into the rock. Rows of small square holes on the peripheries of this feature may have anchored a terrace wall. Mortars, lamp holes, etched game boards, and a small inscription are also found here. The same ramp ascends to a staircase which leads to a terrace (e) above (b) to the west. Here occur the rubble walls of at least two structures. From (e) a path passes through a narrow rocky gap to the summit of the hill (f). There is evidence that this gap was blocked and a ladder led to the top of a large boulder on one side. This uppermost area has segments of walls on all sides, accentuating the

steep drop. In the south half are three circular structures (granaries?) — all greater than 10m. in diameter — consisting of foundation stones (with an upper beehive structure?). Steps lead down into the depression inside two of these structures. Nearby, the tops of the sheet rock and boulders are carved with sockets for three structures (the largest consisting of 7 by 3 sockets).

Below (f) to the east is a narrow shelf (g) with evidence of structures; a small shrine occurs amid boulders on the west. Below (f) to the north are two terraces. The higher area (h) has several mortars but no evidence of any structures. No path is visible linking this terrace with (f) above; however, a ramp between boulders descends to (i) below. This area (i) has fortification walls on its west, north, and east sides. A square bastion guards a narrow entry leading down to the terraces of XXVII to the north. In addition to several mortars, there is evidence of structures and a shrine on (i).

South and east of X, and mostly confined to the lower level, is enclosure XI. This zone is bounded on the south by segments of walls and a doorway already noted (common with Ia). On its east side, XI is limited by a wall which jogs, demarcating the north alley (road N1). The north limit of XI is provided by walls which abut rocky outcrops and follow a high ridge. On the west, an earth and rubble wall appears to have extended between and over several large boulders which rise to the south. A wall divides the west half (a) from the east half (b). Long rectangular mounds (1, 3, 11) appear to have supported structures; these occur on the high ground to the west, north, and east of (a) adjacent to the enclosure walls. An interior wall extends to the southeast from 1, diverting access from the west alley towards the south wall of (a). From the northwest corner of (a) begins the path (Xa-XIa) that leads up to the various terraces of X. Despite the sharp rise in level, no stone steps or ramps are preserved in place. However, worn and polished slabs slipped from their original position suggest that some such construction occurred here. Adjacent to the path and north of 1 is a boulder carved with images (Hanuman, Ganesha) and sockets which suggest a shrine (2). In the middle of (a) are three circular structures (7, 8, 9); on the boulders and sheet rock, holes and sockets indicate other features (5, 10).

In XIb, rubble and fallen blocks cover the surfaces. Walls of a large structure (1) are found immediately south of large boulders on the north side. A number of courts, platforms, and chambers appears to have been located along the east and south sides. The pedestal for a Vaishnava image is found in a ruined chamber (shrine?) in the southeast corner.

A wall upon a ridge separates XI from XII. From the low point in the northeast, the ground rises to the ridge to the south and, more steeply, to X on the west. Several natural terraces to the south and west, with evidence for structures, are defined (and fortified?) by low walls of blocks and rubble. Two long, discontinuous walls bound the north side of the enclosure. Except at its north end, no wall distinguishes the enclosure from the north alley. Here are found courts, platforms, and chambers. High outcrops, with segments of retaining walls in between, bound the east side at its south end. Further north, a wall extends from a large isolated boulder to the north wall.

Traces of walls (oriented approximately northeast-southwest) are buried beneath the fields in the north half of the enclosure; these may indicate different building complexes. Thick walls with column footings of a substantial (two-storeyed) structure (b/1) are located in the northeast corner overlooking the north entry of the alley.

The north alley between XI and XII (west) and XIII (east) is clearly defined by continuous enclosure walls on its east side, and by segments of walls and structures on its west side. The alley marks the route of the north road (N1). About midway along this alley — at a point coinciding with the wall dividing XI and XII — is a gateway, built in two phases. Still complete with a passageway flanked by mouldings, it also preserves platforms with column footings on the inner (south) side.

ENCLOSURE XIII
(Figure 3.3)

This zone is currently occupied by the tourist canteen compound. Approximately rectangular, though slightly tapering (narrower on the north), this enclosure is defined by walls, well-preserved on the west and north, partly buried on the east (common with XVa), and discontinuous on the south. A modern dirt road cuts through sections of the walls, obscuring the northeast corner. Apparently only one gateway provides access into the enclosure; this example (1a-XIII) is located in the west segment of the south wall. Here a north-south passageway is defined by mouldings and a threshold stone; to the north are a pair of gate posts and a stone trough. On either side are platforms with traces of walls (extended on the west) indicating small chambers, possibly even a shrine (a pedestal is located here). West of the gateway is an area (1) defined by a wall on the north. To the east, another structure (3) is contained by wall fragments. Further east, an L-shaped structure with several chambers (4) can be made out; this incorporates an entrance on the west leading into a court (5). Within the court are the remains of a small square tank defined

by curved slabs (partly buried by the modern road). Another pair of gate posts (10) is seen near the north enclosure walls; nearby are more than a dozen grinding stones for mortar (11). Close to the northeast corner are the outlines of a rectangular feature (12) with walls. A water channel (13) enters the enclosure in the middle of the east side; to the north of this channel is a gap (entry?) in the walls with brick construction.

ENCLOSURE XIV
(Figure 3.9)

Though popularly known as the "zenana" (Longhurst 1917, pp. 78-84; Devakunjari 1970, pp. 33-36), no historical evidence links this zone with women of the court. XIV consists of an irregular enclosure defined by walls on all sides, parts of which are modern reconstructions (see dated blocks on south wall). The east and west walls are comparatively straight, though unparallel; the north wall contains a number of turns creating four intermediate angles between the extreme northeast and northwest corners. On the south the wall is partly curved; the buttresses found here being modern features. This highly distinctive configuration is partly explained by several structures both inside and outside the walls (including two towers) which are clearly earlier than the walls which wrap around them. Access to the enclosure is through small doorways, one each in the east and west walls and three in the north wall. The openings are much rebuilt. (The small gap in the modern stonework of the south wall, serving today as a doorway, may not be original.) Outside the walls, especially to the north and northeast (XXIX and XXX), are related structures.

Within XIV the ground is not level. The highest part coincides with the rocky outcrop to the northeast; from here the ground slopes downwards on three sides. At one of the angles in the north enclosure wall there is a depression (tank?) partly filled with collapsed blocks; traces of walls occur along the east side of the depression. Other rocky outcrops are seen at the southwest.

Various structures stand within the enclosure. Near to the middle is a two-storeyed Islamic-styled pavilion (1) (see Chapter 7). West of this building, near the southwest corner of the enclosure, is a rectangular tank inside which stands a palace structure (2) (see Chapter 6). The heaped rubble on three sides of the tank may be the remains of a surrounding colonnade (?). Dominating the enclosure is the elaborately decorated stone basement of a large north-facing palace structure (3) (see Chapter 6). Evidence of a possible colonnade occurs to the west, while traces of walls indicate a complex of ruined chambers to the east. Close to the northwest corner is a rectangular Islamic-styled building

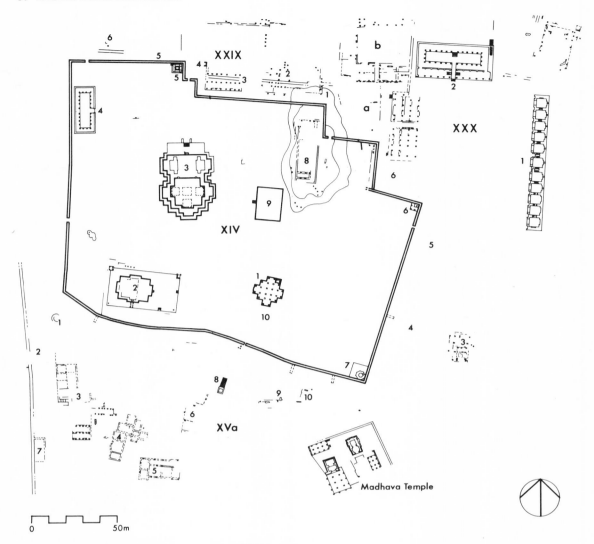

Figure 3.9   Enclosures XIV, XVa, XXIX and XXX.

with a gabled masonry roof (4); the identification of this structure is uncertain (see Chapter 7).

Towers are positioned inside three corners of the walls (see Chapter 7). In one angle of the walls north of palace structure 3 is a square tower (5), while at the extreme northeast corner is another square tower (6), now ruined; an octagonal tower (7) is positioned at the southeast corner. Towers 5 and 7 are clearly earlier than the enclosure walls which abut their outer plastered surfaces; in contrast, tower 6 is built into the walls. These towers overlook the zones outside XIV, through which several principal routes of the city pass (see Chapter 4).

Built upon a rocky outcrop within XIV are the remains of another north-facing palace structure (8), of which only traces are seen (see Chapter 6). The location of this structure partly explains

the angled corner in the nearby walls. Southwest of 8 is a large rectangular tank (9) with steps on the west. The sides of the tank are slightly stepped (renovations?) with stones projecting outward from the walls; the floor is mostly bedrock. Piles of rubble, both within and outside XIV near the northeast and southeast corners, appear to be from collapsed walls. The small well (10) south of the two-storeyed pavilion has an earlier (lower) portion. Other visible features — water channel, circles of stones around the trees, and roads — are modern.

ENCLOSURE XV
(Figures 3.3 and 3.9)

South of XIV and east of XIII is enclosure XV, through which the northeast road (NE) passes.

On the south, XV is bounded by walls common with XVI, but no limit is seen on the east. The zone is characterized by mounds and depressions in which traces of various structures can be made out.

In XVa — the north and west parts of the enclosure — the remains of many buried structures are discovered. To the northwest (near the southwest corner of XIV) is the outline of a circular structure (Islamic-styled tower?) (1). South of this feature are fragments of rubble walls and plaster floors (2), partly exposed by the modern path. Portions of several other structures (3-6) are found to the south and east. Here, earth and rubble walls, and regularly aligned column footings appear to divide the structures into small chambers. Noticeable is the lack of alignment between these different features, though there may have been some interconnecting courts (between 3 and 4, for example). One chamber in 3 has sloping water channels which enter through the north wall; this may have functioned as a bath or toilet. Adjacent to the west wall of XV (common with XIII) is a rectangular structure (7). In the middle of the north side is a stepped well (8), the lower portions of which are original. East of the well are traces of a platform preserving concrete and plaster floors; basement remains are also visible (9). Column bases and wall outlines (10) are preserved near the southeast corner of XIV. To the east is the Madhava Temple complex, oriented southeast to face the principal northeast road (NE).

XVb comprises the northeast road and its flanking structures (a continuation of Ic). On the west, this zone is limited by a substantial wall (common with Ic), in which a gateway (Ic-XVb) is positioned. Small shrines and temples line both sides of the road (see Chapter 5). On the north is a colonnade (1) incorporated into an elaborate structure, now collapsed; 2 represents an area defined by mouldings interrupted by a doorway. North of 1 and 2 is an east-facing shrine with a columned hall (3), to the north of which are traces of a wall against which naga stones are placed. A doubled-halled temple (4) is located further east. South of the road are several ruined temples (6, 7, 10) and part of a double-storeyed colonnade (11). Associated with these structures is a small tank (8) and a water conduit (9) encased in a wall. 6-8 are bounded on the south by an enclosure wall (separating XVb from XVI); south of 10 are two north-facing walls. South of 11 is another wall.

No other features are visible along the road until the partly buried Ellamma Temple (5), still in worship, is encountered (see Chapter 5). Nearby to the southeast is a large tank (12), the stepped sides of which are badly collapsed. Like other tanks of this size, it has an L-shaped entrance. Further south several features are discerned in a dirt track; these include portions of rubble walls (13).

ENCLOSURES XVI-XIX

XVI is located south of XVb, east of II, and north of IIIb; it is, however, separated from these last two zones by the southwest alley marking the route of the south road (S1a). Traces of walls of structures can be observed along the west side of the alley; here, one wall partly blocks the passage. A Hanuman image is carved in the west wall facing the east extension of the alley (shrine?). The original walls of XVI are best preserved at the east and west. Few features are seen within XVI, but rubble, and fragments of stone mouldings — reused in the surrounding (modern) walls — tiles, and pottery sherds indicate many vanished structures. In the northeast corner are the outlines of four rectangular features, south of which are large column footings; nearby is a stone trough. Another rectangular feature is seen to the northwest. Near the southeast corner is part of a rubble wall that once supported an aqueduct, a broken fragment of which is still seen. The platform with stone posts to the south is new, but the adjacent water conduit (?) may be original.

South of the east part of XVI, and north and east of IIIc, is enclosure XVII, bounded in places by modern walls; further south is XVIII, limited in part on the south by the remains of an aqueduct. This aqueduct appears to have turned northward where traces are found on the east, north (11), and west (2) sides of a fortified hill. Northwest of the hill, the aqueduct passes by a tank (1) into which water could be diverted. Remains of an earthenware pipe lead westward from the tank, through the enclosure wall where they link with IIIc/5. The aqueduct is buried at the south end of a small valley, but probably led through the east wall of the alley surrounding IV (where traces of brick construction are visible). A well (3) occurs south of 1. At the top of the hill are the remains (long slab basements) of a rectangular structure (7). Below, to the east and north, are the remains of retaining and defensive walls. Exposed areas of sheet rock, particularly northwest of 7, display various steps, mortars, channels, lamps, and a crudely etched linga.

The area bounded on the north and east by an aqueduct, carried in part on rubble walls, constitutes enclosure XIX; on the south, the lowest stone courses of a wall can be made out. On the west side, on an elevated outcrop, occur remnants of a concrete floor and rubble walls (1). To the east and south, steps, mortars and grooves, and footings for walls (2, 3) have been cut into the rock. Remains of walls and shallow mounds indicate structures (platforms?) (4, 5) in low ground to the south of the hill. Sheet rock and small boulders in the middle of the enclosure are carved with various features (6-11). Here have been piled worn blocks of a pavement (road?); here also occurs a square, plaster-lined brick tank (12). A wall (13) extending northward from the south enclosure wall may indicate an entry into the zone. In three large modern pits (middle of the east half; southeast corner) large expanses of thick concrete slabs, plastered floors, sub-floor foundations, and footing blocks have been exposed (16-22). Walls and footings (23, 24) are also evident on the surface north of the largest pit. A modern wall and dirt track separate these features from the partly collapsed aqueduct (25). Segments of fallen rubble walls extend into the enclosure from the aqueduct.

ENCLOSURES XX-XXII

XX comprises the area between the south boundary of XIX and the fortification walls of the royal centre. This zone is dominated by the Islamic-styled square water pavilion (1) surrounded by a deep water channel (see Chapter 7). Some distance to the east is a small cubic building (2) now much restored and filled in; this has been identified as a "water tower" (?) (Devakunjari 1970, pp. 40-41). A partly buried structure (3) abuts the angle formed by the north wall (common with XIX) and west wall (common with the alley surrounding IV).

Located between the alley skirting the south of IV and the fortification walls is enclosure XXI. A small gateway is found in the fortifications (see Chapter 4), north of which is a rectangular platform. Through this zone, and also XXII to the west, passes a modern metalled road. The only feature noted here is a trench, more than 20m. long, flanked by horizontal chlorite slabs carved with circular depressions (dishes?). This feature is locally known as the "bhojana-shala" or eating hall (Devakunjari 1970, p. 43).

Enclosure XXII is continuous with XXI, and is bounded on the north by partially collapsed walls, and on the south and west by fortifications. Near to the modern road several features are seen, including the Islamic-styled octagonal fountain (1) (see Chapter 7). East of the fountain is a raised platform (2) in which earthenware pipes are embedded in thick brick and concrete. North of the platform is a wall along which runs a water channel; the latter leads into a plaster-lined chamber with channels (sluice gates?) (3). Running north from here is a collapsed wall (once supporting an aqueduct?). Due north of the fountain is a pile of brick, concrete, and plaster debris

(4); possibly this is a ruined Islamic-styled structure (fragments of brick and mortar arches, vaults, etc., are seen). Throughout this zone, rubble, sherds, and roof tiles are found.

ENCLOSURES XXIII-XXV

Though XXIII is bounded on three sides by walls (common with V, VI, and XXII), there appears to be no direct communication between these three enclosures and XXIII. At its southeast corner, an opening leads into an alley flanking V on the south (contained within thick walls). No boundary is visible on the west. Mounds of rubble and fragments of basement mouldings throughout the zone indicate numerous ruined structures. Near the northeast corner is an open columned structure (1) consisting of 8 by 8 columns, with surrounding mouldings (incompletely preserved). South of 1 are a small west-facing shrine (2) and traces of rubble walls (3). Some distance to the west is a small well (4).

XXIV is located west of VI and now consists of mounds of rubble partly under cultivation. To the north, a (modern) water channel flows through the zone separating it from XXV.

XXV is separated by (partly modern) walls from VII to the east, and VI to the southeast. The mounds here are thickly overgrown, and cultivation obliterates many original features. Even so, two temples (3, 4), now mostly buried, are located at the east end. The north part of the enclosure is partly cut off from XXVI to the north by rocky outcrops; here, too, passes a modern dirt road. The west of the zone is dominated by the Virupaksha Temple complex (1), entered through a towered gateway (see Chapter 5). To the east of the temple is a recently excavated palace complex (2) (see Chapter 6). The limit of XXV on the west appears to coincide with a modern metalled road and high earthen mounds (washed out fill from fortification walls?). It is not clear if the tank northwest of the temple was located outside the walls.

ENCLOSURES XXVI-XXVIII

Together with part of XXV, XXVI has been recently labelled the "noblemen's palace area" by the excavators currently working here (Nagaraja Rao 1983, p. 14). Rocky outcrops partly separate this zone from XXV to the south; similar boulders are found on the southeast (coinciding with the west side of X) and the west. A gateway is located some distance to the north, flanked by traces of fortification walls, probably the north limit of the enclosure. A road (N2) extends northward to another gate in the wall of the urban core, and southward to XXV. Throughout XXVI are large mounds; here are visible the outlines of several structures, enclosure walls, alleys, and doorways. One large north-facing palace complex (1) has already been exposed (see Chapter 6). Other complexes are currently being excavated. Southwest of 1 is a small temple (2); other sacred structures are found dotted over the zone (3-6) (see Chapter 5).

XXVII is located north of the rocky hill in the royal centre (X, XII); XXVIII occurs to the north of XIII. The north boundaries of XXVII and XXVIII are indicated by fragments of fortification walls. Between XXVII and XXVIII passes the north road (N1), marked by the alignment of several shrines and the alley (between XI-XII and XIII) to the south. In general, both these zones are deeply buried and thickly overgrown, though the foundations of many structures can be traced, especially on the south. Several buried shrines are situated in XXVII (2-6), also one well-preserved temple (1) (see Chapter 5), east of which passes the road (N1). Large structures are indicated by rubble walls in the southeast angle of XXVIII (adjacent to XIII and XIV).

ENCLOSURE XXIX
(Figure 3.9)

Directly north of XIV, XXIX includes features closely linked with XIV according to various doorways in the walls. On the north, XXIX is bounded by traces of (fortification?) walls, and by segments of walls and platforms that line an east-west road. A large columned structure is found at the southeast corner of the enclosure. A central east-west passageway lined with mouldings (many displaced) indicates that this structure is a gateway (XXIXa-XXX). Most of the 4 by 12 column footings of this gateway are still preserved, sometimes to a height of more than 2m., suggesting that the floor was considerably raised (possibly in two storeys). On the west, basement mouldings and a flight of steps are preserved; elephant balustrades (badly smashed) are seen at the northeast. This gateway leads westwards into a court (a) bounded on the north by a second gateway (a-b) with a north-south passageway. Gateway (a-b) has a series of mouldings and several column footings. On the east side of the gate, traces of rubble walls outline several chambers; these abut a north-south wall demarcating the east limit of the enclosure (west of the rectangular structure, XXX/2). Further north is a second large square court (b), partly defined by mouldings and probably entered in the middle of the west side.

Close to one of the north corners of XIV are collapsed blocks, overturned basements, and traces of plaster floors (1); these may have formed the west limit of the first court (a). Running westwards from 1 is a (modern?) rubble wall

passing through a rectangular columned structure (2), where many footings are seen (much displaced). Another similar structure (3) — with regularly aligned (8 by 3) column footings and a central east-west wall — is located further west. (The high footings may indicate double-storeyed buildings.) Northwest of 3 is a ruined Islamic-styled structure (4), possibly a gateway; we note that directly to the south of 4 is a doorway into XIV. Further west, on the north face of the enclosure walls of XIV, is a curious feature (5). Here the exterior plaster coating of the wall is interrupted by a high tapering outline with a curved top representing an abutting north-south wall, now vanished. Again to the west are traces of another wall (6), with fragments of rubble and brickwork nearby. The presence in the debris of mortared masonry suggests an Islamic-styled vaulted structure.

ENCLOSURES XXX-XXXI
(Figure 3.9)

These zones are located to the northeast of XIV. XXX consists of a great open space, possibly reserved for military displays, bounded on the east by the stables (1) and on the north by a rectangular structure (2). Both these Islamic-styled buildings face onto the court (see Chapter 7). On the west, XXX is delimited by the gateway (XXIXa-XXX) already described. South of this feature is a large depression (6) (tank?) contained by two walls of XIV (northeast corner), and now filled in with fallen stones. (Of interest here are the carvings on the outer faces of the enclosure walls — fighters with swords and daggers, and Rama and Sita enthroned, with Lakshmana, Hanuman, and Sugriva in devotion.) The south side of the court is open, except for a large north-south mound (3) with abundant traces of column footings, wall foundations, basement mouldings, concrete, and rubble. This is all that remains of a north-facing (palace?) structure. Surrounding this mound at its south end is a depression filled with piles of displaced rubble and concrete fragments. West and northwest of 3 are two more depressions with structural remains (4, 5), for which no overall plan can be determined. In 5, (arched?) stone fragments are set into mortar, and traces of plaster floor are visible. At its northeast corner, XXX appears to be cut off by an east-west wall.

Many structures of XXXI — further to the northeast — can be made out. Feature 1 is a complex including a columned building with traces of mouldings and plaster floors, as well as a tank at the northeast corner. (This complex is located north of XXX/1.) Further structures extend to the north and east, where column footings and rubble walls are found. Also belonging to XXXI are several shrines to the north, now partly buried (see Chapter 5).

4. BOUNDARIES AND ROUTES

Walls, Gateways, Roads, and Waterworks

Having described the different zones of the city and the various enclosures of the royal centre, we now concentrate on those elements that control the movement of people, animals, goods, and even water. In examining the boundaries and routes of the royal centre, we discover significant architectural differences between peripheral elements (fortifications and defensive entrances) and interior elements (enclosure walls and connecting gateways). Our study of these walls, gateways, and doorways helps to reconstruct the original routes of movement into the middle of the capital, as well as the paths of communication linking the different zones. Also considered here is the fragmentary evidence of an extensive hydraulic scheme.

FORTIFICATION WALLS
(Figure 4.1)

As has already been noted, the royal centre at Vijayanagara is defined by a ring of walls — the innermost circuit — clearly preserved on the south, traceable on the east, but hardly visible elsewhere. In most respects, these walls resemble those containing the urban core — the second circuit — and also those fragmentary arcs separating the sub-urban centres. Characteristic of all these fortifications is the massive masonry construction with a slightly tapering profile on the outer face. The stone blocks are actually wedge-shaped, only the outer surfaces being dressed. The interior of the walls is of earth, usually packed with rubble and now partly eroded. An earth embankment probably formed the inner face. South of the royal centre the stone walls stand to a height of more than 6m. Here may be observed the regular rectangular blocks, and the relatively well finished joints; no mortar is anywhere employed. At intervals, square or rectangular bastions project outwards.

Almost all the visitors to the city remark on these solid fortifications. Domingo Paes notes the "massive stonework" of the walls, while Fernao Nuniz observes the fortresslike towers on the bastions, between which communication was possible (Sewell 1900, pp. 253, 331). Few traces of these lookout towers are seen today.

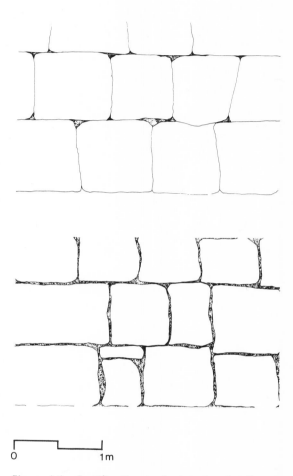

Figure 4.1   Fortification walls, jointing details.

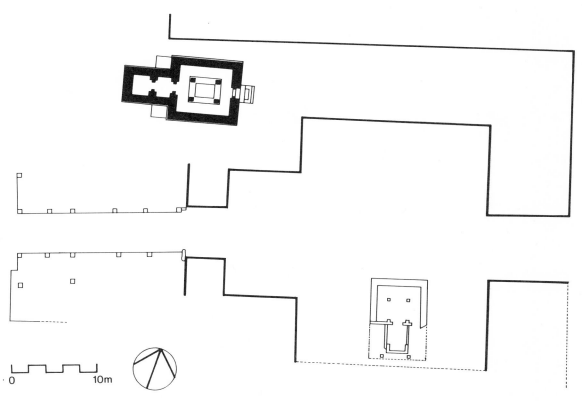

Figure 4.2   Gateway on northeast road, site plan.

DEFENSIVE GATEWAYS
(Figures 4.2, 4.3, 4.4, and 4.5)

Built into these fortification walls are substantial gateways. (Similar gateways in the second circuit of walls are not discussed here.) Despite certain variations in their arrangements, these gateways appear to conform to a fairly standard scheme. Here a doorway, covered by lintels and beams, is positioned between two projecting bastions. Inside the doorway is a passageway flanked by platforms on each of which a colonnade is constructed, sometimes with chambers. Outside the doorways of several examples are large enclosures protected by massive walls. Small shrines are usually located within the enclosure; beyond the gateway, on the outside and/or inside, are other shrines, occasionally free-standing columns also.

Such gateways are often described by visitors. Domingo Paes mentions one "all of stonework, and it makes a bend before you arrive at the gate; and at the entrance of this gate are two towers, one on each side, which makes it very strong; as soon as you pass inside there are two

little temples" (Sewell 1900, p. 254). Such a description may be easily applied to many gateways at Vijayanagara. Within were guards and keepers who, according to Abd ar-Razzaq, "are constantly at their post, and examine everything with a severe inspection" (Major 1857, p. 23).

Our study of the defensive gateways begins with the large example northeast of the royal centre, and then proceeds in a clockwise direction around to the north gateway.

The northeast gateway (NE road) is one of the best preserved on the edge of the royal centre. An inscription (on the ridge to the north) describes it as the main decorated gateway east of the city (Nagaraja Rao 1984). This important gate consists of an east-west passageway flanked by platforms with stone column bases, leading to an east-facing doorway. Skirting the doorway to the north is a recessed passageway (partly collapsed). The two bastions flanking the doorway at the front (east) are linked with tapering walls that create a large rectangular enclosure entered at the east (on axis with the doorway). Within the enclosure on the south are the remains of two small temples (one with a columned hall) facing north; in the

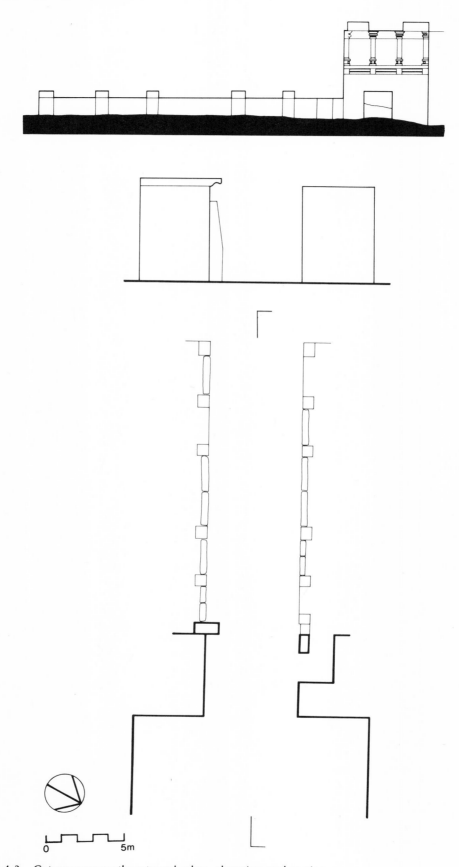

Figure 4.3   Gateway on northeast road, plan, elevation and section.

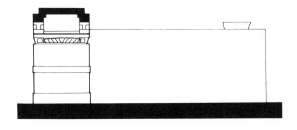

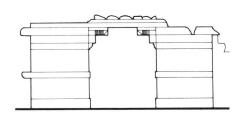

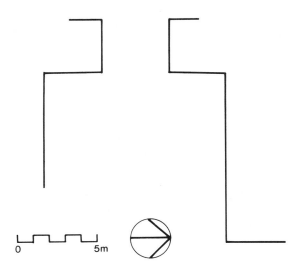

Figure 4.4   Gateway on east road, plan, elevation and section.

middle is a fallen monolithic column. Elevated on the walls near the northwest corner of the enclosure is a well-preserved temple (see Chapter 5). The north and south external faces of the enclosure walls are now missing their stone cladding. Beyond the gateway to the east is another free-standing column and a ruined temple.

A massive basement flanks the platforms of the passageway. Here, the four mouldings are interrupted by blocks. The walls flanking the doorway have four shallow pilasters on a horizontal frieze of basementlike mouldings. Only one projecting corbel is still in situ; its underside has a roll moulding with lotus ornament. The doorway jamb fragment (south side) has bands of lotus decoration rising upon a makara with a foliated tail; beneath is a guardian with a club (damaged). A matching stone fragment — possibly the north jamb — is housed in the Archaeological Museum. This depicts a similar makara and guardian, the latter with a tunic and pointed hat, brandishing a spear (Nagaraja Rao 1983, pl. xliiia). Several blocks on the enclosure walls are carved with images — ascetic, dancer, bull, etc.

Less completely preserved is the east gateway (E road). It, too, is identified by an inscription (on a nearby boulder); it is called the "Monday gateway" (Nagaraja Rao 1984). In this gate a covered doorway facing east is flanked by bastions (south bastion mostly fallen); the passageway is now buried. Inside the gateway to the west are the remains of temples and a free-standing monolithic column. The walls flanking the doorway have a horizontal projecting band. Cornice and eavelike mouldings, with lotus ornament and blocks carved with yalis, support corbels (two on each side). These corbels have angled ends, scrollwork, and roll mouldings, and carry beams and horizontal ceiling slabs carved with a central medallion. Crudely sculptured on the walls are various images — archer, ascetic, yali, goose, elephant, Lakshmi (?), etc. No walls defining an outer enclosure are seen.

Even more ruined is the southeast gateway (SE1 road). Significantly, this south-facing gateway is almost perfectly aligned with the large Jaina temple some distance to the south. Here a north-south passageway is flanked by platforms made up of collapsed rubble and earth walls. The doorway, no longer covered, is set between bastions, the partial outlines of which can be made out. A series of walls, mostly fallen, indicate an enclosure to the south, entered at the southwest corner to create a bent entrance. Inside the gateway are the remains of flanking chambers on platforms. Adjacent to these platforms are shrines; extending to the east and west are partly collapsed fortification walls.

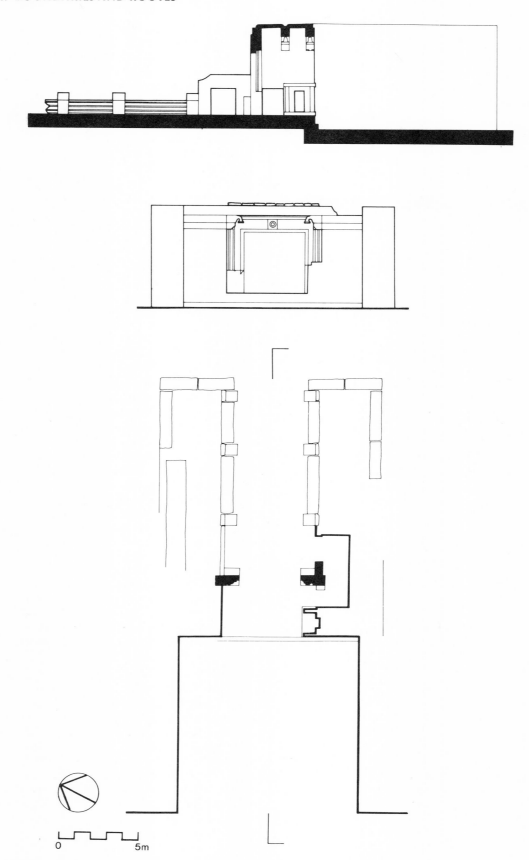

Figure 4.5 Gateway on southwest road, plan, elevation and section.

We come now to an unusual gateway located in the fortifications south of the royal centre (S2 road): this consists of a single opening in the walls without any bastions, jambs, or lintel. To the north are the remains of platforms flanking a passageway (mostly buried).

The southwest gateway (SW road) is positioned between two bastions, but there is no enclosure. Around the west-facing doorway on the south side is a small access corridor, now partly blocked up, as well as a small shrine. Within the gateway (to the east) the passageway is bounded by platforms with tripartite basement mouldings and sculptured blocks; these blocks presumably co-incide with columns (now vanished). The door-way is constructed of long blocks — one for each jamb, another serving as the lintel — carved on the outer face with bands of lotus ornament and scrollwork. Beneath at either side are makaras and damaged (fighting?) figures; a lotus medallion is positioned in the middle of the lintel. The inner (east) face of the doorway has sockets cut into the jambs and lintel (to fix timber or metal?). Above the plain walls project two corbels; the lower is angled, the upper is curved and foliated with pendant buds of different designs (at either side). The beams and roof slabs are plain. Han-uman and an ascetic figure are carved on the blocks of the bastion walls.

Almost the only remaining evidence of the fortifications north of the royal centre is provided by a ruined gateway north of XXVI (N2 road). Here the partial outlines of two rectangular bas-tions flanking a north-facing doorway are seen; to the south, platforms on a simple tripartite basement define a passageway.

Though the defensive gateways in the second circuit of fortifications are beyond our present study, we note here that these are frequently aligned with those of the inner circuit. Such pairs of gateways indicate the principal thoroughfares entering the royal centre. As to the original appearance of these gateways, we observe several more elaborate examples in the peripheral walls of the urban core. The massive gateway (SE1 road) southeast of the royal centre — often known as "Bhima's gate" (Longhurst 1917, p. 45) — has a complete series of corbelled brackets sup-porting horizontal ceiling slabs over the doorway; above are traces of an upper chamber. Elsewhere, these chambers are sometimes provided with Islamic-styled facades (gateway on the NE1 road). The chronology of these gateways is of signifi-cance for the history of the city; unfortunately, no example is provided with a donative inscrip-tion. The two epigraphs already noted — men-tioning the gateways on the northeast and east roads — refer to Vijayanagara as the "City of Bukka Raya." However, it is by no means clear which of the two early rulers of this name is

intended here, nor if the gateways are contem-porary with their rule. Of interest is one gateway beyond the royal centre to the west (SW road). This is coordinated with a small temple dated to the period of Mallikarjuna (1447-1465) — its entrance is axially aligned with the temple. If the gateway and temple are not contemporaneous, the gateway can be no later. This example provides us with a useful chronological clue, since the gateway itself displays features typical of the series and is continuous with the fortifi-cations. Thus, there is the possibility that these walls and gateways may already have been laid out by the middle of the fifteenth century (Michell 1983, pp. 47-49).

ENCLOSURE WALLS
(Figure 4.6)

The overall configuration of walls defining the enclosures of the royal centre has already been outlined; here we examine the specific features of those stone walls which still stand. The basic construction consists of two tapering stone faces, with earth and rubble infill, that meet at the top; throughout, no mortar is used. Like the fortifica-tion walls, the blocks of the enclosure walls are wedge-shaped, only the outer surfaces being dressed. Though now rarely preserved to their full height, some portions of the walls stand almost 7m., including a brick and mortar cap. Perhaps the most remarkable feature of these walls is the range of jointing systems, testifying to many different phases of construction and renovation. As yet, we cannot classify these different wall types into a chronological sequence; however, we note that crudely fashioned walls often appear to be later than those with finer jointing which they abut. An analysis of these wall schemes demonstrates the contemporaneity of construction — or lack thereof — between the different zones of the royal centre. It is unlikely, however, that these jointing systems were always intended to be visible; traces of plaster coating indicate that some walls were once totally covered (and painted?).

The walls defining enclosures V-IX appear to share a common typology. Here the essential characteristics are the relatively small size and uniform shape of the squarish blocks; the joints are interlocking. There is, nevertheless, some variation in the quality of stone cutting, and sometimes small stone plugs are employed. In general, the sizes of the blocks diminish as the wall ascends. At its base the wall is about 1.6m. thick; at the top it tapers to about 45cm., where a small brick and mortar cap is found.

Quite different are the walls bounding enclo-sure IV and its surrounding alley, the east parts of III (b and c), and XIII and XVI; these all display

4. BOUNDARIES AND ROUTES

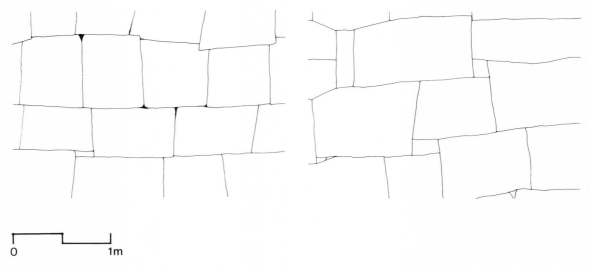

0   1m

Figure 4.6   Enclosure walls, jointing details; left, enclosure V; right, enclosure XIV.

an identical jointing system. Here, large irregular blocks are discovered, often poorly dressed and with inferior jointing (employing stone plugs); quarrying marks are common. At its base the wall is about 2.2m. wide. In some instances, the top of the wall has a horizontal slab upon which is an earth and rubble cap.

Enclosure XIV displays a variety of wall schemes encountered nowhere else in the royal centre. In those part of the walls that appear to be earlier (east and south), the blocks are squarish, well dressed, and tightly jointed. As the walls ascend the blocks reduce in size and regularity. In other parts of the enclosure (north and west) the blocks vary considerably in shape and size, and are laid with a distinctive irregular pattern. The wall is about 1.6m. at the base, tapering to a mere 30cm. at the top, where there is a brick and mortar cap. Holes in this parapet may have been for metal spikes. On some parts of the walls of XIV (north side) large areas of plaster coating are preserved. (Some of the variation in these walls is due to restoration).

Other wall types appear comparatively restricted in their use within the royal centre. Enclosure II is bounded on the south by a wall characterized by long blocks with gently curved, irregular courses. The blocks are well dressed and tightly jointed. (A similar scheme is found in the walls defining the elevated structure abutting the west side of the hundred-columned hall, IVa/1, and the walls supporting the steps on the south side of the same monument.) Exceptional are the walls in the vicinity of the Ramachandra Temple complex. Running northwards from the northwest corner of this complex, at the west end of

enclosure I, is a very thick wall (more than 4m. wide at the base). This has a distinctive stepped profile — of alternating horizontal and vertical blocks — on its east face (serving as seating to overlook enclosure I?). The walls at the east end of I, though now mostly buried, are also of this type. On the south side of I (common with II) is a poorly constructed irregular wall with roughly shaped infill pieces; here the blocks are hardly dressed at all and the jointing is extremely crude. Both these examples contrast with the enclosure walls of the Ramachandra Temple, and also those of other sacred complexes (Madhava and Shaiva Temples). These walls are remarkable for the excellent quality of construction. Here the slabs are large and long, well dressed, and extremely tightly jointed; tie beams are introduced at regular intervals. This wall type is about 1.7m. thick and, unlike other examples, is vertical on both faces. (As the thickness of the blocks is reduced towards the top, the infill of rubble and brick is correspondingly increased.) The wall varies from 3.5m. to 4m. high. Above is a capping horizontal stone, sometimes also a curved brick and mortar cap.

Within the royal centre other walls of inferior construction are discovered in which small and irregular blocks, hardly dressed at all, are laid without any overall jointing pattern. Innumerable small stones are employed as infill. Elsewhere (V and IX, for instance), the walls appear to consist of several courses of stonework at the base, the upper tapering portions being of layered earth often containing stone rubble and pottery sherds, covered with plaster. (The best preserved examples of such walls are seen in a palace complex outside the enclosures, on the south side of the east valley.) In many other cases (Ib, IIIa, IX, XIX, etc.) the earth has completely washed away, leaving only a few courses of stonework.

Relating the enclosure walls to the various monuments is not always an easy task. In some cases (XIV), the walls are obviously later than several structures which they abut, or are built over earlier features (IVa/8, gateways I-II, II-IIIa, etc.). In contrast, other monuments are clearly built upon the (earlier) walls (multidomed structure, 1, in the northwest corner of VII) or into the walls (VIIIa/1).

DOORWAYS IN ENCLOSURE WALLS

Simple openings in the walls provide access into various enclosures (particularly IV, V, and XIV). These openings vary in width from little more than 1m. to about 3.5m., and are usually no higher than 3m. to 3.5m. Such small openings suggest a fairly restricted usage. Over the doorways are plain lintel blocks, occasionally supported on curved corbels (XIV, north and west sides). Sometimes protruding from the inside of the lintels are socket blocks. The original doors, presumably in timber, have vanished. There is, however, one example of a stone door (IIIb/4) imitating timber framing, but its original location is unknown. The jambs of the doorways seem to have been undecorated (unlike those in the gateways); so, too, the thresholds (where preserved).

Certain features are associated with these doorways. We note that, in V, VII, VIII, and IXe, these small openings are screened by secondary walls, creating indirect access routes. On the north of IXe, finely carved granite and chlorite mouldings in the ground appear to belong to an elaborate entrance (in wood?) leading to a small opening.

GATEWAYS IN ENCLOSURE WALLS
(Figures 4.7, 4.8, 4.9, 4.10, and 4.11)

Connecting one enclosure with another are large gateways, now only preserved in their lower stone portions, varying from simple schemes to complex combinations of passageways and courts. Whereas the simpler types appear to be linked with the more public and ceremonial zones of the royal centre (particularly I-IV), the more complicated gateways are obviously related to palace structures and other secular buildings (particularly in V, VIII, IX, and XXIX). In their descriptions of the palaces of the capital, the Portuguese chroniclers mention sequences of heavily guarded alleys, passageways, and gates leading from one court to the next (Sewell 1900, p. 284). The considerable area that these entry complexes occupy within the confined space of

the enclosures suggests the importance of controlling all access.

In their simplest and most monumental form, the gateways consist of two rectangular platforms defined by stone basements, separated by a central passageway. In the middle of this passageway the mouldings are usually interrupted by a recess for the open doors, and sometimes there are indications of door jambs and a threshold; nothing more, however, is usually preserved of these doorways. Abutting either side of the gateways are the enclosure walls. Stone blocks on the platforms indicate regularly aligned columns — generally one row on each side — but none of these have survived in situ. (Since no stone columns are found lying anywhere about, we presume that these were of timber, as were the doorways.) Rubble and earth debris, and also traces of plaster floors, suggest that these platforms were divided by walls into small chambers (for guards?). Various game boards are etched into the stone floors of these platforms.

Reconstructing the original appearance of these gateways is not too difficult. In plan they resemble the entrances to temple enclosures (as in the Ramachandra Temple). We believe that the upper parts of these gateways may also have resembled these temple examples — with rows of columns supporting angled eaves and horizontal roofs, possibly with towers rising above. In the gateways associated with the enclosure walls, though, all these architectural elements would have been in perishable materials.

Several examples of this standard gateway type are found on the periphery of enclosure I, leading into the various adjacent zones (II, IXa, XIII, XVb, and XVI), also between II and III, and between IIIa and IVa. In the largest example (I-II) the passageway is defined by a high tripartite basement, the bottom and top mouldings of which are identical, though inverted, with undecorated medallions. These mouldings are interrupted to create a recess for the open doors (vanished); column footings are positioned on the top course of the basement with blocks beneath. Here there is marked evidence of wilful destruction and burning (exfoliated and cracked stonework). Proceeding southwards, through II and IIIa into IVa, two more gateways are encountered of the same type. Within IVa the gateway is extended by the (later?) addition of two or three platforms to the south (IVa/3), with a different and more complex series of mouldings flanking the passageway. South of this second gateway a brick wall (IVa/4) creates a bent entrance.

One smaller gateway of this type is completely built with stone columns, beams, and roof. (This example is located east of the enclosures, leading to a palace complex north of the octagonal bath.) The dilapidated structure has 4 by 3 columns with

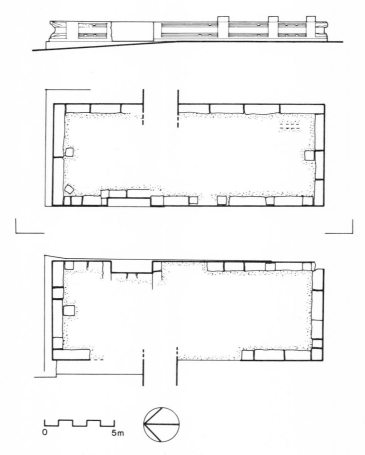

Figure 4.7   Gateway Ic-II, plan and section.

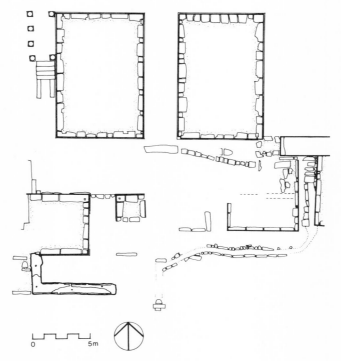

Figure 4.8   Gateways in IVa, plan.

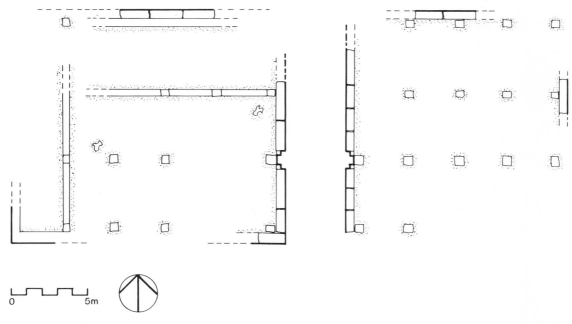

Figure 4.9   Gateway IXb-c, plan.

a central east-west passageway defined by a tripartite basement. The column brackets support beams with angled ends to take a sloping eave (partly preserved on the north and west). The central beam over the passageway has socket blocks and a lotus medallion.

Different gateway schemes are found within enclosure IX, and between XXIX and XXX. Two examples (IXa-b, b-c) have the platforms on either side of the elevated passageway expanded to create large columned structures raised above the level of the court. Here column footings are preserved in situ, set into earth and rubble wall foundations. (Where the foundations have been eroded, the column footings, consisting of blocks piled one upon the other, are revealed.) The basement mouldings demarcating the central passageway are more elaborate than the schemes already described, and even incorporate blocks carved with rearing yalis. The largest of these examples (XXIXa-XXX) has 4 by 12 columns with extremely high (more than 2m.) basement mouldings. A flight of steps ascends to the (vanished) floor level. The gateway VIIIa-IXa preserves traces of 4 by 3 column footings on its south side, where porches face both inwards and outwards. To the north, there is only an inner porch.

Within VIII and IX, other related gateway complexes are discovered, now mostly ruined. Here the gateways begin with an outer rectangular court or covered porch with a plastered floor in which stone column footings are set; access to

this court is by one or more steps. On three sides are platforms with basement mouldings and column footings. In the middle of the long side the basement is interrupted by a passageway leading into an interior court. Characteristic of all these schemes are the alternating sequences of un-aligned passageways and courts — creating many changes of direction — and the small scale of the passageway.

Better preserved examples of such entryways are seen in V (northeast of palace complex 1) and XXVI (north of palace complex 1). Here, small interior courts have plaster floors, access steps ascending to the platforms, column footings, and even the lower portions of walls defining small chambers.

Within the royal centre there is an exceptional example of an Islamic-styled gateway, now only partly standing. Built across the northeast road (NE), this gateway (Ic-XVb) incorporates two platforms with column footings on the inside (west). On the outside the enclosure walls abut the gateway; here a doorway was originally covered by an arch. (The lower portion of an arch in two planes can still be observed on the south pier.) Arched niches are found at either side; within the niche deeply recessed on the south is a carving of Hanuman beneath Vaishnava emblems.

Another possible gateway of a completely different type is found in the valley east of the enclosures. Now mostly buried and incompletely

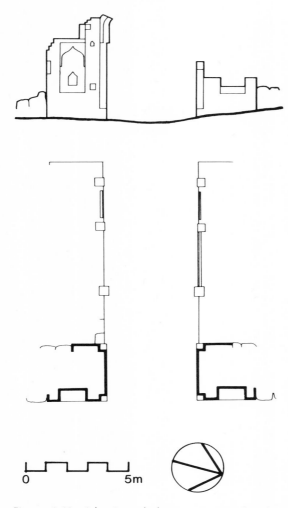

Figure 4.10   Islamic-styled gateway Ic-XVb, plan and elevation.

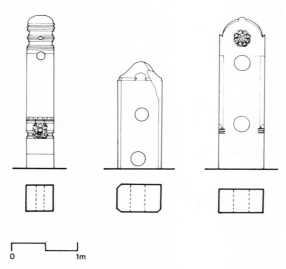

Figure 4.11   Gateposts; left, in enclosure III; centre, near gateway Ia-XIII; right, in enclosure XIII.

preserved, this gateway seems to consist of four platforms, each with 3 by 3 columns, defining two intersecting passageways.

Associated with one gateway (Ia-XIII) is a small pedestal and a fallen column, suggesting the presence of a cult image. Indeed, some of the small chambers in these gateways may have functioned as shrines. More curious are the pairs of finely carved stone posts of different shapes, some of which may not be in their original position. One of these pairs stands inside a gateway (Ia-XIII), another is near a gateway (IIIa-IVa), and a third pair is found at the north end of XIII (10). These posts have delicately incised foliate medallions or scrollwork, moulded and curved tops, and two circular holes. Obviously poles (of wood?) were set into these holes (as barriers?).

Access to the various terraces of X is through natural openings in the rock, sometimes provided with stone staircases and ramps (Xa-XIa, Xb-e); in several instances, stone flights of steps are cut into the rock. Ladders or earthen ramps, now vanished, may have ascended to elevated steps and platforms (west alley - Xc; Xa-d, Xd-f).

MOVEMENT INTO THE ROYAL CENTRE
(Figure 4.12)

We have already noted the system of movement within the capital, pointing out the different radial, ring, and linear roads; here we focus only on those roads within the royal centre. Since the radial and linear roads pass around the enclosures — significantly, there is no direct movement across the royal centre — we are mainly dealing with a converging system (Fritz 1983). Here, the location of defensive gateways in the fortifications, other gateways in the enclosure walls, and also the alignments of sacred and secular structures, are the chief indicators of routes; only a few traces of road surfaces, steps, etc., are visible.

We begin our examination with the various gateways on the periphery of enclosure I: No other space within the royal centre has such a concentration of gateways, suggesting that here converged the principal roads of the city. Three of these routes are easily traced. From the north alley, a road (N1) enters I, while to the east there are two gateways, through one of which (Ic-XVb) passes the northeast road (NE). This latter route is the longest street in the royal centre (almost 1km. to the peripheral gateway), and inscriptions on nearby monuments provide it with various names — "main bazaar," "bazaar of the pan-sellers," etc. (Nagaraja Rao 1983, pp. 57-59). Facing onto this road are numerous temples and shrines, many now ruined or partly buried. The concentration of sacred structures along this road is remarkable; no other street in the royal centre

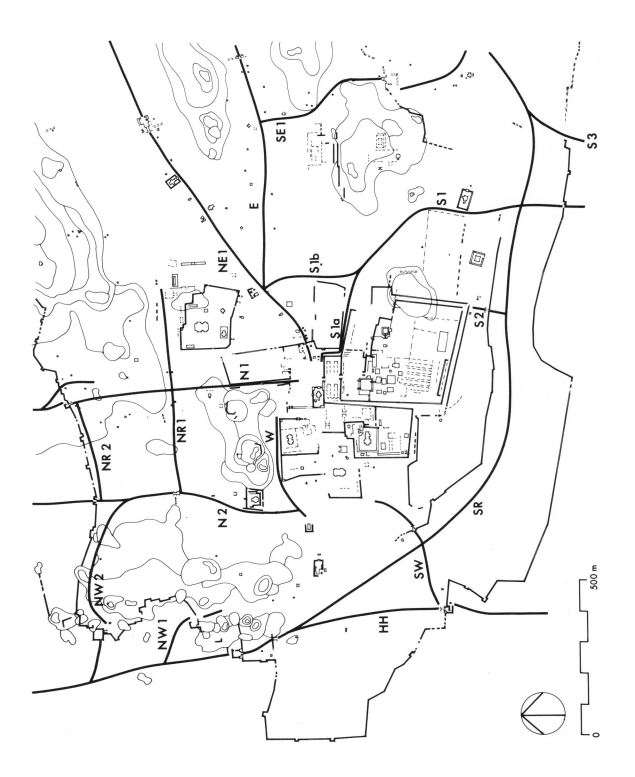

Figure 4.12   Roads leading into the royal centre.

— or, for that matter, anywhere else in the city — has such a density of different temples continuing for such a long distance. Domingo Paes notes that there are "temples in every street, for these appertain to institutions like the confraternities . . . of all the craftsmen and merchants" (Sewell 1900, p. 256). In the southeast corner of I, a branch of the south road (S1a) enters the enclosure, having passed through the southeast alley.

Various arteries converge on the great northeast road within the royal centre. Beyond the gateway Ic-XVb, several roads from the south (S1b), southeast (SE1), and east (E) — each demarcated by a defensive gateway in the fortifications — join the northeast road. Their point of meeting may have occurred south of the Madhava Temple complex, overlooked (and controlled?) by the octagonal tower in the southeast corner of XIV.

In the southwest of the royal centre, another road (SW) finds its way into XXIII, but from then on its route is unknown. We have little indication of major roads entering the enclosures from the west. North of XXVI, a gateway marks the presence of a road (N2) which proceeds southwards, flanked by several shrines, a well, and a palace complex. Its ultimate destination, however, is by no means clear. The unusually small gateway in the fortifications south of the enclosures has already been noted. Despite the fact that this must have provided some sort of access, it seems unlikely that a principal road was linked with this entrance; rather, there may have been some connection with the ring road system skirting the royal centre beyond the fortifications. To the north, a ring road (NR1) may have followed the south side of the fortifications.

MOVEMENT WITHIN THE ROYAL CENTRE
(Figure 4.13)

Here we are primarily concerned with the system of alleys, walls, gateways, and doorways indicating movement between the enclosures, and even between subdivisions within each enclosure. One of the most strongly defined routes in the royal centre leads from enclosure I towards IVa, passing through four gateways (already noted) into an area of platforms between which are small courts and alleys. This route is characterized by the decreasing size of gateways (north to south) and the avoidance of any precise alignment of passageways. With its various subdivisions, enclosure III includes the north-south route just described, but there are also other movements. The flight of steps leading up to the great platform (IVb/1) provides evidence of a connection between IIIb and IVb. Further east, IIIc joins the alley that surrounds IV on three sides. Bounded by high walls, this alley is linked with the

enclosure only by a single small doorway (west side of IV).

Within IV no obvious route seems to have existed between the various zones. In the northwest quadrant (IVa), courts and alleys suggest only confined movement between various structures which are crowded together. One sequence of raised basements and paved courts (IVa/21, 23) appears to connect with IVb, where several water structures are positioned in an open space. Much more regular are the north-south alleys of IVd, onto which face long columned structures (1-12).

Running north-south, the alley west of II, III, and IV, and east of V and IX eventually arrives at the small doorway in the south enclosure wall of the Ramachandra Temple. The walls of this alley act as a barrier to any east-west movement between these zones. This boundary is continued by the west wall of the temple complex, and another wall terminated by a gateway (Ia-IXa). Only through this gateway is movement possible southwards or westwards.

Moving south, through gateways demarcating the boundaries of IXa, b, c, d, and e, the route eventually turns westwards and northwards before reaching enclosure V. Thereafter, this route continues to change direction, passing through the courtyard of structure V/2, an entryway complex, and finally arriving in the courtyard of palace complex V/1. Only movement in VIII displays such a tortuous route. Within V the various palace structures are bounded by courtyards with subsidiary walls; there is little suggestion of routes of movement from one zone to another. However, along the west of the enclosure, probably on the north as well, access corridors are provided. One of these was probably aligned with a small doorway in the south wall.

Proceeding westwards from gateway Ia-IXa, another route passes through at least three entrances and five courts (VIII/a-e) with many changes of direction; the ultimate destination is probably the palace structure VIIIf/1. A small doorway between VII and VIII is screened by walls on both sides creating narrow access corridors. Similarly, the door in the west wall of VI leads to a corridor running between the walls and a large cellular structure. The probable entry on the north of VII was screened on the outside (north) by a long colonnaded structure. A wall with column footings on the inside (south), close to the enclosure wall (east half), also may have continued across the opening.

As for the other routes of movement within VI, VII, and elsewhere in VIII, these are by no means clear; no internal gateways or alleys are visible. The walls bounding the north sides of VII and VIII do suggest an east-west route (through the west alley) outside the enclosures (perhaps co-

Figure 4.13   Movement within the royal centre.

inciding with the modern road) leading from the zone to the west (XXV) through the walls and platforms of XI, through a doorway, into enclosure I (road W). The multidomed structure (VII/1) may have overlooked the meeting of this east-west route and the north road (N2).

Other gateways on the periphery of I suggest entries into confined areas. On the south are the two gateways leading into the Ramachandra Temple complex. To the southeast a gateway provides access into XVI, while to the northeast another gateway is linked to XIII. We also note the small opening in the walls between Ib and XVb.

XIV has several doorways in its outer walls;

interestingly, there are no gateways. If we coordinate these openings with the layout of structures within the enclosure, it may be possible to discern one or more routes. Outside to the northeast is a gateway complex (XXIXa-XXX) leading into the rectangular court onto which face a rectangular structure and the elephant stables (XXX/1-2). Quite possibly, this space was also linked in some way to the northeast road, which passes nearby to the south, and also to the north road (N1), which passes to the west. The alignment of walls, platforms, small temples, and shrines north of XXIX and XXX suggests a probable east-west route (NR1).

4. BOUNDARIES AND ROUTES

WATERWORKS
(Figure 4.14)

Throughout our description of the individual enclosures of the royal centre we have noted numerous hydraulic features — channels, aqueducts, pipes, tanks, wells, etc. — often closely associated with various water structures. Though these features are now only observed as isolated and usually fragmentary elements, their presence within the royal centre testifies to a complex hydraulic system, now mostly vanished. In fact, the travellers often remark on the many gardens and groves of fruit trees within the city. Domingo Paes specifically mentions "many conduits of water," "lakes," and "tanks" (Sewell 1900, pp. 256-257).

As yet, we cannot be certain about the principal sources of water, other than the river and its tributaries as the ultimate origins. Judging from the general lie of the land, water must have been conducted into the royal centre from the south and west (elsewhere are elevated ridges). Even today there is a great tank to the south (near Kamalapuram); the water channels deriving from this reservoir probably follow an ancient scheme. (We have already observed the channels in the irrigated valley to the north; other channels may be seen in the agricultural zones between the sub-urban centres beyond the urban core.)

Within our area of investigation (excluding IV; see below), we begin with the longest features — the aqueducts. These are created of plaster-lined stonework or brickwork in a U-formation, generally supported on rubble walls. Such an aqueduct (XIX/25), now mostly collapsed, passes west of the Shaiva temple complex southeast of the enclosures, and north of the square water pavilion (XX/1). As already noted, this channel probably passed around three sides of a hill in XVIII, crossed the alley, and linked up with a stone aqueduct within IV (described below). A similarly collapsed aqueduct is detected near the octagonal fountain in XXII. Traces of another aqueduct are seen leading into a rectangular tank within the courtyard of palace structure XXVI/1. Smaller aqueducts consist of stone channels cut into long blocks. Examples occur in Ic(17), IIIa, and XVIb(9).

Other hydraulic features include lines of earthenware pipes, one fitted into another. Fragments of such pipes are found embedded into thick brick and mortar east of the octagonal fountain (XXII/1), also within V (courtyard walls of palace complex 1). Other fragments occur in III (b/3, c/5), XV (b/9), and XVIII(1). Vertical pipes are discovered fixed into the enclosure walls of XIV (abutting tower 5), or descending from a small plaster-lined tank built into the granite shelf over the rock-cut temple (east of the enclosures). In

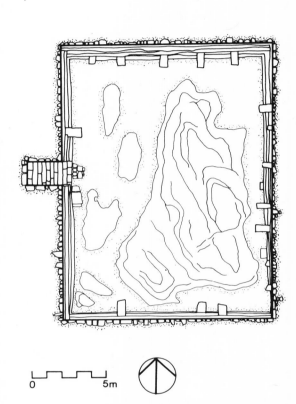

Figure 4.14 Stone-lined tank (XIV/9), plan and section.

at least two examples we find the remains of structures with plaster-lined angled channels. XVa/3 is a bath or toilet, while XXII/3 may have functioned as a water regulator (with sluice gates?). Also connected with the movement of water are plaster-lined channels, sometimes covered with stones and usually set into the ground. Those within IV are described below, but here we note many other fragmentary examples in I, III, V, VI, VIII, and elsewhere, suggesting an elaborate outlet system. Stone channels are found projecting out of the enclosure walls of a palace (XXVI/1) and sacred structure (Ramachandra Temple complex).

Plaster-lined tanks are common: these vary from small and medium-sized examples (in II, III, V, and elsewhere), to large stone-lined tanks entered by flights of steps (in V, VI, XIV, XV, and XXV). These tanks are usually rectangular, and in at least one instance (northwest of the Virupaksha Temple complex) utilize columns to support a projecting balcony. Other tanks (in Ic, IIb, IIIa, and XIII) have curved stone slabs on four sides. Here, too, we note the stone-lined tank of the water palace (XIV/2). Stone tanks are sometimes partly cut into boulders (VI/7) or make use of natural rocky crevices (Xb). Monolithic stone troughs are associated with two gateways (I-XIII, IIIa-IVa), and also occur within several enclosures (II, IIIa).

Wells are also an important part of the water supply. These range from examples with well-finished stonework (courtyard of palace complex XXVI/1) to small openings with rotated square tops (in Ic, IXb, and elsewhere), or simple stone coverings (west alley).

HYDRAULIC FEATURES OF ENCLOSURE IV
(Figures 4.15, 4.16, 4.17 and 4.18)

No other part of the royal centre displays such a complex series of waterworks as this zone. We have already observed that the enclosure is divided into four unequal quadrants by a partly preserved stone aqueduct. Water apparently entered the enclosure from a channel in the middle of the east side, now only preserved in fragments. At first laid on the surface and then, as the ground falls away, raised as a U-shaped stone channel on piers (broken by the modern road), the aqueduct proceeds westwards until it meets a well (IVa/33) in the middle of the enclosure. Before this well is reached, however, a secondary branch leads southwards towards the great tank (IVc/1); this branch, made of plaster-lined concrete, is supported on a masonry wall, now collapsed. Further along the stone aqueduct another secondary channel turns southwards, though only a fraction of this survives. From the middle of the enclosure the aqueduct divides into two parts. That part continuing westwards is only preserved for a short distance, the line of supporting stone piers soon disappearing. That part turning northwards, though, is still to be seen. Descending to ground level, this channel flanks several structures (IVa/28, 34); joins two secondary branches leading eastwards (towards IVb/3, 4); turns through a courtyard (IVa/23); and then divides into a west branch (passing south of IVa/13-14) and two northeast branches (passing beneath IVa/16 and eventually linking up in courtyard 9). The channels ultimately vanish beneath the enclosure walls to the north.

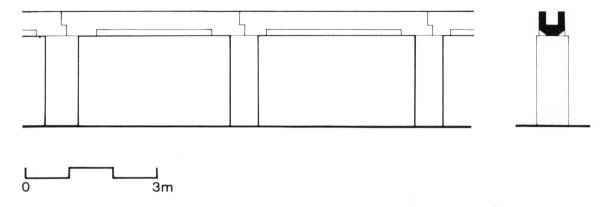

Figure 4.15   Aqueduct in enclosure IV, elevation and section.

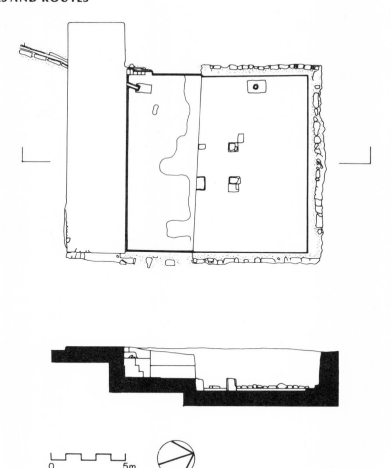

Figure 4.16 Plaster-lined tank (IVb/3), plan and section.

Associated with the various structures of IV are several plaster-lined channels set into the ground and covered with roughly shaped stones (south of IVa/5, west of IVa/13). More finely finished stone channels covered with dressed blocks appear to be linked with the principal water system described above. Some of these originally led to various stone basins (IVa/24, IVb/2) and plaster-lined tanks (IVb/3). South of IVa/14, three channels pass over each other at different levels.

Numerous tanks of different shapes and sizes are found throughout this enclosure, particularly in the northwest quadrant. These tanks vary in size from small, irregularly shaped basins with plaster lining (IVa/14, 18) or cut rock (IVb/5), to square basins with plaster lining (IVa/23), and finely finished carved stone basins with moulded sides (IVa/24, IVb/2). In one example (IVa/32), a tank with stepped sides is created in plaster-covered brickwork. The largest plaster-lined tank

(IVb/3) is located west of the great platform and is divided into shallow and deep areas. Four brick piers in the middle of the tank indicate the presence of a central structure, now vanished. Steps and a carved stone spout are visible at the southwest corner. A few wells, too, are found (northeast of IVa/10, 31), and there is at least one instance of what may be a toilet pit (southwest corner of IVa/11).

The great tank (IVc/1) in the middle of the southeast quadrant of the enclosure is the largest hydraulic feature in the royal centre. Here, stepped stone courses and massive concrete, stonework, and brickwork create an immense rectangle (the water basin measures 67m. by 22m.). In the middle of each side narrow platforms are created, each with four stone columns, now mostly fallen; the columns on the north are carved with rearing animals. A flight of stone steps on

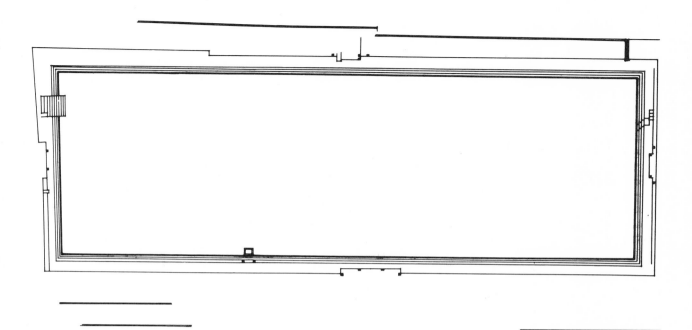

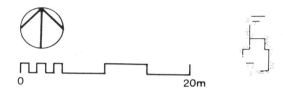

Figure 4.17   Great tank (IVc/1), plan.

the west leads down to the water; on the east, narrow plaster-covered brick steps are seen. In the northeast corner a spout once conducted water into the tank. On the south is a stone-covered drain set into the plastered floor of the tank; associated with the drain is a sluice gate forming part of the stone sides of the tank. Surrounding the tank is a plaster-covered walkway.

Also remarkable is the monumental aqueduct (IVd/17) running parallel to the south enclosure walls of the southwest quadrant, surrounded on three sides by walls. The channel here is partly set into a natural rocky crevice. At regular intervals along its length, stone beams supported on piers are laid across the channel. Water appears to have entered from the east, where it may have been conducted after passing out of the great tank; beyond the west end of the enclosure, though, the aqueduct disappears.

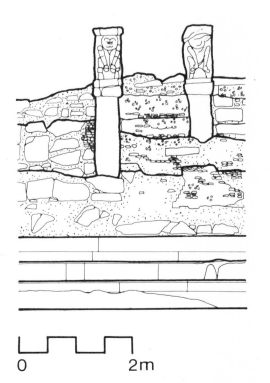

Figure 4.18   Great tank (IVc/1), detail of stone, brick and rubble lining.

5. SACRED ART

Temples, Shrines, and Sculpture

Though the royal centre at Vijayanagara never functioned as a holy place — comparable to the various locations along the Tungabhadra River and on the rocky outcrops nearby — a great number of temples is, nevertheless, found in this zone (Figure 5.1). Two sacred complexes within the royal centre appear to be of particular importance — the Ramachandra Temple located in the middle of the enclosures, and the Virupaksha Temple about 500m. due west. We note the contrasting affiliations of these two temples, one Vaishnava the other Shaiva. The road (NE) proceeding northeastwards from the Ramachandra Temple is lined with numerous temples and shrines, all the way to the gateway in the fortified walls. Here are found Shaiva and Vaishnava shrines, two Jaina temples, and even one sanctuary currently in worship dedicated to an aspect of Devi. In the valleys east and southeast of the enclosures many temples are found, often ruined and partly buried, lining the principal roads; to the north and northeast are additional shrines, extending onto the granite ridges. One of the largest sacred complexes is found to the southeast; nearby to this is the Tiruvengalanatha Temple.

EVOLUTION OF TEMPLE ARCHITECTURE

Though the development of temple architecture within the royal centre cannot be isolated from the overall evolution of sacred styles at the capital — and, indeed, from that throughout the whole empire — this chapter focuses only on those examples in or near the royal enclosures. The earliest temples at the site go back to the pre-Vijayanagara period, and are built in styles typical of Deccan architecture of the tenth and eleventh centuries. Characteristic of these early examples — which continued to be built at the site up until the fourteenth century — are basement and cornice mouldings with uncut angled blocks, plain walls, open porches with balcony seating and angled eaves, columns with delicately worked shafts and capitals, and pyramidal stone superstructures. Elements from such a typical pre-Vijayanagara structure appear to be incorporated into an underground chamber (IVa/22) within the royal centre (see Chapter 6). Here are found the chlorite columns and brackets of a typical earlier temple; however, we know nothing about the original location or dedication of this monument.

Possibly the earliest sacred building to be erected in the royal centre is the shrine dedicated to Virupaksha (XXV/1) west of the enclosures. Though now almost completely engulfed by a series of later extensions, the principal sanctuary and adjoining open porch with seating and angled eave (now walled in) seem to be closely related to these pre-Vijayanagara period temple traditions. The details of the basement, columns, eaves, and doorways suggest a fourteenth-century date. No other structure in this early style is known in the royal centre, and we believe that the Virupaksha Temple is the oldest intact sacred monument surviving in this zone, possibly erected soon after the establishment of the dynasty. That this was a royal chapel of continuous significance is demonstrated by the numerous additions up to the sixteenth century.

The first temples at the capital to be constructed in what may be termed a "proto-Vijayanagara" style appear to be Jaina. Two examples — one on the northeast road, the other southeast of the royal centre — are dated to 1385 and 1426, within the first century of the dynasty's career. According to the epigraphs on these monuments (*South Indian Inscriptions* I, nos. 152-153), Jainism was royally acknowledged and patronized. Even the locations of these temples — one outside an important gateway, the other facing onto a principal thoroughfare — proclaim the importance of these monuments within the capital. Architecturally, the temples are impressive for their large scale and massiveness. Though utilizing many of the elements of previous temple styles, these buildings are both larger in scale and less ornamented. Their plain walls, stepped stone superstructures, and carved columns and doorways are typical features. Nor is this style an isolated phenomenon at the site; several other examples are known in the sacred centre and elsewhere in the capital. What is striking about these temples is their dependence on earlier Deccan tradition, thus suggesting a degree of archaism (Michell 1984a).

Perhaps more characteristic of the Vijayanagara style is a group of small temples that employs a common repertory of basic elements — tripartite basements, plain walls, overhanging cornices, and brick superstructures on the exterior; columns with carved blocks and curved or angled brackets, ceilings of rotated squares, and doorways with

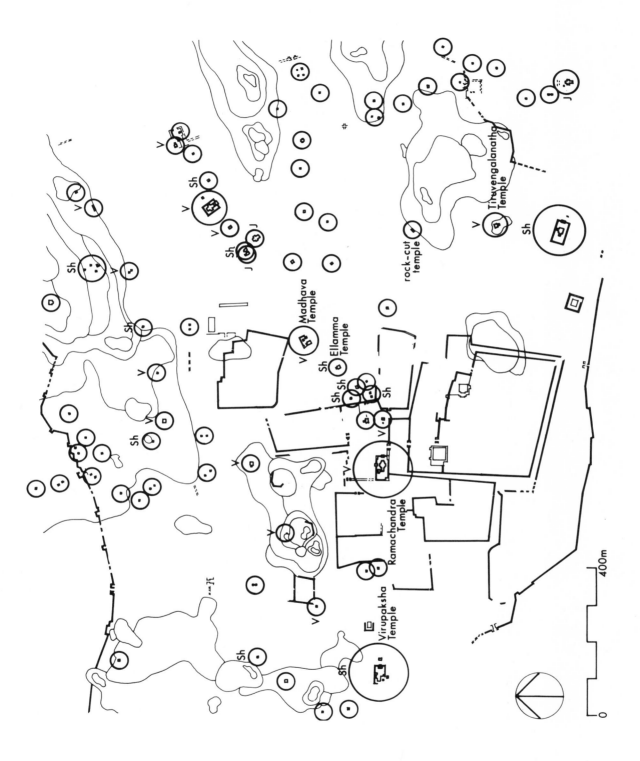

Figure 5.1 Location of temples (circled) within the royal centre, indicating wherever possible Shaiva (Sh), Vaishnava (V) or Jaina (J) cults.

carved bands on the interior. Judging from one dated temple outside the royal centre to the west (Michell 1983), this style was current in the middle of the fifteenth century. In almost all their features, these temples are still dominated by local Deccan traditions, evidently retained at the capital for smaller sacred buildings.

However, for temples of outstanding importance, it is clear that a southern-influenced idiom was adopted, possibly from the beginning of the fifteenth century. The Ramachandra Temple may, in fact, be the first major construction at the capital in the "southern" style. Despite the lack of a dated donative inscription, the shrine of this temple is inscribed with a Sanskrit verse referring to one of two early fifteenth-century rulers named Devaraya (*South Indian Inscriptions* IV, no. 252). The temple must have been worked on by the finest artisans and sculptors of the day, and probably served as a state chapel. Its architecture and art reveal a style very different from the temples already noticed. The external elevation has a complex series of basement mouldings, a wall that projects and recesses rhythmically, full-height and secondary pilasters, the latter framing deep niches, and ornamental pilasters standing in pots. The wall is overhung by a deep cornice, while above rises the brick and plaster superstructure arranged in tiered storeys and capped by a square-to-dome roof. All these elements are easily identified with the "southern" style; that is, they appear to derive from building projects of the Late Cholas and Pandyas in the centuries immediately preceding the Vijayanagara era. Certain Deccan features, though, are also subtly integrated: columns with carved blocks, ceilings of rotated squares, and the projection on the east face of the tower (not retained in later temples at the city). The inclusion of sculptured blocks between the pilasters of the outer walls, and the carved decoration of the basement and cornice, are also characteristic of the southern style.

But not all fifteenth-century sacred structures at Vijayanagara were so lavishly decorated as the Ramachandra Temple; later schemes — such as the Madhava and Tiruvengalanatha Temples, and an unidentified monument (XXVII/1) — exhibit an absorption of southern influences into a simpler and more massive style. Typical of these temples are the plain walls, moulded basements and cornices, and elaborate brick and plaster superstructures surmounted by part-spherical roof forms. Perhaps also belonging to this phase — to be dated to the second half of the fifteenth century, possibly even extending into the early sixteenth century — is the Shaiva complex southeast of the enclosures. Here the principal double-sanctuaried shrine is set in a courtyard surrounded by a rectangle of enclosure walls. The exterior of the building displays an effective integration of

southern-derived elements to create a low and massive elevation. The superstructures of the two sanctuaries are dwarfed by the towered gateway to the east, the latter anticipating the grandiose projects of the sixteenth century. Here, the ascending brick tiers of the tapering storeys culminate in a rectangular vaulted roof decorated with exuberant plasterwork. No doubt, the towered gateway of the Vaishnava complex on the northeast road, now greatly ruined, was similar.

With the reigns of Krishna Raya and Achyuta Raya (1509-1542), sacred architecture at the capital reaches its most ambitious and monumental phase. Belonging to this period are a number of large-scale temples; significantly, none of these are found within the royal centre. In this zone there are only extensions to earlier constructions (Virupaksha, Ramachandra, and Madhava Temples) and a few isolated small shrines (on the northeast road). Characteristic features of temple architecture of the sixteenth century are the elaborately moulded and doubled basements, composite columns incorporating rearing beasts, double-curved overhanging eaves, and brick and plaster parapets; the ornamentation of the interiors is greatly increased, with friezes carved on beams, ceilings, and doorways. The great sixteenth-century sacred complexes — Virupaksha, Krishna, Tiruvengalanatha, Vitthala, Raghunatha, and Pattabhirama — are all located outside the royal centre. According to the testimony of their inscriptions, most of these temples benefited from the direct sponsorship of the Vijayanagara kings, ministers, and generals. The architecture and sculpture of these building projects incorporated the most advanced and sophisticated artistic techniques of the era. Nor did this practice cease after the abandonment of the capital in 1565: throughout the sixteenth century, and even well into the seventeenth century, the Vijayanagara temple style continued to evolve under royal patronage at many of the great sacred centres in the south.

VIRUPAKSHA TEMPLE COMPLEX (XXV/1)
(Figures 5.2, 5.3, 5.4 and 5.34)

Functioning as the nucleus of this confusing cluster of shrines, columned halls, colonnades, porches, altars, and gateways, is a small temple, probably the earliest intact structure in the royal centre. The complex is contained in an irregular and incomplete rectangle of enclosure walls, outside of which is another hall and gateway. The surrounding retaining walls which give this temple its "underground" appearance (Longhurst 1917, p. 89; Devakunjari 1970, pp. 43-44) are not original, nor are the various water channels that run through the complex. Built in a number of successive phases spanning the whole Vijayanagara period, the temple is dedicated to Virupaksha

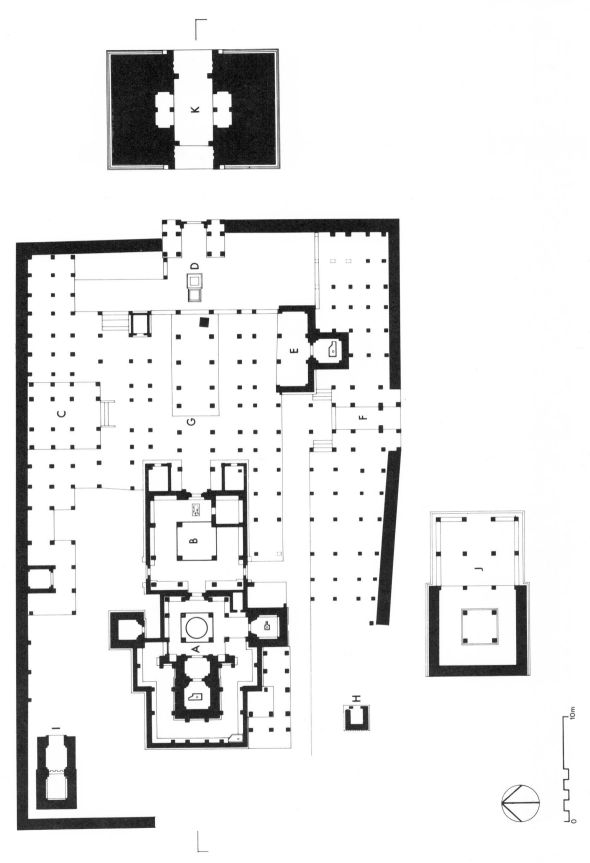

Figure 5.2   Virupaksha Temple, plan of complex.

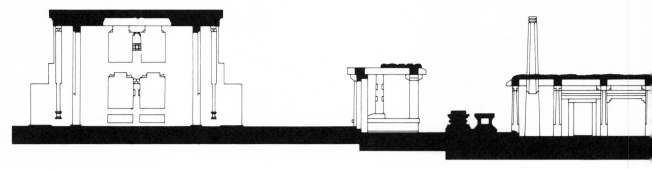

Figure 5.3   Virupaksha Temple, section.

according to an epigraph recording a grant of Krishna Raya in the detached hall (J) to the south (*South Indian Inscriptions* IX/II, no. 491).

The principal east-facing temple (A) originally consisted of a sanctuary, antechamber, and open columned porch; the porch had seating all around and an extension on the south. At a later date this open porch was enclosed to create a hall with a doorway on the east; two small shrines were added, one within the hall and the other outside to the north; columns and walls were built around the sanctuary on three sides to form an enclosed passageway. Within the sanctuary is a buried pedestal, and above is a ceiling with rotated squares. The shrine doorway displays a Lakshmi icon over the opening, with a frieze of miniature roof forms above, and potlike caskets beneath at either side. In the walls flanking the antechamber doorway deep niches are positioned; above rise ornamental roof forms. The four columns in the middle of the hall are raised on a floor area inscribed with a large circle. These columns are of an early type, with basement blocks, double capitals, and partly curved brackets; some of the columns against the walls are similar. Of interest are two lathe-turned columns flanking the south entrance to the hall (blocked by a later shrine). Over the central bay is a ceiling of rotated squares. The outer walls of the sanctuary, now enclosed by the surrounding passageway, preserve traces of basement and cornice mouldings, characterized by angled uncut blocks. Also to be seen are portions of the sloping eave of the original porch, and the lowest courses of the stepped stone superstructure above the sanctuary.

The first extension to the east (B) consists of a square hall, once an open porch with four columns in the middle and twelve on the periphery with seating slabs in between. Walls on four sides with doorways may be later additions. Near

to the east doorway is a Nandi image (probably not in the original position), delicately carved and polished in black basalt. A small (later) shrine is built into the southeast corner of the hall. Extending to the east is a porch with two free-standing columns and seating; at some later date, small shrines were added here. Possibly also associated with this phase is the free-standing monolithic column to the east, now contained within a later colonnade (G) and protruding above its roof. The doorways, columns, beams, and ceilings of this hall are very similar to those of the first phase, though, in general, not as finely carved. The sloping eave of this hall and porch is clearly visible on three sides; even the parapet with angled uncut blocks can be seen.

Abutting the enclosure wall to the north is a colonnade (C) consisting of 4 by 4 columns. Flanking the access steps to the south are yali balustrades. Two rows of columns have blocks with carvings and curved brackets; the other columns are plain. This colonnade is linked by beams and ceiling slabs to (later?) colonnades on three sides. The various changes in level result in clumsy joints and inclined beams. Some distance to the west is a small shrine.

East of the principal temple and its columned extension are two square altars with contrasting basements, and a gateway (D). The gateway has an east-west passageway, stepping down to the west. Either side of this passageway are platforms with columns supporting beams and horizontal roof slabs; a sloping eave is only partly preserved. Meeting the north and south sides of the gateway, but not aligned, are the enclosure walls.

To the southeast is a small shrine (E), now surrounded by colonnades but originally free-standing. This small north-facing shrine has a square sanctuary adjoining a rectangular porch enclosed on three sides with two free-standing columns. The columns have miniature basements

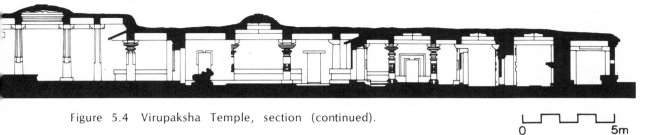

Figure 5.4 Virupaksha Temple, section (continued).

0   5m

and double capitals. On the south of the enclosure is an open columned gateway (F), consisting of a north-south passageway stepping down to the north. This passageway is flanked by two platforms, each with 4 by 2 columns. Between the second pair of columns flanking the passageway is a doorway facing south. In the middle of the lintel is an icon of Lakshmi, now much worn. Projecting beams take a sloping eave on three sides. East and west of the gateway are the enclosure walls; these abut the gateway on the south. Built against the north face of these walls is a colonnade: on the east this continues until it meets the outer walls of a shrine (E); to the west it is four columns deep and continues for several bays before breaking off abruptly.

Also found to the east of the principal temple and its extension is an open colonnade (G) linking many of the features already described. Judging from the abutment of the ceiling slabs of the colonnade with these features, it is clearly a later addition. Eight of the columns (on the principal axis of the temple) are raised on an elaborate basement. Four of these have tapering sixteen-sided shafts, and support a ceiling with an enlarged medallion and delicately incised foliation; elsewhere, the columns have tapering octagonal shafts. The colonnade wraps around the north and south ends of the hall extension (either side of the porch). One bay at the northeast is converted into a small shrine facing west.

Detached shrines are found at the southwest and northwest corners of the enclosure. These east-facing sanctuaries do not preserve any columned halls, though the northwest example (I) incorporates a small antechamber. Above the southwest shrine (H) rises a ruined brick superstructure, the upper part of which is square-to-dome. The stone tower of the northwest shrine has collapsed.

Outside the enclosure walls to the south is a well preserved hall (J) within which is an inscribed slab recording Krishna Raya's grant (referred to above). On the west the hall is enclosed on three sides; on the east it becomes an open porch. In the middle of the enclosed hall is a raised floor area with four columns; two more columns are positioned at the step that leads down into the porch. This porch has 4 by 2 columns with (seating?) slabs positioned between the outer columns; it is entered in the middle of the east side. The basement of the hall is doubled, and the walls (much reconstructed) are plain except for a curved frieze of petals and a cornice. At the open porch the basement is shorter. Within, the step separating the porch and the hall is defined by a carved basement. The interior columns have carved blocks and curved brackets; similar brackets high up on the walls support beams with friezes of petals. Over the raised floor is a ceiling with an enlarged medallion surrounded by dancing girls, scrollwork, and yali heads. Within the porch, beams divide the ceiling into two bays; outside is a double-curved eave, deeply undercut.

Beyond the enclosure walls to the east is a large incomplete gateway (K). Here an east-west passageway is flanked by chambers at two levels. The outer walls are elevated on a double basement; at each doorway this basement is terminated in (mostly) uncarved blocks. Full-height pilasters alternate with secondary pilasters standing in pots. Above the wall is a cornice, projecting slightly over the entrances. Probably no superstructure was ever built (no brick or plaster debris is seen nearby). The high doorways within the gateway employ bands of foliation; icons of Lakshmi (west) and Ganesha (east) appear in the middle of the lintels, with guardians beneath at either side (west doorway only). Flat elongated pilasters are positioned on the side walls flanking the doorways. Within the gateway are columns with octagonal and sixteen-sided shafts, and brackets with roll mouldings.

5. SACRED ART

RAMACHANDRA TEMPLE COMPLEX
(Figure 5.5)

Located in the middle of the enclosures, this temple is the most completely preserved sacred building in the royal centre. The complex consists of a rectangular courtyard — with gateways in east and north walls (leading into I) and a small doorway in the south wall (providing access to the alley) — within which is a principal shrine, a minor shrine, and several columned halls and colonnades. Though popularly known as "Hazara Rama," this temple was dedicated to Ramachandra according to epigraphs on the principal shrine and northeast columned hall (*South Indian Inscriptions* IV, nos. 251 and 253). No foundation date is known for the temple, but an inscription on the basement of the east wall of the principal shrine (*South Indian Inscriptions* IV, no. 252) mentions the ruler Devaraya (I, 1406-1422, or II, 1424-1446 ?). Thus the establishment of the temple can be no later than the first half of the fifteenth century. Venkataramanayya (1945) argues that this epigraph belongs to an earlier building phase; the Ramachandra Temple, he proposes, was constructed by Virupaksha II (1465-1485).

PRINCIPAL SHRINE
(Figures 5.6, 5.32, 5.33, 5.36, 5.37, 5.38, and 5.39)

Located in the middle of the courtyard, this east-facing shrine has a square sanctuary linked by a doorway to a rectangular antechamber. Another doorway leads to a rectangular transitional bay opening directly into the square hall. This hall has four free-standing columns on a central raised floor area inscribed with a circle. A narrow shelf runs around the walls, while engaged columns flank doorways on three sides. Two narrow openings, perhaps also functioning as doorways, are positioned in the west wall. The north and south porches each have two columns and two wall projections framing the doorways. (Curved slabs for seating may be later insertions.) The original east porch has four columns raised on a high basement flanking the principal doorway. At a later stage this porch was extended and 2 by 4 columns added. To the east is a small altar.

With the exception of the projecting walls containing the north and south porch doorways, the basement runs continuously around the temple. A curved spout emerges out of an open-mouthed yali on the north. At the north and south porches, the basement begins higher up and is reduced in scale; another basement series is utilised for the east porch. Either side of the three hall doorways the basement is terminated by carved blocks. Pairs of full-height pilasters demarcate the projections and recesses on the outer walls of the sanctuary and antechamber. Secondary shorter pilasters frame the niches in the middle of three sides of the sanctuary; above are miniature cornices and rectangular roof forms. Flanking these niches are ornamental pilasters emerging out of pots, also provided with miniature roof forms. Sculptured panels in two rows fill the spaces between the pilasters on the sanctuary and antechamber walls. On the walls of the hall, three rows of panels appear between full-height pilasters; here there is no change of wall plane. The doorways in the west wall of the hall are framed by pilasters, and the lintels have foliate arches rising from makaras with flowing tails. Within the arches are an icon of Lakshmi (north) and a *Ramayana* scene (south). The walls are terminated by an overhanging cornice with large medallions decorated with foliation and yali heads. Above the sanctuary walls the cornice is deeply undercut and is provided with ribbing; partly concealed by the cornice is a frieze of flowing brackets. Over the hall walls, however, the cornice has no ribs and there is a row of ganas beneath. Upon the cornice is a frieze of lions and yalis.

Rising upon the sanctuary is the square brick and plaster superstructure with a projection on the east side coinciding with the antechamber beneath. The superstructure is divided into three storeys. The lower two storeys have three principal projections on each side (continuing those of the walls below) framing recesses in which smaller secondary projections are located. The pilasters defining the projections support a miniature roof form — square at the corners, rectangular in the middle, and arched in between. The central projections are higher than the others, and inside are secondary niches of the same scheme but at a smaller scale. The third and uppermost storey is elevated on a short wall supporting a square-to-dome roof form, now much restored. The projection on the east has an enlarged arched form on its front (east) decorated with exuberant plaster decoration — makaras, tufts of foliage, flamelike motifs, and a capping yali head. Within the arch is a miniature niche with its own cornice and rectangular vaulted roof form. On the sides (north and south), the curved vault is plainly visible.

The (original) porch columns on three sides have double capitals and curved brackets. The deeply overhanging eave is double-curved and decorated with foliate medallions. The porch doorways (missing on the south) are defined by bands of foliation and other motifs. Sculptured panels in three rows continue from the outer walls into the recessed entrances of the north and south porches. The eight columns constituting the porch extension to the east are of a different type, being greatly elongated and without capitals.

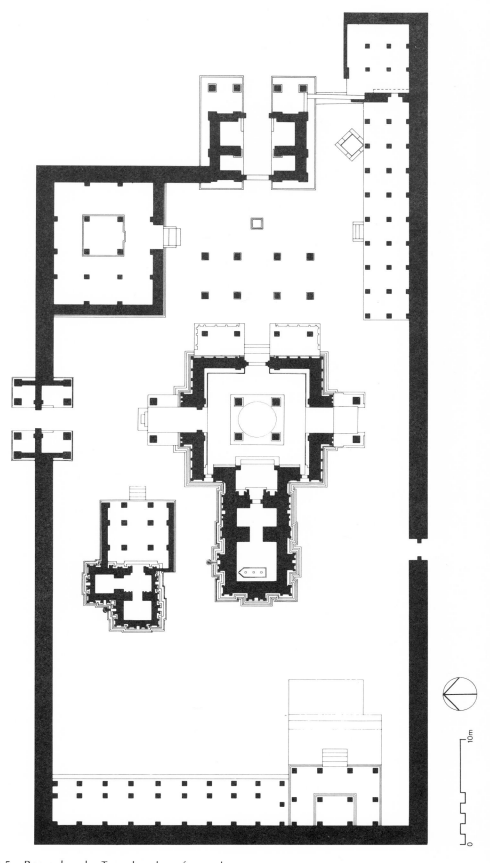

Figure 5.5   Ramachandra Temple, plan of complex.

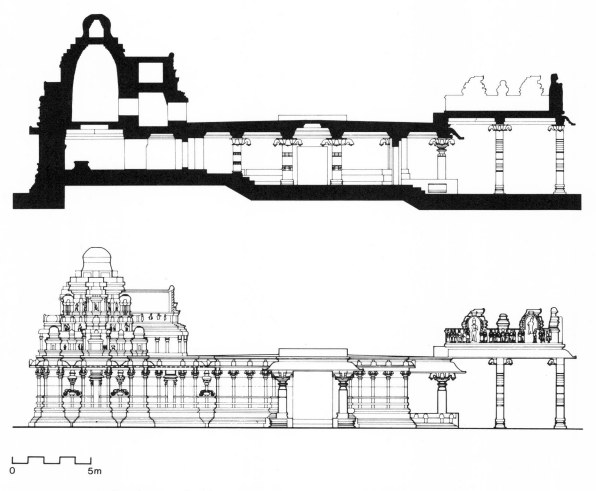

Figure 5.6   Ramachandra Temple, elevation and section of principal shrine.

The beams support an undecorated overhanging eave within which is a triple curve. Rising above a frieze of yalis and other beasts is a brick and plaster parapet with figural sculpture, now much damaged. Enlarged figures are contained within arched niches, carried on pilasters and elaborately decorated with makaras and foliation. Smaller projections are partly concealed by rows of attendant figures. Above these niches and projections, mouldings culminate in rectangular roof forms (clearly observed on the north).

Inside the sanctuary the walls are plain, except for the shelf against the back (west) wall. The ceiling has rotated squares with a central medallion. The rectangular pedestal has three small square holes to fix cult images (now missing). Half-pilasters and ornamental pilasters in pots frame the transitional doorways, which have bands of foliation with guardians beneath. The west wall of the transitional bay has niches flanked by half-pilasters elevated on a basement. Two steps (replacements?) lead down to the hall.

The principal decoration of the hall is provided by the central four columns of highly polished basalt, carved with considerable delicacy. Sculptured icons on the three blocks of each column are framed in miniature niches; there is an elaborate basement beneath. Here are found the 24 forms of Vishnu as well as most of the incarnations; also Durga, Ganesha, attendant courtiers, devotees, sages, and guardians. The curved brackets support beams with petalled friezes. Above the central bay is a raised medallion within rotated squares. The engaged columns have simpler designs and are carved with various Vaishnava icons and decorative themes. Medallions are found on the ceiling slabs in front of the north and south doorways.

SCULPTURAL PROGRAMME OF MAIN SHRINE

The most important sculptures on the exterior of the principal shrine of the Ramachandra Temple comprise a *Ramayana* series carved on the outer walls of the hall. The panels are arranged in three rows, beginning at the north part of the west wall of the hall. (The niches are numbered in a clockwise direction; see Figure 5.7).

In the bottom series the story begins; Dasharatha seated with a sage (1); Dasharatha stands in devotion before another sage (2); Agni emerges from the sacrificial fire performed by the deer-horned sage, Rishyashringa, who gives the offering to Dasharatha (3); Dasharatha presents the offering to his three queens (4); Dasharatha seated with his four sons (5); Vishvamitra (6); Rama shoots Tatike (7); Vishvamitra with young Rama (8) and two sages (9); Rama releases Ahilya from the stone (10); Vishvamitra performs the sacrifice (11); Rama kills Subahu and Maricha (12); Vishvamitra with Rama and Lakshmana is received by Janaka (13); Rama breaks Shiva's bow (14); Janaka with his four daughters (15); Rama and Lakshmana with Janaka (16); Sita garlands seated Rama (17); Janaka blesses the marriage ceremonies (18-20); four couples ride in chariots to Ayodhya (21-22); Rama strings and shoots Parashurama's bow (22-23); couples ride on elephants to Ayodhya (25, 27); four brothers seated with their wives (28); Dasharatha seated with his queens (29-30); Dashikubja discusses Rama's forthcoming coronation (31-32); Kaikeyi demands the promised boon (33); Rama worships before the coronation (34); Dasharatha and Kaikeyi order Rama to leave Ayodhya (35); Kaikeyi garlands Sita (36).

The middle series of panels begins with the exile to the forest: Rama, Lakshmana, and Sita (1); three forest sages (2); Rama shoots a demon (3); Rama kicks a fallen demon (4); sages welcome Rama, Lakshmana, and Sita (5, 7); Lakshmana with bow (6); Rama and Sita with Agastya (8); Rama and Sita with Lakshmana (9, 12); Lakshmana cuts off Shuparnakha's nose (11); Rama in battle with a demon riding a chariot (13); two demons with swords and shields (14); Ravana in his chariot battles with Rama (15); another demon battles with Rama (16); Sita requests the golden deer (17); Rama leaves Sita to find the golden deer (18); Rama chases and kills the deer (19-20); Lakshmana meets Rama (21); Ravana in ascetic disguise approaches Sita (22); Ravana rides with Sita in his chariot (23); Jatayu fights Ravana (24); Rama and Lakshmana meet wounded Jatayu (25); Rama kills Kamba (26-27); Rama and Lakshmana meet Hanuman (28); seated Rama meets Sugriva (29); Rama kills Vali by shooting an arrow through seven palm trees (32); Rama meets dying Vali (33); Sugriva stands before Rama (34); Lakshmana deputes Hanuman to search for Sita (35; repeated on south wall of antechamber); monkeys in devotion (36).

The story is concluded in the top series of panels: monkey in devotion (1); Rishyashringa with monkeys (2); Sugriva with wife (3); Rama with monkeys (4-5); Hanuman jumps over the ocean (8); Hanuman sets fire to Lanka (9); Hanuman breaks off a jackfruit (10, 12); Hanuman fights demons (13); Hanuman shows Rama's ring to Sita (14; repeated on north wall of antechamber); Hanuman grapples with demons (15-16); Indrajit arrests Hanuman (17); Hanuman seated on tail before Ravana (18); Hanuman reports to Rama (19);

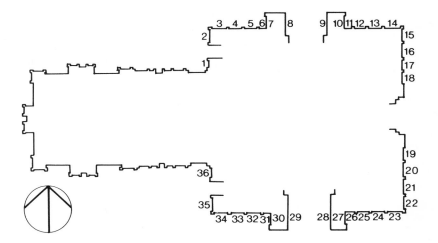

Figure 5.7   Ramachandra Temple, key to Ramayana sculptures on principal shrine.

5. SACRED ART

Sugriva with monkey attendants (20); Rama and Lakshmana carried by monkeys (21-22); monkeys in devotion (23-24); Sugriva and Hanuman with Rama and Lakshmana (27); monkeys construct bridge to Lanka (28); Lakshmana kills demon (29); Rama kills Ravana (30); people of Ayodhya watch Lakshmana reward Hanuman (33-34); Rama and Sita enthroned, with Lakshmana, Hanuman, Sugriva, and monkeys standing in adoration (above doorway between 35 and 36).

Less systematically organized are the sculptures on the outer three walls of the sanctuary and antechamber. Here, the deep niches (now empty) are flanked by guardians with clubs and Vaishnava emblems, female chauri-bearers, Hanuman and Garuda. Beside the *Ramayana* episodes already referred to, there are several related depictions of Rishyashringa, Sugriva, Rama, Sita, and monkeys. Vaishnava icons, often repeated several times, include seated Narasimha, seated and standing Jina figures (replacing the Buddha incarnation), and four-armed Vishnu, sometimes with Lakshmi or receiving the respects of Gajendra. Krishna figures, too, are found — dancing with sweets, crawling, subduing the serpent, or in a multi-armed form playing the flute accompanied by cows and gopis.

MINOR SHRINE
(Figure 5.8)

North and slightly west of the main shrine of the Ramachandra Temple is this smaller temple, a curiously asymmetrical structure combining two sanctuaries with a single antechamber and hall, the latter being a later addition. No original cult icons are preserved in this temple, nor are there any inscriptions.

Two sanctuaries (rectangular on the west, square on the north) open off a small rectangular antechamber. These elements constitute the original structure, as defined by the elaborate basement that runs around the walls on all sides, partly obscured by the abutment of the plain (later) walls of the hall. Within the hall are 3 by 2 free-standing columns (originally constituting an open porch), with (later) walls and engaged columns to the north and south. The hall is open to the east.

The basement running around the two sanctuaries and antechamber has a double series of mouldings with elaborately carved ornament. Notable is the variation of mouldings beneath the wall projections. The short vertical courses within the basement are divided into panels carved with both Ramayana and Krishna episodes. The former includes Hanuman prostrated before Rama (south), and Hanuman carrying the mountain, monkeys in devotion, and Rama shooting the bow (west); the latter depicts Krishna pulling the mortar (east), dancing on the serpent, fighting the crane and

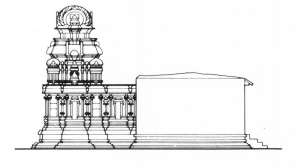

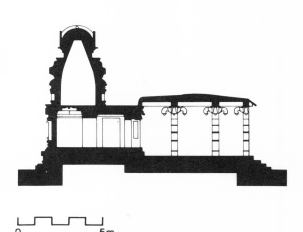

Figure 5.8 Ramachandra Temple, elevation and section of minor shrine.

elephant demons, dancing with sweets, crawling, and eating butter (south), and Krishna hiding up the tree with gopis beneath (north). As well, there are three scenes illustrating the rescue of Gajendra (east).

The outer three walls of each sanctuary have pilasters framing projections and recesses. The shorter secondary pilasters flanking the deep niches (now empty) in the middle of each side support a miniature cornice and rectangular roof form, complete with medallions and finials. Ornamental pilasters on ribbed pots are positioned in the recesses. On the wall projections, *Ramayana* panels are carved in two rows on the south, west, and north sides. The episodes illustrated here — especially the scenes showing Rama and Sita before the sacrificial fire, and travelling together in the chariot — complete the *Ramayana* series of the principal shrine. The final panel (north) shows Vishnu sleeping on the serpent. On the east wall episodes from the Narasimha story are found (south to north).

The outer walls of the temple are overhung with a highly decorated cornice within which are ribs. Above the west sanctuary rises a brick and plaster superstructure, now much restored. Rectangular in plan, the tower repeats the same scheme as that of the main temple; it is divided into three storeys and is capped by a rectangular vaulted roof with arched ends. There is, however, no projection on the east face. Little of the original sculpture can be made out, except for a seated Narasimha (south). Plaster makaras with long tails, foliate decoration, and flamelike tufts are seen on the capping roof. No superstructure appears to have been erected over the north sanctuary.

Both sanctuaries have plain interiors, except for ceilings of rotated squares. The doorways to the west sanctuary (not preserved on the north sanctuary) and antechamber are defined by bands of foliation. The antechamber walls are plain, but those flanking the west doorway have pilasters elevated on a moulded basement. Carved on the short walls in which the antechamber doorway is recessed are panels of royal devotees with offerings, and one of the Narasimha scenes. Either side of the doorway the walls continue those of the exterior.

The walls of the hall are plain, and the columns have carved blocks and curved brackets; there are no capitals. At the east end is an angled eave.

SUBSIDIARY STRUCTURES

Within the courtyard of the Ramachandra Temple complex are two columned halls and two colonnades. South of the east gateway a small square tank is set at an angle. The paving stones are modern.

Positioned in the northeast corner of the courtyard is a rectangular hall, the walls and columns of which abut the enclosure walls, obscuring several carved panels. Clearly, this hall is a later addition. A donative inscription on the outer wall is dated 1513 (*South Indian Inscriptions* IV, no. 253). The plain walls are elevated on a basement, interrupted on the south by yali balustrades and steps leading up to the single doorway. Either side of the doorway are bands of foliation issuing from makaras; the lintel is carved with a row of ganas and yalis. The walls are terminated by bands of curved brackets and jewelled petals; above is a cornice with foliage medallions. The interior of the hall has 3 by 2 free-standing columns, four of which are elevated on a raised floor area aligned with the doorway. This floor area is defined by a short basement. The four columns here have carved blocks, double capitals, and curved brackets. However, the other two free-standing columns and the engaged columns against the walls have no capitals. Over the central floor area, an enlarged medallion ceiling is raised on eight carved blocks with intermediate open spaces. Built against the west enclosure wall near the southwest corner of the courtyard is another open hall. This consists of 4 by 3 columns on a simple basement. The four central rear columns are further elevated on a second basement. The curved brackets of the columns support friezes of dancers and musicians; above the front bay is a raised ceiling slab with an enlarged medallion surrounded by dancers and geese. An angled eave is now only preserved on the east.

Colonnades at the west and south appear to be later additions. Running along the west enclosure wall are two rows of free-standing columns and a single row of engaged columns. The angled brackets of these crudely finished columns support an angled eave on the east (only partly preserved). Another colonnade abuts the south enclosure wall. This is raised on a basement with a flight of steps flanked by yali balustrades in the middle of the north side. The two rows of free-standing columns have uncarved blocks; angled brackets support a sloping eave that returns along the west end of the structure. At the east end, the colonnade is partly blocked off by a wall; here a doorway once led to a square chamber with four central columns, now much dilapidated. This chamber is built into the south enclosure wall and the massive basement of the nearby gateway (Ic-II), and may have served as a kitchen (Filliozat 1983, p. 9).

GATEWAYS
(Figure 5.9)

Aligned with the east porch and doorway of the principal shrine of the Ramachandra Temple,

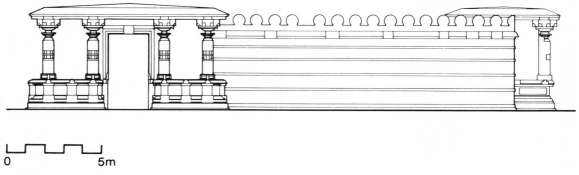

Figure 5.9   Ramachandra Temple, elevation of east gateway and enclosure wall.

the east gateway consists of a passageway with two doorways flanked by platforms. An open porch is found to the east, while infill walls on the north and south define interior chambers. The crude abutment of these infill walls with the four columns flanking the passageway suggests that this gateway may once have been a completely open structure. A high basement runs continuously around the gateway, interrupted only by the enclosure walls to the north (but not on the south), and by the recess for the door frames within the passageway. In the middle of the basement are projecting blocks with a variety of sculptures. The four columns on the front (east) have double capitals; similar columns on the north and south are now partly concealed by infill walls. Of interest here are the various carvings, especially icons of Bhairava and Durga on two columns within the passageway. Angled brackets support beams with angled ends to take a sloping eave that continues around the building on four sides. The brick and plaster parapet (visible in the nineteenth-century photograph) has now completely vanished. The doorway facing east is defined by foliate bands that continue over the lintel with a Lakshmi icon in the middle; above is a cornice with medallions divided into three projections. Flanking the doorway are engaged columns with inverted bell-like capitals and curved brackets. The doorway facing west (obviously a later addition) reproduces the same scheme as that on the east, except that a lotus medallion appears in the lintel. The threshold stone, also an insertion, is carved with a medallion. Within the gateway, the ceilings are horizontal and undecorated. The early photograph shows walls flanking the north side of the gateway; these have now disappeared. Further east is a detached panel carved with a Hanuman image (not in its original position).

Similarly aligned with the north porch and doorway of the principal shrine, the north gateway of the complex is smaller and simpler than the east example. Here open porches on the north and south, separated by a doorway, each consist of two free-standing columns and two engaged columns connected by walls. The columns are elevated on a basement, interrupted by the abutting enclosure walls to the east and west, and by the central recess for the door frame. The columns are similar to those on the east porch. Angled brackets support petalled friezes; above is an inclined eave on four sides. The north-facing doorway in the middle of the gateway is flanked by engaged columns, the shafts of which have foliation and pots. The doorway itself has petalled bands and a Lakshmi icon in the middle of the lintel.

ENCLOSURE WALLS
(See Endpapers)

Containing the Ramachandra Temple in a rectangle are high enclosure walls; these are discontinuous around the courtyard. Two types of wall are easily distinguished. The first runs north of the east gateway, along the north and west sides of the enclosure, and along the south side until it meets the small doorway. This wall is constructed of massive but finely jointed masonry (see Chapter 4), with drainage outlets set into the foundation course. The outer faces of these walls are divided by raised horizontal bands into long friezes of courtly reliefs (not found on the south wall). The inner faces of the wall on the east and north side (the latter east of the gateway) have narrative *Ramayana* panels. The walls are capped by a plain cornice with uncut medallions on the outside and narrative panels on the inside. Above the *Ramayana* panels is a parapet consisting of part-circular blocks carved (on the outer faces) with yakshas, geese, yalis, ascetics, and even an icon of Krishna dancing on the serpent.

The second type of wall is found on the south side of the enclosure, running eastwards from near the small doorway until it meets the gateway (Ic-II) southeast of the complex (across which it partly continues). The granite blocks of this wall are roughly finished; probably it is a later addition (or replacement?). A foundation course is seen south of the east gateway, but no wall is preserved.

On the outer faces of the enclosure walls are continuous reliefs; these run in a clockwise direction around three sides of the temple, terminating at the east gateway. The five sculptured friezes diminish in height as they ascend (coinciding with the stone courses). The bottom (first) frieze consists of a procession of elephants, mostly with riders and attendants with sticks. The elephants hold trees, branches, or bundles of grass in their trunks; between the animals are trees. In the second frieze, horses are led by attendants, many of whom have pointed beards and cloaks (Muslims, according to Goetz 1966). On the west and north, some of the horses rear and jump. Seated royal figures are also seen (at the corners and next to the gateways), leaning on cushions inside "palaces," sometimes with attendants or bearded supplicants. At the south end of the west wall, niches frame images of Karttikeya and a yaksha blowing a conch (later incorporated into small shrines — IXa/1-2).

The third frieze presents a large variety of military displays and martial arts. Here are found sword-fighters, stick-fighters, wrestlers, and acrobats; musicians play horns, flutes, drums, and other musical instruments; lines of soldiers carry bows, sticks, swords, shields, curved daggers, etc. Cavalry, too, mounted on horses, elephants and even camels (north), are depicted. In some scenes men bend bows. The figures have varied costumes and hair styles (especially on the north). Courtly riders also appear, accompanied by parasol-bearers and mace-bearers; seated figures face military supplicants and musicians, or observe fighting matches. Images of a yaksha and seated Ganesha are found on the west.

Dancing women in various postures form the subject of the fourth frieze. Here girls hold sticks and beat drums. Male drummers and musicians are also occasionally included. The fifth frieze introduces mythological scenes taken from the Krishna story. Here Krishna pulls the pestle (north and east), hides in a tree with naked gopis beneath (east and west), and embraces Radha or dallies with her while the gopis look on (north). In addition to attendant gopis, courtly women beat drums and even squirt each other with water (north). At the north end of the east side, two figures in chariots (?) fight each other with bows and arrows.

Within the courtyard, the enclosure walls display an extensive series of *Ramayana* reliefs. This series is preceded by several panels illustrating the Shravanakumara story (carved onto the east side of the north gateway, abutting the enclosure walls). This "prelude" to the *Ramayana* depicts (from bottom to top): Shravanakumara carrying his old and blind parents in baskets and collecting water; Dasharatha accidentally shooting Shravanakumara; Dasharatha being cursed by the parents; and, the suicide of the parents.

On the enclosure walls, the *Ramayana* reliefs are distributed in panels on six horizontal courses, partly concealed by the walls, columns, and (modern) buttresses of the hall built into the northeast corner of the enclosure. Though these panels do not exactly reproduce those of the principal shrine, there are only a few variations. The story begins on the north wall (east of the north gateway), and proceeds eastwards until the northeast corner; thereafter, southwards until the east gateway. The first course is mostly uncarved. On the second course is found the opening scenes — the sacrifice of Rishyashringa, the exploits of the youthful Rama, and the marriages of the four brothers. The third course illustrates the arrival at Ayodhya, the banishment of Rama, Sita, and Lakshmana, and the arrival in the forest. The fourth course is devoted to the various forest episodes, including the abduction of Sita, and ends with Rama instructing the monkeys. The fifth course depicts the exploits of Hanuman and concludes with the battle between Rama and Ravana. The sixth course has no panels, the continuous frieze proceeding in the reverse direction. Here is shown the death of Ravana, the trial of Sita by fire, and the return to Ayodhya. In the final scene (east of the north gate), the people of Ayodhya, together with Hanuman and Garuda, worship Vishnu sleeping on the serpent.

LAMP COLUMN AND SHRINE
(Figure 5.10)

More than 80 m. east of the Ramachandra Temple complex, and precisely aligned with its east gateway, are the remains of a lofty stone lamp column (Ic/14), the broken parts of which lie scattered about. The column consisted of a tapering octagonal and sixteen-sided shaft, with the upper part decorated with petals. The capital was in two parts, a circular section with a projecting octagon, and a square section. Only the stump of this column still stands, surrounded by a mass of concrete and the outline of a square platform.

Further east and also aligned with the temple gateway is a shrine (Ic/13), probably intended to house an image of Garuda or Hanuman, and

5. SACRED ART

now much dilapidated. Here a small sanctuary is attached to a rectangular porch with two free-standing columns. Angled brackets supported a sloping eave, a fragment of which survives.

TEMPLES ALONG THE NORTHEAST ROAD

Beginning north of the shrine just described is the northeast road (NE), lined on both sides with shrines and temples until it meets the defensive gateway almost 1km. away. These structures are oriented southeast or northwest so as to face onto the road. (Cardinal directions are assumed in the following descriptions.) These monuments are examined in sequence along the road, commencing with the small cluster of shrines either side of the Islamic-styled gateway (Ic-XVb).

SHRINES NEAR THE ISLAMIC-STYLED GATEWAY (Figures 5.11, 5.12, and 5.13)

Ic/2 consists of a square sanctuary and rectangular antechamber linked to a square hall. This hall has engaged columns against the walls (the four free-standing columns have vanished) and doorways on the east and south. Wall niches are positioned either side of the doorway to the antechamber. The outer walls are elevated on a basement and have a projecting course, carved on the south with meandering scrollwork; no cornice is seen. Columns flank the south entrance (doorway is missing), while pilasters emerging out of pots are seen at either side of the antechamber (also missing its doorway). The adjacent wall niches have pilasters supporting a miniature cornice and square-to-dome roof. Angled brackets and fragments of the ceiling are found fallen within the hall. Of interest here are the traces of original plasterwork.

East of the Islamic-styled gateway on the north side of the road is the colonnade XVb/1. This consists of 2 by 4 columns at the east end of a thick pile of fallen stones. The colonnade is raised on a basement and the columns have unusual projecting brackets with pendant hemispheres. On the east side a sloping eave is still in place. To the north the colonnade is broken off, while to the south another (later?) basement, with a frieze of elephants, defines a rectangular raised area extending westwards. Here are found overturned and broken basement courses, composite column shafts, brackets, and double-curved eaves. (Some of these are still standing in the nineteenth-century photograph.) A fragmentary Bhairava image is discovered in the rubble.

Further east is a Shaiva temple (XVb/4) with two columned halls, separated by a wall with a connecting doorway. To the west, a small square sanctuary is surrounded on four sides by a colonnade, including 4 by 4 columns to the north,

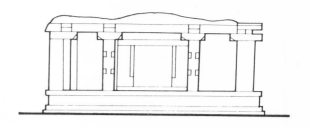

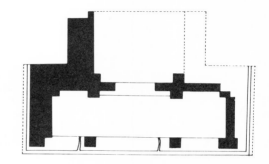

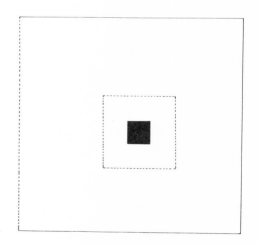

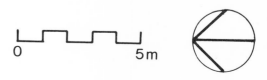

Figure 5.10 Lamp column and shrine east of Ramachandra Temple, plan and elevation.

70

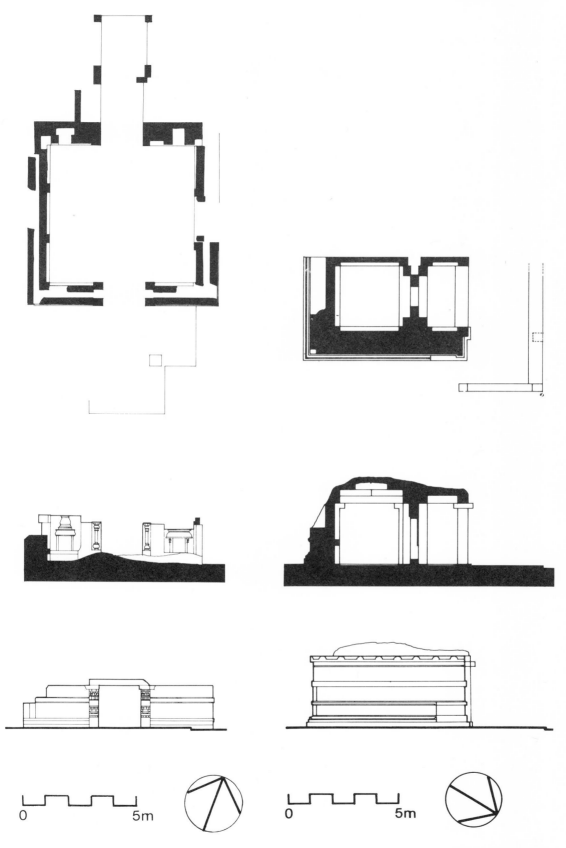

Figure 5.11   Temple Ic/2, elevation, section and plan.

Figure 5.12   Temple XVb/6, elevation, section and plan.

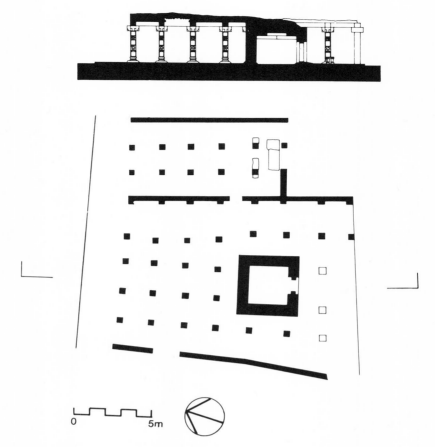

Figure 5.13   Temple XVb/4, plan and section.

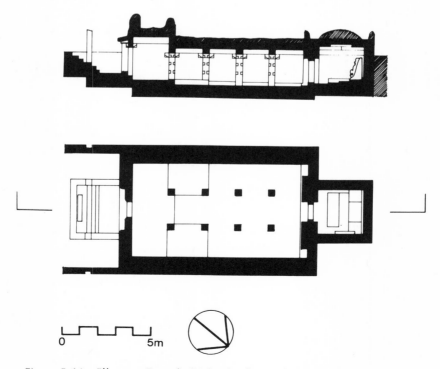

Figure 5.14   Ellamma Temple (XVb/5), plan and section.

and three stone footings to the south. Walls are only preserved on the east and west. The east hall has no shrine but 2 by 6 columns; a doorway is on the south. Almost the only notable feature of the sanctuary is the doorway with an icon of Shiva and Parvati over the opening, and guardians with Shaiva emblems beneath at either side. In front of the doorway is a loose chlorite fragment carved with the foot of Durga and part of the speared buffalo. The free-standing columns in the west hall have an unusual variety of carved images and emblems.

On the south side of the road is another series of shrines. XVb/6 consists of a square sanctuary and rectangular antechamber with walls and column bases to the north indicating a rectangular columned hall or porch, now vanished. The walls are plain except for a projecting cornice. Within the sanctuary is a broken Virabhadra sculpture. The doorway has petalled bands, above which is a frieze of dancing women; beneath at either side are enlarged makaras. The doorway is set within a second larger frame with icons of Durga (right) and Bhairava (left) beneath.

To the east is a shrine (XVb/7), of which only the sanctuary and antechamber are still partly standing. Five columns in front (north) suggest an open porch with extensions to east and west; either side of the doorway the walls are also extended. A fragmentary naga stone is found here. Even more ruined is the next shrine (XVb/10) with only part of the sanctuary walls still standing. The most easterly of this group is the two-storeyed pavilion (XVb/11), apparently part of a colonnade. The lower level has six columns; above are four columns of a different design, with carved blocks and curved brackets. A sloping eave, originally on four sides, is found only on the east. The brick and plaster tower still visible in the nineteenth-century photograph is not preserved. Of interest is an inscription carved on one of the upper beams which records that this pavilion was constructed by a mercantile guild for the god Raghunatha (Nagaraja Rao 1984).

ELLAMA TEMPLE (XVb/5)
(Figure 5.14)

Dedicated to an aspect of Devi, this temple is still in worship and has been much renovated. Facing southeast onto the road, the temple consists of a square sanctuary linked by a doorway to a long hall. The hall has 2 by 4 columns with an open porch to the south (now mostly filled in) with four columns. Little of the outer walls of the original temple can be made out due to the rise in ground level and the various additions. At the south, angled beam ends support a sloping eave; the wall above may incorporate an original parapet. Inside the temple, the columns, ceilings, and

doorway have been overpainted and almost no original carvings can be made out. Within the sanctuary there is a seated four-armed deity, possibly an original cult image (Devakunjari 1970, p. 38). At the south end of the hall, the floor and horizontal ceiling are raised up.

MADHAVA TEMPLE COMPLEX
(Figures 5.15 and 5.16)

This group of two shrines, associated colonnades, and enclosure walls (near the southeast corner of XIV) faces southeast onto the road. Laid out approximately in a square, the enclosure walls with a plaster-covered brick parapet are only partly standing on the north and east. To the west is a modern retaining wall. The principal shrine is found on the west side; behind, in the northwest corner, is an open hall of 3 by 5 columns. A second shrine, now missing its roof and inner walls, stands to the east; in front (south) are the remains of an elaborate columned hall.

The principal shrine consists of a rectangular sanctuary and antechamber; these are connected by a doorway to an open hall of 4 by 4 columns, possibly a later addition. Within the hall to the northwest is a Hanuman image carved on a gigantic panel (2.7m. high) leaning against a short wall. Between the outer columns of the hall on the west and south are modern retaining walls; here is found an inscription identifying Madhava as the deity to whom the shrine is dedicated (*South Indian Inscriptions* IV, no. 248).

The sanctuary and antechamber are elevated on a basement with a yali spout on the east. The walls are plain except for a vertical recess demarcating the junction of the sanctuary and antechamber within, and a cornice. Above the sanctuary rises the rectangular brick and plaster superstructure, now much ruined. The lower two storeys of the tower each have three or five projections with pilasters supporting miniature cornices and roof forms. The plaster sculptures have mostly disappeared; traces of supporting timbers are seen. The rectangular roof form is apsidal at both ends; on four sides are miniature niches with roof forms. Within the sanctuary the only feature of interest is a rectangular pedestal with a miniature basement. Though the original doorway is obscured by modern buttresses, guardians with clubs and Vaishnava emblems are visible. The outer columns of the hall once supported a sloping eave, now vanished.

To the east is the square sanctuary and rectangular antechamber of another shrine. The outer walls of this structure are more or less intact, though leaning dangerously; the interior is now a mass of collapsed walls, ceiling slabs, and brickwork. The exterior walls are elevated on a high double basement which rhythmically projects

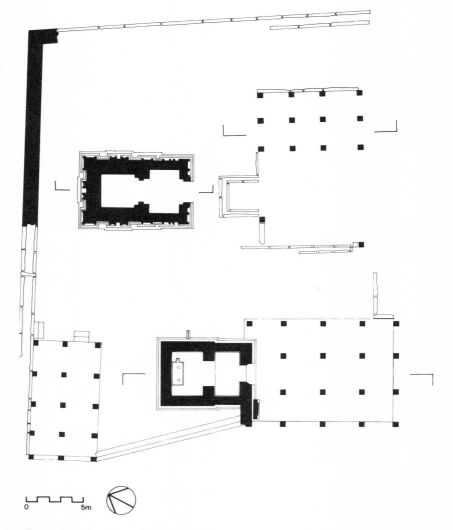

Figure 5.15   Madhava Temple, plan of complex.

and recesses; the upper basement varies beneath the central projections of the sanctuary. A curved spout is seen on the east. On three sides of the sanctuary the walls have three projections framing two recesses. Full-height pilasters define the projections, and in the middle of the central projection on each side are niches (now empty) created by secondary pilasters supporting miniature cornices and rectangular roof forms. In the recesses, single pilasters stand in pots. The south doorway is formed by carved blocks that terminate the basement mouldings, and by full-height pilasters; the lintel has fallen. On either side are carved panels and miniature niches surmounted by roof forms. The wall is terminated by projecting friezes of petals, curved brackets, and ganas.

South of this shrine is a colonnade with 4 by 3 columns still standing in their original position. Everywhere around are the heaped remains of collapsed and broken columns, brackets, beams, ceilings, and eaves; pieces of concrete roof and brick infill are also found. Parts of the walls that enclosed the hall are seen on the east; on the west, stone courses are set into the ground. Possibly, the hall may have consisted of 6 by 6 columns, with three north-south aisles, each of three bays. One inner bay (2 by 4 columns) is still completely preserved. The columns here have carved blocks and curved brackets. Above is a beam with petals and jewels, and an overhanging cornice with ribs and foliate medallions. This cornice supports a recessed frieze of yalis, dancers, courtly ladies, and various Vaishnava icons. The latter include some of the incarnations, a four-armed Vishnu figure inside a miniature niche, three scenes from the Narasimha story, and several Krishna episodes. Projecting brackets with seated yalis (doubled at the corners) carry another

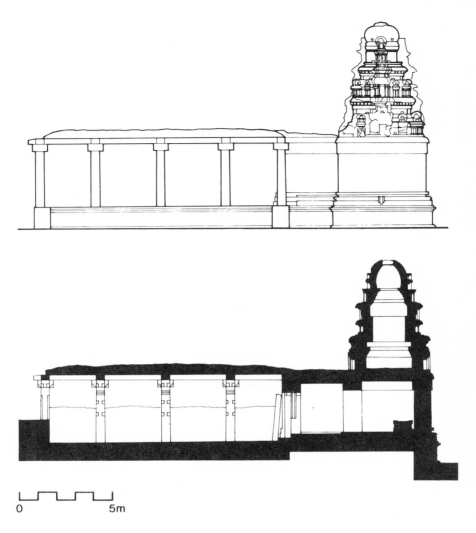

Figure 5.16   Madhava Temple, section and elevation of principal shrine.

beam carved with yalis, ganas, and geese on the side, and scrollwork underneath. The horizontal ceiling has a central medallion surrounded by bands of flowers and scrollwork.

ADJACENT JAINA AND SHAIVA TEMPLES
(Figure 5.17)

These two buildings stand close together, facing southeast onto the road. The Jaina temple consists of a square sanctuary and antechamber, each with a doorway, adjoining a hall with four columns in the middle on a raised floor area (mostly missing). A second doorway leads to a porch on the south, with 4 by 2 columns, probably a later addition. The walls are partly fallen on the east and west, and completely on the south. Little of the original exterior of the temple is seen. Within the sanctuary is a ceiling of rotated squares and an overturned pedestal with a carved basement. The antechamber doorway has a meditating Jina figure carved over the opening. The hall columns have basement blocks, double capitals and angled brackets. Of interest is the raised ceiling panel supported on slabs with ingenious interlocking joints.

The adjacent Shaiva temple to the east has a long rectangular sanctuary connected by a doorway to a hall with four free-standing columns. Either side of the doorway a passageway begins, but is only partly preserved on the west. Almost nothing of the original exterior is visible except the plain walls. Above the open end (south) of the hall, fragments of a brick parapet are seen. Over the doorway is a block carved with a seated female divinity (?), now damaged; beneath at either side are guardians with Shaiva emblems.

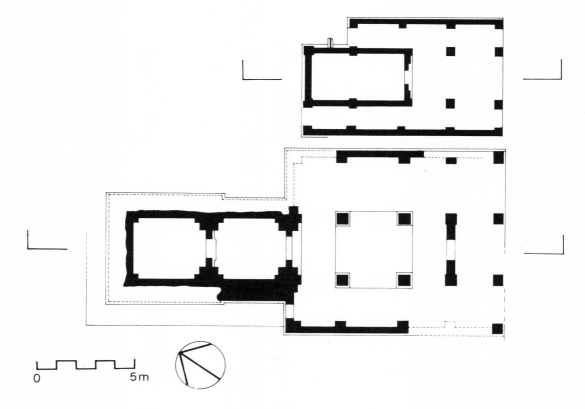

Figure 5.17   Jaina and Shaiva temples on northeast road, plan.

DATED JAINA TEMPLE
(Figures 5.18 and 5.35)

This large structure is oriented northwest, almost opposite the pair of temples just described. An inscription incised on the walls of the north porch is dated to 1426, and proclaims the royal patronage of Devaraya II (*South Indian Inscriptions* I, no. 153).

At the south end of the temple a square sanctuary is entered through a doorway. A transitional bay leads into a large (inner) hall with four columns in the middle, and twelve on the periphery, separated from the walls by a narrow shelf. The walls are mostly missing to the east and north. A connecting doorway leads to a second (outer) hall which repeats the same scheme of the inner hall, though on a slightly larger plan. In the middle of the west wall is a second sanctuary, now without its doorway. In the middle of the east and north sides, doorways give onto two porches. The east porch has two free-standing columns and two engaged columns linked by raised seating (now partly missing). The north porch has double the number of columns

with a few slabs supporting balcony seating. Further north are several columns and a doorway, clearly later additions.

Now partly buried, the exterior basement consists of a simple tripartite scheme. The walls of the sanctuary have a central projecting horizontal course, and vertical bands at the corners and at the junction of the sanctuary and transitional bay within. Above is a cornice with large uncut medallions. (The walls are partly fallen or concealed by modern buttresses around the two halls.) The columns of the porches have polygonal shafts and double capitals. The angled ends of the beams here support a sloping eave (preserved only on the north). The principal (north) doorway is elaborately ornamented with foliate bands; beneath at either side are makaras and elephants, while in the middle of the lintel is a Jina figure seated within a decorated niche. Inside the temple the sanctuaries are plain except for the ceilings of rotated squares. The doorway of the south sanctuary is similar to that on the porch. The hall columns are squat and have polygonal shafts and double capitals. Rotated ceilings with raised medallions are found in both halls.

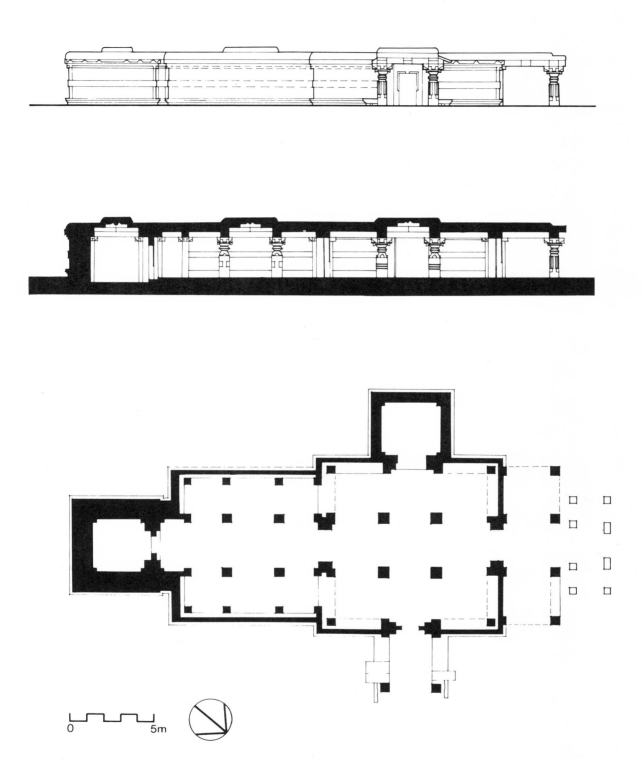

Figure 5.18   Dated Jaina temple on northeast road, plan, section and elevation.

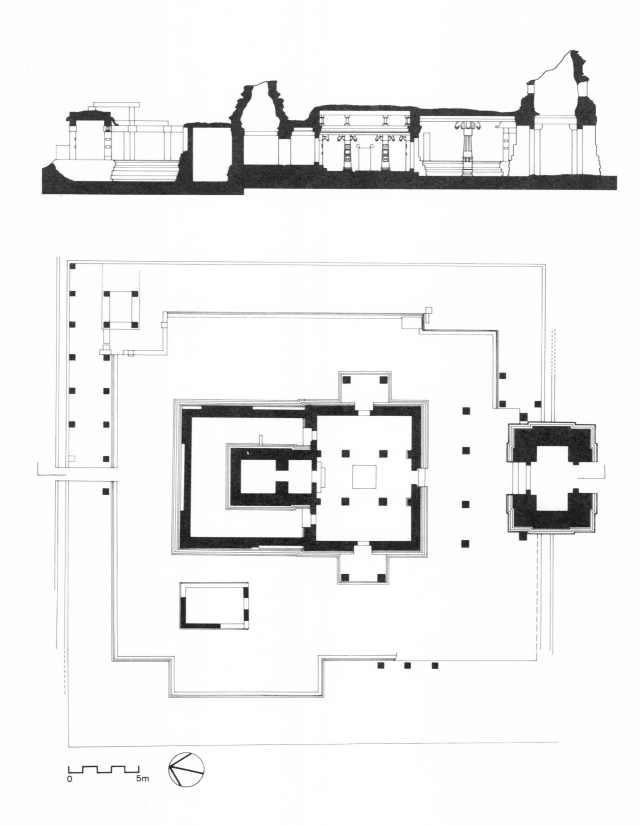

Figure 5.19   Vaishnava temple complex on northeast road, plan and section.

VAISHNAVA TEMPLE

Further along the northeast road is a small temple facing southeast. Only parts of the walls and brick infill of the sanctuary stand; however, the hall, with its 3 by 2 columns in the middle and row of four columns on the open (south) side, is still preserved. Two openings in the north wall of the hall may have led to a passageway surrounding the sanctuary. On the exterior, little of the basement is seen, and the walls are plain with a cornice above. The principal interest within the hall is provided by the columns, beams, and ceiling. The four columns defining the central bay to the north have carved blocks and curved brackets. These support friezes of dancing girls and potlike drums. The ceiling has an enlarged medallion surrounded by bands of dancing girls. The two columns south of this bay have their shafts completely covered with an ascending series of miniature "facades," each with niches, cornices, and roof forms. At the open end of the hall, the central columns are of the composite type with enlarged rearing yalis; the corner columns have clusters of colonettes. Elaborate mouldings constitute the capitals and brackets of these columns. Above is a double-curved eave, now mostly collapsed, with delicately incised scrollwork and upturned elements at the corners.

VAISHNAVA TEMPLE COMPLEX
(Figures 5.19, 5.20 and 5.30)

A short distance further along the northeast road is this southeast-facing sacred complex. This consists of a temple in the middle of a rectangular courtyard surrounded by a colonnade; within the courtyard is a minor shrine. On the south a towered gateway is linked by a covered walkway to the south doorway of the temple.

The temple comprises a square sanctuary and rectangular antechamber divided by piers, opening onto a hall on the south. Here, four free-standing columns create a central aisle with a raised ceiling. Either side of the antechamber, two openings lead into a passageway that runs around the sanctuary on three sides. Doorways within the hall to the east and west lead to porches; the doorway to the south provides access to a covered area with four free-standing columns in the middle and two more near the corners of the gateway. Further south is the gateway with a central walkway between platforms (now mostly buried). The colonnade of the courtyard, now much dilapidated, has two rows of columns with recesses on the east and west (not aligned). Fragments of enclosure walls abut this colonnade on the north. A small shrine facing south is located within the courtyard west of the temple.

Above the moulded basement of the temple only portions of the exterior walls survive. These are plain except for shallow niches flanked by pilasters on each side of the passageway (preserved only partly on the west). A cornice terminates the wall. Over the sanctuary rises the brick and plaster superstructure, now much ruined. The square lower storey has three projections on each side, each capped by a miniature cornice; above is a circular drum and a fragment of the hemispherical roof form. No plaster sculpture has survived. The east and west porches are raised on basements but the access steps have vanished. Columns have carved blocks and curved brackets supporting a triple-curved eave and a plain parapet. Within the porches, the doorways and ceilings are plain. The covered area to the south employs six elongated columns with tapering sixteen-sided shafts; the brackets are curved. Only part of the double-curved eave is preserved on the east. The south doorway is badly damaged; it is partly framed by blocks terminating the upper mouldings of the basement.

Within the temple the sanctuary and antechamber are plain; the former is now missing its ceiling slabs. The doorway to the hall has bands of foliation with an icon of Lakshmi in the middle of the lintel; beneath at either side are guardians with Vaishnava emblems. All the other doorways are undecorated. The columns have blocks with carvings and curved brackets. Over the central north-south aisle, these carry beams and friezes of male drummers, female dancers beating potlike drums, and figures in coracles; projecting blocks are sculptured as seated yalis. The ceiling slabs are unadorned. To be noted is a large square slab in the middle of the floor incised with the outlines of a large lotus. In the passageway the moulded basement and plain walls of the sanctuary and antechamber are visible; the horizontal ceiling slabs (partly missing) are cut into angled segments at the corners.

The colonnade is now mostly collapsed and greatly overgrown. It is raised on a basement, and the columns resemble those of the temple porches. Portions of a double-curved eave, horizontal ceiling and concrete roof are seen to the north and south; elsewhere fragments of these are strewn around. At the northeast corner additional bays are introduced, with several plain columns and a doorway; one bay is double-height. The minor shrine is now mostly collapsed, but the doorway still stands; in front is a pile of debris, perhaps a fallen porch.

The outer walls of the towered gateway are raised on a double basement. At the entrances on the north and south this basement is terminated by carved blocks. The walls on four sides have a central projection carried through the basement up to the top of the walls; on the east and west these projections are partly uncarved to take abutting enclosure walls. Pilasters demarcate the projections, corners and intermediate piers; secondary pilasters in pots are found in the recesses. A frieze of petals and a flattened cornice terminate the walls. The doorways are deeply recessed and have foliate bands around the openings with medallions in the middle of the lintels. Beneath at either side are guardians (now buried). The doorway jambs have ladies clutching foliated branches with meandering stalks that continue onto the underside of the lintels. The brick and plaster tower rising above is greatly ruined. The lower storey (best preserved on the south) has an enlarged central projection with niches surmounted by miniature cornices and roof forms. Plaster figures are only preserved in fragments; these include devotees and male divinities (?) with female attendants in arched niches.

THREE SMALL TEMPLES

Continuing along the northeast road, we discover several more shrines at either side. The first example to the east is separated from the Vaishnava complex just described by the remains of a large tank. This temple comprises a sanctuary, portions of an antechamber, and a mass of fallen stones and a column indicating a square hall, all facing southeast. The sanctuary doorway has petalled bands and guardians with Shaiva emblems beneath. Only part of the lowest storey of the brick and plaster superstructure survives.

The next two examples face northwest. Here, square sanctuaries adjoin antechambers and columned halls, now mostly ruined. The interiors of the sanctuaries have their ceilings still in situ; the pedestals, though, are displaced.

TEMPLE IN NORTHEAST GATEWAY

This east-facing temple is built on the north bastion of the fortified gateway through which the northeast road passes (see Chapter 4). Here a small square sanctuary and antechamber adjoin a square hall with four columns in the middle on a raised floor area (now mostly missing). Two raised areas (extensions?) are found north and south of the antechamber. Parts of the temple walls have now fallen, revealing the brick infill. Above the sanctuary rises the square brick and plaster superstructure, well preserved in its lowest storey. This consists of three projections on each side defined by pairs of pilasters and surmounted by miniature roof forms; the central deep niche is an enlarged arch decorated with foliate plasterwork. The hall doorway has bands interrupted by an icon of Lakshmi in the middle of the lintel; beneath are guardians with Vaishnava emblems. Within the temple the sanctuary and antechamber are plain; the doorways resemble those of the hall. The columns have carved blocks and angled brackets. Rotated squares, with a central medallion in the hall, form the ceilings.

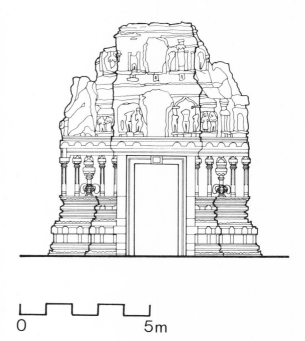

0   5m

Figure 5.20   Vaishnava temple complex, elevation of gateway.

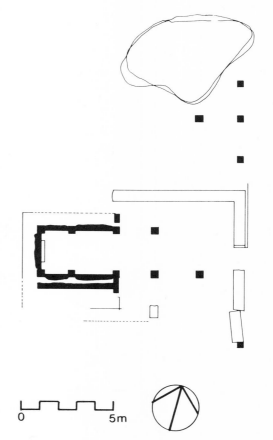

0   5m

Figure 5.21   Temple XXVI/2, plan.

TEMPLES NORTH OF THE ENCLOSURES
(Figures 5.21 and 5.22)

Within the zones in the north part of the royal centre (XXVI-XXXI) there is a considerable number of small shrines, now mostly ruined and buried beneath accumulated soil. A marked variety of temples is found here: some sanctuaries have no attached columned hall while others have elaborate arrangements of columns; several shrines are built up against boulders carved with sculptured icons; a few examples preserve only their columned halls.

Due north of the Virupaksha Temple complex is a curious rectangular structure (XXVI/3) built on a rocky shelf. Here, 4 by 2 free-standing columns are surrounded by an outer row of 6 by 4 columns with infill walls on four sides; an entrance is on the west. Walls, beams, and ceilings are all roughly hewn; the exterior projecting beams once carried a sloping eave (vanished). Curiously, there is no sanctuary.

Some distance to the northeast is a small ruined temple (XXVI/4) built against a rock carved with a fine image of Virabhadra (Nagaraja Rao 1983, pl. xliva). The icon is framed by pilasters and has a lobed arch with a yali head at the apex. In front is a square pedestal and several (original?) naga stones. The small sanctuary, with walls and a ceiling of horizontal slabs, is open to the south with columns to the east and west. Raised on the rock behind, four columns support horizontal slabs and brickwork.

Near to the southwest corner of the palace complex XXVI/1 is a ruined east-facing temple (XXVI/2). The sanctuary and antechamber are now missing their doorways; within the sanctuary is an overturned pedestal. To the east, three (out of four) central columns of the square hall still stand. The outer walls of this hall are preserved in their lower courses, and here can be seen doorways on the east and south. Immediately north of this temple is a boulder carved with icons: four-armed Harihara; Rama and Sita with Lakshmana; and Hanuman and Garuda holding hands over a vertical naga (Nagaraja Rao 1983, pl. xliib). East of the temple, traces of a colonnade are seen.

A fairly well preserved temple (XXVII/1) is located north of XII, facing east onto the north road (N1). This temple is built in two phases: to begin with, the sanctuary, antechamber, and rectangular hall; later, an east extension to the hall at a lower level. The upper hall has two free-standing columns, and was reached by steps flanked by balustrades, now fallen. The lower hall has 3 by 2 columns in the middle, two columns at the open east end, and doorways on the north and south. An inscription on the inner wall of the hall mentions Achyuta Raya (Nagaraja

Rao 1984). Stone rubble north and east of the temple may be the collapsed remains of enclosure walls; to the south are indications of minor shrines.

Parts of the outer walls of this temple are now fallen, revealing the brick infill. The basement is doubled around the sanctuary and antechamber, the lower series continuing onto the walls of the upper hall, returning inside the hall to define the change in level. The walls are plain except for small niches in the middle of three sides of the sanctuary. These niches are surmounted by curved arches with makaras, and yali heads at the summits; they frame icons of Lakshmi. The doorways are surrounded by recessed bands with Lakshmi in the middle of the lintel (north) and guardians with Vaishnava emblems beneath at either side. Over the sanctuary rises the square brick and plaster superstructure; the projections on the two lower storeys have pilasters and miniature roof forms, now much damaged. Above is the circular drum and a portion of the hemispherical roof form. A few plaster sculptures are partly preserved; these include musicians, devotees, and a seated couple (Vishnu and Lakshmi?). Within the temple the sanctuary is now missing its ceiling. The doorway is surrounded by bands and there is a Lakshmi icon in the middle of the lintel; beneath at either side are guardians with Vaishnava emblems. The columns have carved blocks and curved or angled brackets. Above the columns at the open (east) end are angled beams carrying a sloping eave.

Northwest of this temple are several dilapidated and overgrown shrines, one of which (XXVII/2) consists of an open colonnade of 4 by 4 columns within which is a sanctuary facing north. To the north of this example are two open columned structures built close together, and now partly buried. That to the east (XXVII/3) has a sanctuary and a small antechamber. Within the shrine is a carved Hanuman slab; a detached Ganesha sculpture is found nearby in the hall as well as fragments of doorways (for additional shrines?). The ceiling slabs over the central aisle of 3 by 2 columns are raised. The brick superstructure above the sanctuary is now greatly ruined. The west structure (XXVII/4), now almost inaccessible, has 4 by 4 columns.

Overlooking enclosure XIV from the northwest is a temple (XXVIII/1) elevated on a large boulder, beneath which is a spacious rock shelter. Two retaining walls on the south and a wall on the west define a court within which is a well (now filled in). Beyond the walls to the southwest are the heaped slabs of a fallen staircase. Stone slabs on the east indicate a collapsed construction (?). The temple consists of a sanctuary, entered on the east, surrounded on four sides by a passageway (narrower on the west) with a doorway on

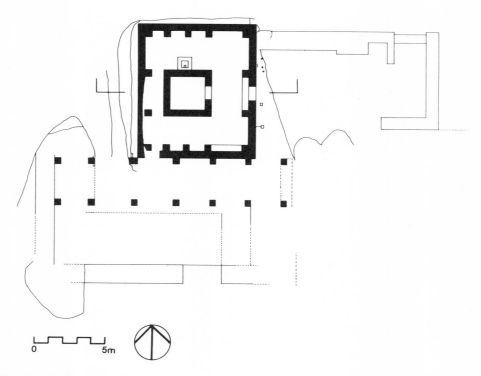

Figure 5.22 Temple XXVIII/1, plan.

the east. Another smaller opening in the south wall leads to an open colonnade of 2 by 7 columns on the south extending westwards. The unadorned walls of the temple have projecting blocks on the outside (brackets of the interior columns); above is a plain cornice. The east doorway has undecorated bands and a Lakshmi icon over the opening; beneath at either side are guardians with Vaishnava emblems. Carved on the rocky step in front is an enlarged image of a devotee. Within the temple the construction is massive, the sloping natural rock serving as a floor. The sanctuary walls are of stone infill between columns, partly covered with plaster; the ceiling has rotated squares and a medallion. An overturned long pedestal is seen here, also a sculptural fragment (?). Emerging from the middle of the north side of the sanctuary is a spout curving over a small hole cut into the rock and framed by carved mouldings. Nearby is a detached pedestal with elaborate mouldings. The passageway has undecorated square columns set into the walls with brackets projecting on four sides (even through the walls). The beams and horizontal ceiling slabs are plain.

Northwest of the temple just described is a small pavilion (XXVIII/2) built against a rock sculptured with a Bhairava icon. Above the icon is a curved arch with a yali head at the summit; pilasters are at either side. Further east is another

small shrine (XXIX/7) built against a boulder, the underside of which provides a natural crevice for the sanctuary. Only some small naga stones are now found here. The hall has 2 by 4 columns, but is only partly enclosed on the east and west. Outside the hall to the south, and on axis with the sanctuary, is a free-standing monolithic column with a tapering part-octagonal shaft. Some distance to the northeast is a dilapidated temple (XXXI/4) with a crudely constructed sanctuary abutting a rock carved with two nagas and a linga. An open hall with 4 by 2 columns still stands to the east. Here, again, a free-standing monolithic column is found on axis with the sanctuary to the east. South of the temple just described are two ruined shrines; that to the east (XXXI/2) is better preserved. This consists of a south-facing sanctuary housing a Hanuman image, and a hall with four free-standing columns and walls on the east and west (partly collapsed). Carvings of a donor couple and a seated Ganesha are found near the doorway. Proceeding northeastwards, two ruined colonnades are discovered, but without any associated sanctuaries. Nearby is a large rock carved with Vaishnava icons — Vishnu with two consorts, and two images of Narasimha.

Flanking the northeast valley are several shrines on the north ridge. These include a rocky shelf carved with icons of the incarnations of Vishnu,

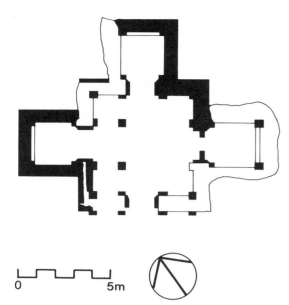

Figure 5.23 Triple-sanctuaried temple east of enclosures, plan.

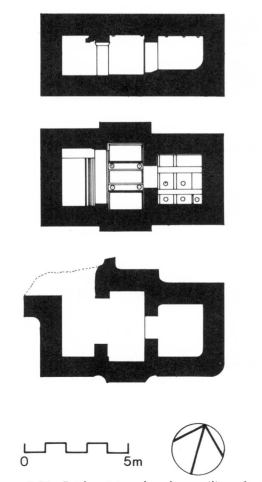

Figure 5.24 Rock-cut temple, plan, ceiling plan and section.

with additional scenes from the Vamana and Narasimha stories; also donors and ascetics (Nagaraja Rao 1983, pls. xlvi-xlvii). The colonnade sheltering the rock is now partly collapsed. To the south is a retaining wall; access steps are cut into the rock.

TEMPLES EAST OF THE ENCLOSURES
(Figures 5.23 and 5.24)

East of XVI is a small ruined temple consisting of a square east-facing sanctuary and a small antechamber, now mostly ruined. A basement is preserved but the plain walls with an intermediate projecting band are only partly standing; nothing survives of the superstructure. One of the engaged columns at the open (east) end still stands, and here many collapsed stones (of a porch?) are seen. Some distance to the northeast is a group of eight columns, all that survives of an open hall (of 4 by 4 columns); there is no evidence of any associated sanctuary. The central columns have carved blocks. Not far away is a small gateway, apparently unattached to any other structure, with two columns and a lintel.

Proceeding along the east road (E) towards the fortified gateway, we encounter many ruined and partly buried temples. Here is an unusual triple-shrined temple, the three sanctuaries facing east, south, and west into a columned hall. The sanctuaries are square, and each has a ceiling of rotated squares. The hall had four free-standing columns standing but the roof has collapsed; the doorway in the middle of the south side has disappeared. No external features of this temple are visible. Other nearby temples have small single sanctuaries, sometimes with an intermediate antechamber, adjoining halls of 4 by 3 or 4 by 4 columns (many of which are now missing). Near to the east gateway is a cluster of shrines, including a hall of 3 by 4 columns aligned with a free-standing monolithic column. Opposite, facing south onto the road, is a ruined temple with the remains of a finely carved doorway.

Not far away is the only example of a rock-cut temple, excavated into a granite outcrop on the south edge of the east valley. Here, a small irregularly hewn sanctuary is linked to a rectangular hall on the west by a doorway. Piers separate this hall from a porch, which extends to the north where it is sheltered by an overhanging rocky shelf. On the ceiling and upper walls of the sanctuary and hall, shallow pilasters and "beams" are carved. The shrine doorway has a Lakshmi icon over the opening; sun and moon emblems are found on the walls at either side. Above the opening linking the hall and porch is a sloping "eave," complete with medallions and a rib on the underside. Filling in the natural crevices are traces of masonry and brickwork.

5. SACRED ART

SHAIVA TEMPLE COMPLEX
(Figures 5.25, 5.26, 5.27 and 5.31)

Southwest of the enclosures is one of the largest sacred structures in the royal centre. Though clearly a Shaiva shrine, there is no epigraphical or iconographic evidence to suggest any specific dedication for this complex. Even so, it is usually known as the Chandrashekhara Temple (Deva-kunjari 1970, p. 40). This double-sanctuaried temple stands in the middle of a rectangular courtyard, defined by enclosure walls on four sides. In the southeast and southwest corners are the remains of columned halls; in the middle of the east side is a towered gateway.

The temple has sanctuaries on both the west and north. The principal (west) sanctuary is square and adjoins a square antechamber. The rectangular secondary (north) sanctuary and antechamber are smaller. Doorways from both antechambers lead into rectangular transitional bays that step down into the hall. Here are found four central columns on a raised floor with engaged columns against the walls. Access steps (modern replacements) descend from the doorway on the south; to the east a doorway leads to an open porch of 6 by 3 columns.

On the exterior of the temple the basement is doubled, the uppermost moulding being interrupted by wall niches. Spouts protrude from yali heads on the outer walls of both sanctuaries. The walls of the shrines have vertical recesses (carried through the basement) demarcating the junction of the sanctuaries and antechambers within. On three sides of both sanctuaries, pilasters are positioned at regular intervals; secondary pilasters emerge out of pots. Shallow niches in the middle of each side have pilasters supporting miniature cornices and rectangular roof forms. The niches on the antechamber walls have arches springing from pairs of makaras; yali heads are located at the summits. Within these arches are miniature icons of Lakshmi. The walls of the hall repeat the same basic scheme. Above the walls is a cornice with uncut medallions. The doorways (east and south) are set in entrance frames partly created by carved blocks, some of which terminate the upper series of basement mouldings. The upper portions of the frames are flanked by half-pilasters; above the lintels are miniature cornice mouldings. The doorways are surrounded by bands of foliation, with a lotus medallion over the opening, and guardians with Shaiva emblems at either side.

The towers rising above the two sanctuaries are of brick and plaster, and are quite well preserved. The lower two storeys are divided into five projections; the central projection being enlarged and doubled. The projections are defined by pilasters and carry miniature cornices and

square-to-dome, arched, or rectangular roof forms. Above rises a short wall with Nandis (incomplete) at the corners. Plaster figures — devotees, musicians, attendants, and deities (too damaged to identify) — are only partly preserved. The third and uppermost storey of the west sanctuary consists of a circular drum with projections supporting a hemispherical roof. Over the north sanctuary there is a rectangular vaulted roof form, the arched ends of which are surrounded by exuberant plaster decoration — tufts of foliation and an enlarged yali head at the summit. The projection within the arch, now damaged, is fashioned as a miniature shrine. On the long (curving) sides are the arched tops of three intermediate niches, also covered with this decoration.

The porch is elevated on a lower tripartite basement. The columns of the central (east-west) aisle have carved blocks and angled brackets; the other columns are plainer. Over the central aisle the ceiling slabs are raised and there is a carved medallion. The sloping eave is a mostly modern replacement.

Within the temple, both sanctuaries are plain. Here the ceiling slabs are missing, revealing the hollow corbelled interiors of the brick towers. The antechambers and transitional bays are also plain and massive. The doorways have foliate bands, and medallions (only discernible in the north) in the middle of the lintels; beneath at either side are guardians with Shaiva emblems. The hall columns have carved blocks and curved brackets. The beams above support a raised horizontal ceiling with a medallion.

At the southeast corner of the courtyard six out of 4 by 4 columns on a simple basement still stand. At the southwest corner, balustrades and basement mouldings define a square plan; in the middle is another square area with two (out of four) column footings.

The towered gateway is rectangular with a central east-west passageway at ground level flanked by platforms with columns. The doorways are similar to those on the temple, though enlarged; the guardians beneath have no emblems. The outer walls of the gateway are raised on a double basement, reproducing that of the temple. At the two entrances the basement is terminated in carved blocks which continue all the way to the cornice. Full-height pilasters, secondary pilasters standing in pots, and the frieze and cornice above, repeat the same scheme as the temple. On the north and south there are uncut portions to take the abutting walls. Above rises the brick and plaster superstructure, higher and more complex in all its details than those over the sanctuaries. Three diminishing storeys support a rectangular vaulted roof with arched ends. The lower two storeys have a series of projections treated

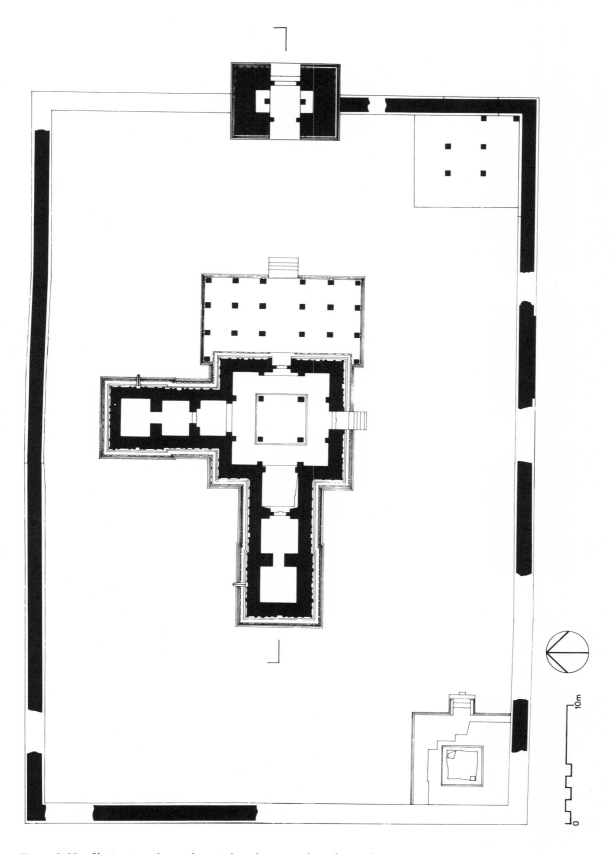

Figure 5.25   Shaiva temple southeast of enclosures, plan of complex.

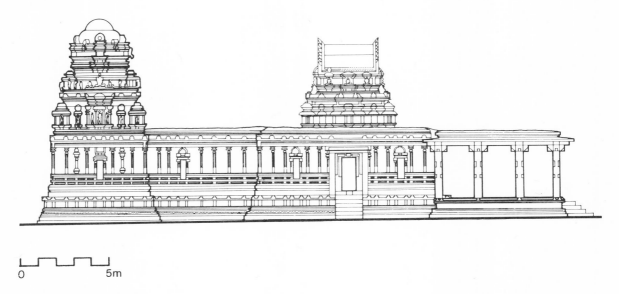

0   5m

Figure 5.26   Shaiva temple, elevation of shrine.

as niches with a variety of roof forms — square, arched, and rectangular. The central projections are enlarged and have pilasters supporting miniature eaves beneath which are secondary projections. Above are long rectangular roof forms with several extensions and arches; these coincide with the principal eave terminating each of the lower two storeys. Beneath the eave is a series of foliated brackets and a vertical wall. The windows positioned in the middle of the east and west sides do not preserve their original plaster decoration.

The third and uppermost storey is raised on a short wall. At the arched ends (north and south) there is exuberant plaster decoration. Here rows of yalis, geese, and ganas are supported on makaras with upturned heads; surrounding these rows are bands of flamelike tufts with an enlarged yali head at the summit. Within the arch is a niche with a rectangular roof, flanked by figures. On the curved long sides, enlarged projections display arches on a miniature series of mouldings; smaller projections are at either side. The stumps of finials are seen above.

The plaster sculpture on the tower is comparatively well preserved except that the heads of most figures are lost. Here are found standing devotees and guardians, male and female deities (unidentified except for a seated figure of Narasimha), and also seated ganas and Nandis at the upper corners of the second storey.

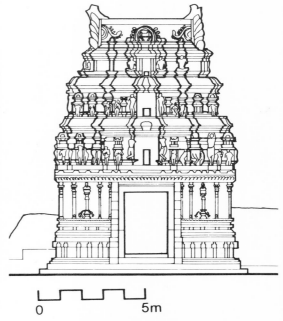

0   5m

Figure 5.27   Shaiva temple, elevation of gateway.

Only portions of the stone layers and brick infill of the enclosure walls, and fragments of the plaster-covered brick parapet, still stand.

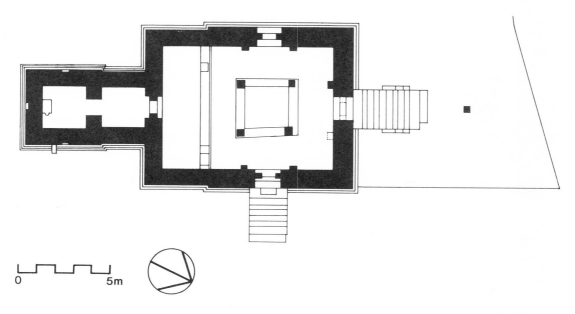

Figure 5.28   Tiruvengalanatha Temple, plan.

TIRUVENGALANATHA TEMPLE
(Figures 5.28 and 5.29)

Though known as the Sarasvati Temple (Deva-kunjari 1970, p. 40), an inscription dated 1554, inscribed on the basement of the sanctuary, indicates that this shrine was originally dedicated to Tiruvengalanatha (*Annual Report on South Indian Epigraphy* 1936, no. 337).

The north-facing temple is built upon a large granite boulder. It consists of a square sanctuary and antechamber, with a doorway leading to a columned rectangular hall. This hall is in two levels, divided by a single step, with 3 by 2 free-standing columns. Doorways on three sides are reached by steps (missing on the west, original balustrades on the north). The retaining walls to the north are reconstructions.

On its exterior, the temple has a basement raised on a vertical course; on the east protrudes a spout. The sanctuary walls are plain except for small niches on three sides. These niches are surmounted by curved arches with yali heads at the apexes. Inside the arches are Hanuman (west), seated figure (?) (south), and dancer (east). Also carved on the walls are a tortoise, fish, and snake (east and south). A cornice terminates the wall. Over the sanctuary rises the well preserved brick and plaster superstructure. The lower two storeys have five projections framing intermediate re-cesses; each projection is flanked by pilasters,

miniature cornices, and roof forms. In the middle of the central projection on the lower storey is a recessed arched niche. The crowning circular drum and hemispherical roof have projections on each side, now missing much of the original detail. Plaster figures, mostly headless, are found on all sides; these include devotees, seated Nara-simha (south), and other seated deities (?). The walls of the hall have small projections coinciding with the change of floor level within, but are otherwise plain. The doorways (preserved only on the east and west) have bands of foliation with icons of Lakshmi in the middle of the lintels; beneath at either side are guardians with Vaish-nava emblems. The jambs and undersides of the lintels have meandering scrollwork and medal-lions. Above the walls (east side) is a brick parapet, now missing almost all its plaster deco-ration. Over the east doorway the parapet has an enlarged niche, now empty, with traces of plaster decoration.

Within the temple, the sanctuary and ante-chamber are plain; the former is now missing its ceiling slabs. The rectangular chlorite pedestal has delicate mouldings; on the central projection there is an icon of Garuda. The doorway to the hall repeats the same scheme as those on the outer walls. The hall columns have carved blocks and curved brackets (central four columns only); above is a ceiling with rotated squares. A small medallion is carved on the south ceiling bay.

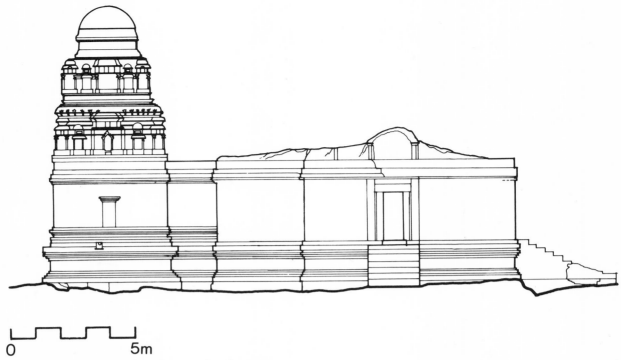

Figure 5.29   Tiruvengalanatha Temple, elevation.

BASEMENTS
(Figures 5.30, 5.31, 5.32 and 5.33)

A progression of basement mouldings, from simple to complex schemes, is observed in the temples of the royal centre. The simplest type is discovered in the principal shrine of the Virupaksha Temple complex and in the dated Jaina temple on the northeast road. Here the basement is tripartite; the bottom and top mouldings are identical through reversed, and the central course is plain and vertical. The Virupaksha Temple basement (partly buried by later additions) has angled uncut blocks; the Jaina example has quarter medallions at the corners. This latter form — with angled or curved mouldings, sometimes employing intermediate and corner medallions — is common in many of the temples, especially those with simpler designs or more crudely executed columns and walls. The larger temples, however, introduce more complex basements; frequently, several variations of the basement are found in the same building. Usually the most complicated series of mouldings appears beneath the sanctuary walls, while projecting porches and halls display simpler basements.

The principal shrine of the Ramachandra Temple, for example, has a bottom curved moulding (upana) with flowing petal decoration, above which are a vertical course, a part-octagon, two short vertical courses separated by a plain band and, at the top, an inverted upana, smaller than the one beneath. Other basement mouldings on the same building introduce an intermediate curved element with ribs, presenting a potlike contour, or an overhanging cornice (kapota), complete with medallions often decorated with foliation and yali heads.

Further elaboration is seen in the doubling of temple basements, where two series are superimposed, one stepped back over the other. In the shrine of the Shaiva temple complex, for instance, the lower series consists of an upana with petals, a projecting band, a vertical course, and an overhanging kapota with medallions. The upper series is plainer and shorter; it displays a vertical course, a part-octagon, two vertical courses separated by a band, and an inverted upana. Similar, though not quite identical schemes are found in the Tiruvengalanatha Temple, also in the gateways of the Vaishnava Temple complex on the northeast road, the Shaiva complex southeast of the enclosures, and the Virupaksha Temple complex.

No temple basements, however, can compare with the rich detail and complicated carvings of those of the two shrines of the Ramachandra

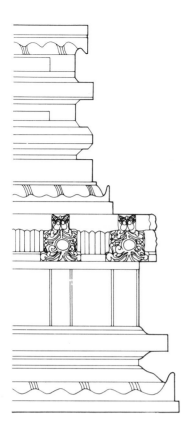

Figure 5.30   Basement, Vaishnava temple complex.

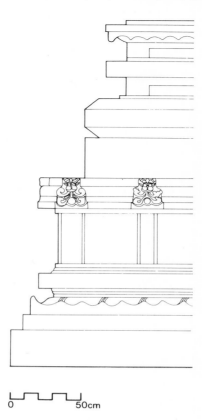

Figure 5.31   Basement of shrine, Shaiva temple complex.

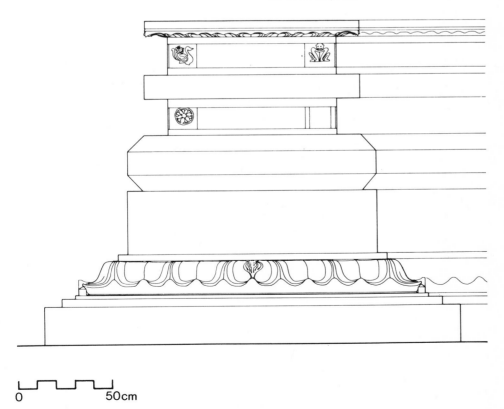

Figure 5.32   Basement of principal shrine, Ramachandra Temple complex.

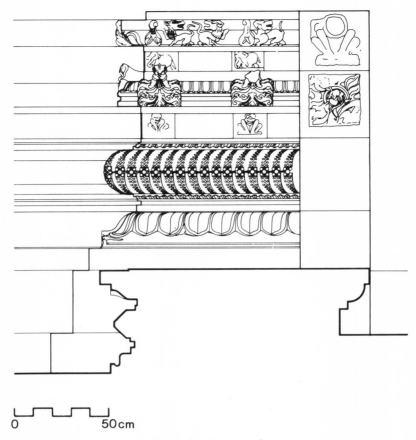

0   50 cm

Figure 5.33   Basement of principal shrine, Ramachandra Temple.

Temple. Here an amazing variety of foliate, animal, and figural sculpture is included; each element itself being highly elaborated. Thus, the upana has petals and foliate medallions, the ribbed curved elements have bands of jewels, and the overhanging kapota has rows of petals with highly decorated medallions. Miniature animals and figures are positioned at the corners. The mythological scenes and icons found here have already been noted.

Also associated with the basements of temple sanctuaries are curved spouts, usually emerging out of open-mouthed yali heads. Yalis also form the principal decoration of balustrades flanking steps, but few of these are completely preserved.

COLUMNS AND PILASTERS
(Figures 5.34, 5.35, 5.36, 5.37, 5.38 and 5.39)

A considerable variation in typology and decoration is also seen in the columns of temples within the royal centre. Probably the earliest

column form is found in the inner hall (originally open porch) adjoining the principal shrine in the Virupaksha Temple complex. Here, the columns are raised on a separate block carved with a miniature tripartite basement. In the middle of the square column shaft are octagonal and sixteen-sided sections; the upper portion tapers inwards and becomes circular. The capital is in two circular (lower) and projecting square (upper) parts, with many intermediate mouldings; the brackets are gently curved. This basic column form persists into the early fifteenth century, as can be seen in the dated Jaina temple on the northeast road. Here, the separate basement block is retained, though somewhat simplified. The squat square shaft has two square blocks separated by octagonal and sixteen-sided bands. The double capital emphasises the circular and projecting square elements; the brackets are angled. Variations are observed in the porch columns of the same temple where octagonal and sixteen-sided shafts are employed. A more decorated version of this column type is found in the gateway porches of the Ramachandra Temple complex. Here the central bands on the shaft, carved with friezes of foliation, are provided with upturned petal motifs at the corners, each raised on a miniature basement. Panels of geometric and foliate ornament, and also figural carvings, are positioned on the square blocks. An even more elaborate version of this scheme with a double capital is seen in the porches of the main shrine of the same complex. Here the upper part of the shaft has curved flutings providing a transition to the lower circular part of the capital. The brackets are curved with pendant buds.

However, the most common column type found in the fifteenth- and sixteenth-century temples dispenses with the capital. Here a flattened basement moulding, usually of the tripartite form with small medallions, is carved onto the base of the shaft itself. As the shaft tapers upwards it is divided into three blocks, usually of diminishing size, with carved figures and ornamental motifs on each side. Separating these blocks are octagonal and sixteen-sided sections, with ornamental upturned petal motifs and pendant buds. The brackets curve outwards and are terminated in pendant buds. In some sixteenth-century examples

0   50cm

Figure 5.34   Columns of inner hall (A), and hall extensions (G and J), Virupaksha Temple complex.

(east porch extension to the Ramachandra Temple, hall (J) to the south of the enclosure walls of the Virupaksha Temple), this scheme is considerably ornamented. Here the basement mouldings are increased, and double projections introduced. The foliation between the blocks is expanded, and the upturned petal motifs come to be supported on miniature basement mouldings, often in triple projections; even miniature shrines with roofs are incorporated. The brackets have flowing lines incised onto their projecting blocks, and the pendant buds are attenuated.

But the most highly ornamented version of this scheme may not be one of the latest. Inside the hall of the principal shrine of the Ramachandra Temple are four columns of polished black basalt, exquisitely carved. Here the basement has five elements, with miniature medallions and animals at the corners. Each sculptural panel on the three blocks of the shaft is set within a frame of half pilasters and foliate arches with yali heads at the summits. Separating these blocks are upturned petal motifs on miniature basements, friezes of foliation on octagonal and sixteen-sided bands, and pendant buds. The curved brackets extend outwards, curving down into pendant buds.

Another column type displays a long tapering sixteen-sided shaft rising out of lower square and octagonal sections. A simplified version of this scheme is discerned in the fragments of the fallen column east of the Ramachandra Temple complex; inside one of the porch extensions (G) of the Virupaksha Temple sixteen-sided columns rise above elaborate carvings. One column form is found only in a single example in the royal centre (XVb/1). Here the column shaft is plain except for grooves at the top interrupted by pendant leaflike motifs; the undersides of the projecting cubic brackets have pendant hemispheres (uncarved lotus buds?).

Of the composite columns typical of sixteenth-century temple architecture, only one structure (Vaishnava temple, on the northeast road) in the royal centre preserves this type intact; fragments of similar columns, however, are discovered elsewhere (XVb/1). Here the central shaft is of the standard type with carved blocks; in front are rearing enlarged yalis or three-dimensional colonettes with circular or sixteen-sided shafts. The series of mouldings above includes miniature cornices and animals. Another sixteenth-century column form — hardly known in the royal centre, except for the Vaishnava temple already noted — is the type which superimposes miniature "facades" one upon each other. Each facade has its own basement, niches defined by pilasters, cornices, and square or rectangular roof forms.

Defining the projections and recesses of the walls of several temples and gateways are slender full-height pilasters; similar pilasters, though

mostly with halved shafts, capitals, and brackets, flank the deep niches in the sanctuary walls. In general, the pilasters are of a uniform type, being miniature versions of full-sized columns. The shafts have square or part-octagonal sections, the upper portions curving inwards with a potlike contour. The capitals are double — part-octagonal and part-square — and support miniature curved brackets with pendant buds. Small sculptures and foliate motifs often decorate the pilaster shafts. Few examples, however, can match the ornamentation of the pilasters on the principal shrine of the Ramachandra Temple complex. Here the capitals are part-octagonal and the brackets are tripled; delicately incised foliation and jewelled motifs cover almost every element.

Shorter pilasters are often positioned in the intervening recesses. These sit in ribbed pots, with jewelled tassels on the sides flanked by sprays of foliation issuing from makara heads. The upper part of the shaft tapers inwards, and a part-octagonal capital supports curved or animal brackets and a miniature cornice. Above rises a pyramidal arrangement of elements, surmounted by a square-to-dome or rectangular vaulted roof form, complete with medallions and finials.

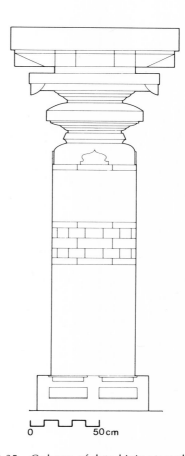

Figure 5.35   Column of dated Jaina temple.

Figure 5.36   Hall column of principal shrine, Ramachandra Temple (height 3.05m.).

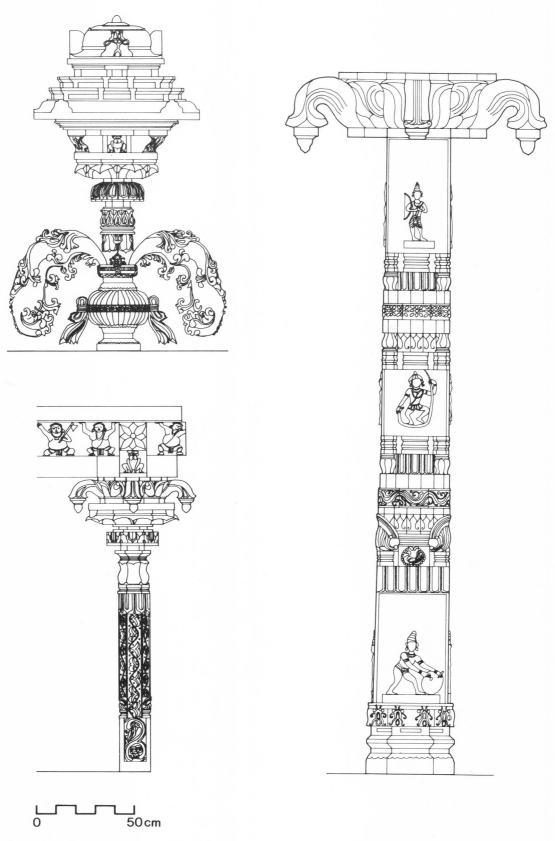

0   50cm

Figure 5.37   Pilasters on outer walls of principal shrine, Ramachandra Temple.

Figure 5.38   Porch column of principal shrine, Ramachandra Temple. (height 4.52m.).

94

ICONOGRAPHY OF COLUMN CARVINGS

In many temples of the royal centre the sculptures of chief iconographic interest are found on the square blocks of the hall and porch columns. These sculptures display a considerable variety of themes. In general, it is possible to determine the cult dedication of the temple from these carvings, despite the fact that Vaishnava and Shaiva emblems often appear together. (In general, though, Vaishnava motifs appear to predominate.) There is usually a marked overlap of themes and sharing of common motifs. No precise sculptural programme seems to have been followed, though some overall principles of organization may be discerned: royal devotees and donors usually appear on the central columns; dancing girls, ascetics, crouching yalis, and animals are mostly confined to the lower blocks; cult emblems and deities are often positioned in the upper blocks. There are, however, many exceptions to this scheme.

The principal Vaishnava cult emblems are the conch, discus, and namam; in Shaiva temples lingas are common, often on a pedestal, sometimes with a serpent curling around the base or rearing over the linga, or even being tenderly licked by a cow. Royal devotees, too, sometimes worship lingas with a rearing serpent. Sun and moon motifs are also known. Icons of Vishnu include Vitthala, with two arms hanging down, and standing or seated four-armed images, occasionally mounted on flying Garuda. More unusual are the 24 forms of Vishnu (hall columns of the principal shrine of the Ramachandra Temple); however, the incarnations of Vishnu are fairly common. Fish and tortoise forms often include human torsos. Varaha is only rarely depicted. Narasimha is frequently shown seated in yogic posture or even grabbing the hair of his victim. Vamana appears with his parasol, sometimes transformed as Trivikrama with his leg raised high. Parashurama is unusual. Rama is often found, with bow and arrow, sometimes accompanied by Lakshmana, or seated on a throne, often with Sita. Buddha is rare (sometimes replaced by a Jina figure), as is Kalki. Krishna scenes are common: the god is shown dancing, often on the serpent, crawling, tied to a pestle, holding or tasting sweets; more unusually, Krishna hides the clothes from the gopis or plays the flute.

Shaiva icons include images of the god dancing, or seated with Parvati. Bhairava appears with a dog, or even dances. Other gods are also sometimes illustrated, including Surya holding two lotuses with a disc behind his head, and Brahma. Lakshmi is often found, usually seated with lotuses in her hands and sometimes with elephants above. Durga is occasionally depicted, slaying the buffalo or standing on the severed head of the animal (both in the Ramachandra Temple gateway and on the porch columns).

Ganesha is a favorite icon, either dancing or seated; while Karttikeya is also occasionally seen. Garuda and Hanuman often appear. Garuda stands in devotion or flies through the air, while Hanuman with his curling tail is one of the characteristic Vijayanagara mottos. He strides forwards or flies through the air (carrying the mountain); elsewhere he stands in devotion, sometimes with Sugriva and other monkey attendants.

Other themes depicted on temple columns include warriors with swords, shields, tridents, bows or arrows, even mounted on elephants. Guardians, usually with clubs, hold cult emblems. As for dancers and musicians, these are ubiquitous. Thus, drummers, horn players, and flute players; dancers with tambourines, snakes, staffs, daggers, and drums; female dancers with pleated skirts and sticks, their arms often held high; and pairs of male and female dancers, often in knock-kneed postures. As well, there are wrestlers and acrobats, the latter sometimes balancing on poles.

Attendant females include ladies holding bows and arrows, dishes with offerings, candelabras, parrots, fly-whisks, mirrors, and books; naked women are found with snakes, holding their robes, or clutching branches; some women even display their sexual parts. Copulating couples are rare. But perhaps the most interesting of all these human representations is the large range of ascetics and saints, particularly well illustrated in the columned hall of a Shaiva temple (XVb/4) on the northeast road. Here are found ascetics, seated and standing in meditation, or holding rosaries, water pots, flags, staffs, drums, musical instruments, parasols, and other items. Sometimes their outstretched arms or folded limbs are supported on stands. In an unusual instance, a bearded ascetic wearing a meditation band is seated on top of a column. Also popular is the saint Matsyendranatha crouching on a fish. The variety of hair style and costume of these ascetics is marked. As well, figures are found with reed cloaks, also shepherds with cloaks covering their heads leaning on sticks.

Courtly devotees are a significant theme. Standing or walking towards the shrine, these devotees have their hands brought together in adoration. They wear high hats, turbans, tasselled costumes, or long tunics, evidently the contemporary fashion. Sometimes these courtiers are seated on thrones leaning on cushions, or stand inside multilobed "palace" entrances.

Of the celestial and mythical guardians there are yakshas, mostly with lotus flowers, blowing conches, or holding conches and maces. Ganas are seated with flowers, conches, horns, tridents, or drums, or dance with sticks and staffs. Flying figures with musical instruments, axes, or flowers appear above the clouds, or in aerial chariots. Among the animals are various hybrid creatures — combinations of bulls and elephants, centaurs, makaras, birds with yali heads, makaras with bird bodies, yakshas with yali heads, etc.

Animals and birds are common. Thus: tortoises, cows, seated Nandis, walking elephants, seated and squatting monkeys, monkeys in devotion, geese with foliated tails (one of the most common motifs of all), and peacocks. More unusual are pairs of knotted snakes, elephants squirting them-selves, and coiled rearing snakes. Mythical beasts include yalis and stylized lions, the latter in various postures — particularly crouching, walk-ing with one paw raised, seated with the head turned around, or dancing with snakes.

Among the foliate motifs are square and round medallions, carved on almost all columns. Panels of foliation and scrollwork are popular, also curved branches with foliation. Flamelike tufts appear, as well as geometric stars and medallions, interlocking triangles, and rotated squares.

Figure 5.39   Porch column of principal shrine, Ramachandra Temple (height 2.68m.).

6. PLATFORMS AND PALACES

Remains of Secular Buildings

Now greatly ruined, the various platforms and palaces described here constitute a significant element in the architecture of the royal centre, and indeed of the whole capital. Though the precise functions of these platforms and palaces are still unknown, we may be confident that most of these buildings were connected in one way or another with the public and private activities of the king and court.

These ceremonial, administrative, and residential structures are closely related in building technique. Here, carved granite basements, packed with earth and pottery sherds, support square and rectangular floors covered with plaster; access is by flights of stone steps. Stone footings set into the floor indicate the arrangement of columns, presumably in timber. Traces of earth and rubble walls with plaster coating have been uncovered in recent excavations; from these fragments it is possible to determine the internal spatial divisions for several larger palace structures. We note the overall resemblance of plan types and stone basement and balustrade details to temple architecture, particularly the columned halls of sacred complexes. But whether the upper portions of these secular buildings — the columns, eaves, ceilings, roofs, or towers — also imitated sacred architecture is not known.

ORIGINAL APPEARANCE

As to the overall appearance of these structures, contemporary courtly literature and the accounts of the various travellers provide only a few clues. According to the *Madhuravijayam*, for instance, the palaces of Vijayanagara were like the "clouds of autumn," "coloured like gems"; "the sun caught in the heights of the city's palaces produced the illusion of a golden jar" (Sridhara Babu 1975, pp. 138-139). Such poetic metaphors emphasize the high towers and metallic and jewelled surfaces. (It is to be admitted, however, that such descriptions are fairly conventional in Sanskrit literature; Ramanujan 1970, p. 232.) Travellers' reports give little more precise information. In his description of the capital, Duarte Barbosa notes that "the king . . . has great and fair palaces . . . with many enclosed courts and great houses very well built, and within them are wide open spaces, with water tanks in great numbers" (Dames 1918, p. 202). Domingo Paes also de-scribes the new palaces laid out by Krishna Raya as having "only one floor with flat roofs and towers . . . which go from storey to storey. They have pillars, and are all open, with verandahs inside and out" (Sewell 1900, p. 246).

Another source of information that may be relevant to the appearance of these buildings are relief carvings on temple walls (see Figure 6.1). These sometimes depict figures, both divine and human, in "palaces." Here, the god or king, usually accompanied by his consorts and attendants, sits on a throne inside an elaborate structure; towers occasionally rise above. On closer examination, all the elements depicted here — basement mouldings, columns and brackets, overhanging eaves, etc. — are familiar in temple architecture. But whereas temples were constructed entirely of masonry, secular buildings generally utilized perishable materials.

In our study of these monuments of Vijayanagara we have to imagine a whole series of vanished wooden elements — columns, brackets, beams, ceilings, overhanging eaves, and towers — decorated with plaster and painted, perhaps brightly. Other materials, too, must have been employed. The excavators have recovered broken roof tiles as well as iron nails and braces and hooks, and even burnt ivory finials (Thapar 1982, p. 45). As for other materials —silver and gold covering the various architectural elements, and elaborate hangings (with silver and gold thread?) decorated with painted images — these did not survive the abandonment and destruction of the capital. Such metallic and textile elements — particularly gold plates inlaid with jewels, silk cloths, and wall paintings — are noted by the travellers (Major 1857, p. 38; Sewell 1900, pp. 250, 285). We know that south Indian royal ceremonial architecture of the nineteenth century utilized metal columns, canopied thrones, painted hangings, and rows of flags and banners to adorn various reception halls (Appadurai-Breckenridge 1978); such ephemeral ornamentation may still be observed today in India. Thus we have to imagine these buildings at Vijayanagara rising above their stone basements in one or more storeys. Brightly painted and highly polished, probably decorated with precious metals and gorgeous cloths, these gleaming towered structures must indeed have been spectacular creations worthy of their royal and courtly inhabitants.

6. PLATFORMS AND PALACES

Figure 6.1   Carved representations of typical "palace" designs (from the Ramachandra Temple).

TYPOLOGY AND FUNCTION

Several distinct types are found within this group of secular buildings. We believe that this typological variation may be linked with functional differences; as yet, though, we do not clearly understand the connection. The first category seems to be structures with a definite ceremonial-ritual purpose. Here belongs the great platform (1) of enclosure IVb, usually associated with the mahanavami festival. This monument may have been exclusively used for the ceremonies of this outstanding annual event. Certainly, the successive phases of construction of its elevated stone basements suggest renovation and expansion over a substantial period of time. Whether the other great monument nearby — the hundred-columned "audience hall" (IVa/1) — was also primarily a ceremonial monument is not known.

More difficult to estimate, however, are the functions of the various multicolumned and multiroomed structures in enclosure IV. Mostly confined to the northeast quadrant (a), these structures vary in shape, with different columnar arrangements and spatial divisions. Whether these structures are to be assigned an administrative and/or a bureaucratic function depends on how we interpret the role of the king in the daily life of the capital. More curious are the very long and regular structures currently being exposed in the southwest quadrant (d). These uniformly laid out buildings may have housed residential, administrative, or ritual activities; or indeed, even combinations of these purposes. We note that no other structures of a comparable typology are found elsewhere in the royal centre.

Another category of structures is distinguished by the stepped outlines of the plan, and the series of ascending floor levels with one or more chambers at the top. Some of these structures are set within courtyards, surrounded by subsidiary buildings. Dotted all over the royal centre, both inside and outside the enclosures, these structures may have functioned as residences and/or sites of reception and entertainment for prominent members of the royal family and court. (The partly residential character of these structures is suggested by the mortars and grinding stones that have been discovered in the excavations.) For convenience we label these buildings as "palaces," by which term we mean to indicate the wide range of activities that may have taken place here — public or private, ceremonial or utilitarian, etc. Foreign travellers to the capital often mention palaces: Duarte Barbosa, for instance, reports that here lived "all the great lords and governors" (Dames 1918, p. 202).

Other building types found within the royal centre are associated with intermediate courts and entryways, and may have functioned as waiting areas, enroute to the main zones of activity. Here we note the four rectangular platforms in II (similar examples in IIIc), coordinated in a symmetrical scheme; these platforms are defined by a single course of stone, with traces of rubble walls on four sides. Another rectangular platform is seen in IXe; in IXd, walls on three or four sides contain rectangular floor areas at different levels. In other zones, platforms with colonnades are built against enclosure walls.

GREAT PLATFORM (IVb/1)
(Figures 6.2, 6.3, 6.16, 6.19 and 6.20)

Rising above the elevated ground in the northeast corner of IV, this platform clearly dominates the enclosure, and indeed the whole royal centre. Traditionally, the platform has been associated with the annual mahanavami ceremonies; as a result, it is usually referred to as the "Mahanavami Dibba" (Longhurst 1917, p. 56). According to Domingo Paes, during this festival the king ascended a building with "two platforms one above the other, beautifully sculptured, with their sides well made and worked." At the top was a "throne of state" for the king (Sewell 1900, pp. 264-265). Probably, it was this description that led Longhurst to label this monument as a "throne platform" (1917, p. 56). The significant location of this platform in respect to processional routes within the royal centre, its unique architectural character, and the nature of the friezes carved on its stone basements, all reinforce the connection between this monument and the rites of the mahanavami.

Only the stone basements of this square structure have survived; these support a floor area more than 22m. square, raised 10m. above the ground level (on the south), with access steps on three sides. On the south and west the platform faces towards a complex of smaller structures

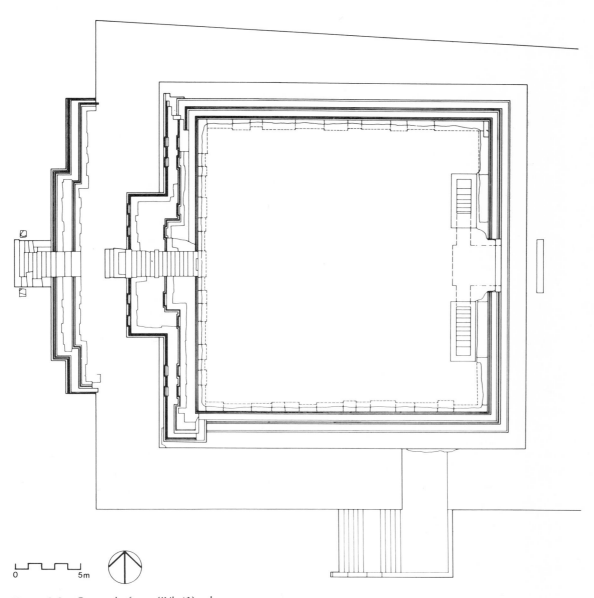

Figure 6.2   Great platform (IVb/1), plan.

and also tanks and aqueducts. On the north and east the ground level is much higher (natural boulders are visible); here retaining walls incorporate many carved blocks taken from the monument.

An examination of the architecture of the platform reveals three distinct phases of construction. We believe that the earliest stage of construction (phase one) may be dated to a time soon after the establishment of the royal centre in the fourteenth century (Michell 1982b). Certainly, the monumental simplicity of the basement and the vitality of the carvings of this first phase are unique. In contrast, the latest stage of construction (phase three) displays many features common with sixteenth-century temple architecture. Thus, the monument may span the whole history of the capital.

PHASE ONE

This first building phase of the great platform comprises the two lowest granite basements forming two immense squares (about 38m. and 28m. on a side). The sides of each stage are in one plane, slightly tapering as they rise, almost completely covered with shallow relief carvings except for some of the lower portions. Characteristic of this first phase are the massive blocks — irregularly cut but finely finished — with gently curved and often interlocking joints. On the north and east the ground level rises, obscuring the lowest basement completely; the upper basement, too, is greatly reduced on these sides. Portions of the massive boulders on which part of the platform is built are seen on the south; these are also partly carved with reliefs. The extensive rebuilding of the lower basement at the east end of the south wall almost completely conceals the southeast corner.

Projecting away from the south side of the lower basement is a monumental staircase facing west, bounded by walls on the south and east. Here the stones are smaller and more regularly cut; possibly, the staircase is a later addition. In the middle of the east side of the upper basement, blocked-out, uncarved stones indicate the presence of access steps. Several such stones lie nearby, set into the ground.

Three closely related sculptural styles, sharing a common iconography, may be detected in the carved friezes of this first phase. (1) On the lower basement walls the sculptures are characterized by flat carving, angular outlines, and lively compositions. The subjects run across the joints from one block to another. (2) The upper basement has smaller stones with more densely packed compositions. Each block has raised bands along its peripheries defining a central carved area. (3) The walls of the projecting staircase have horizontal bands framing regular friezes. At least one carved yali balustrade is misplaced here.

All the subjects found on this first phase of the platform are devoted to illustrations of the varied aspects of courtly life. Processions of animals include elephants, camels, and horses, with riders and attendants; elephants often have their trunks wrapped around trees. Rows of geese are also found, together with undulating lotus ornament. One popular theme is concerned with hunting and the forest. Hunters are shown with bows and arrows, shooting deer and boar, and spearing lions and tigers; they are accompanied by dogs on leashes, or carry animals on their shoulders. Of interest are the occasional enlarged (royal?) hunters. Also found here are huntresses with bows and arrows. In the forest scenes, deer are mating, lions and bulls fight together, and monkeys sit beneath trees. Another common subject is the display of martial strength — mounted warriors, footmen with shields and swords, stick-bearers, and men carrying banners.

More urbane in spirit are the diverse musicians and entertainers. These include male drummers, cymbalists, players of reed instruments, dancers with pointed beards and conical caps (Muslims, according to Goetz 1966), and wrestlers. There are also female dancers, often with sticks, drummers and other instrumentalists, and acrobats; women sometimes carry pots or hold parrots. Perhaps the most significant scenes are those that represent enlarged (royal?) figures seated on couches with attendants. Before these seated figures, visitors pay their respect, including "foreigners" (Muslims?) with conical caps, beards, and long tunics. These seated figures are also entertained by wrestling matches, dancing, and acrobatic displays.

An indication of a possible sculptural programme is seen on the south side (west of the staircase). From bottom to top the themes are: royal reception and processions of soldiers, hunting scenes, rows of horses and camels, and elephants.

PHASE TWO

Completely different in style is the second phase of construction of the great platform. Here a moulded basement in two tiers rises upon the upper basement of phase one, to support the square floor area above (see Figure 6.16). The mouldings at the bottom of the lower tier have a stone course carved with elephants, geese, dancers and musicians, separated by flat bands or pilasters. Above, the mouldings are finely carved and deeply cut. On the enlarged vertical course of the basement, pilasters frame medallions, geese, pots, and miniature shrines, all in flat relief. Iron clamps secure the uppermost stones of both tiers of mouldings.

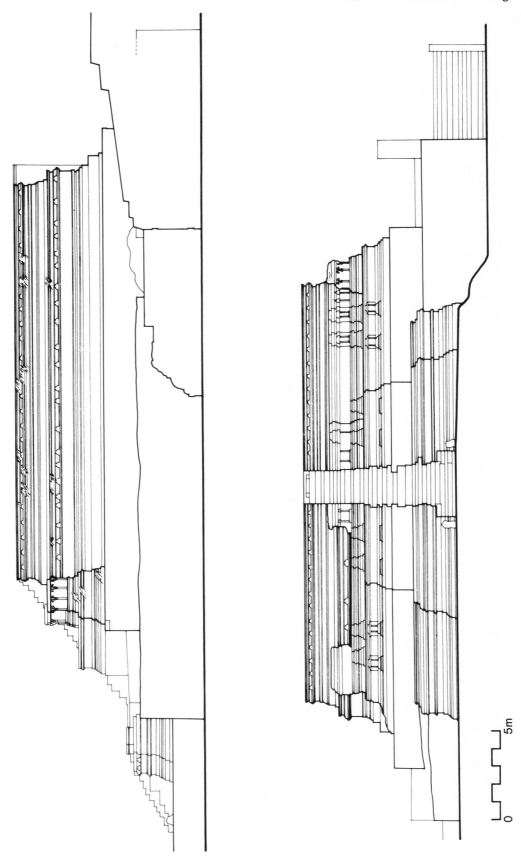

Figure 6.3   Great platform (IVb/1), south and west elevations (top and bottom, respectively).

6. PLATFORMS AND PALACES

In the middle of the east side, the basement of phase two is interrupted by a chamber open to the east. Carved on the wall at the back (west) of this chamber are friezes of dancers and drummers, guardians with clubs, hunters with elephants, and processions of animals. From here two flights of steps (north and south) concealed within the fabric of the structure ascend to the upper floor. These steps are roofed with stone slabs on curved brackets. Nothing remains of the original plaster floor on top of the platform, which is now covered with concrete.

PHASE THREE

Abutting the west side of the great platform is the third and last phase of construction. This consists of a triple-tiered basement, completely built in chlorite. These chlorite mouldings flank a central flight of steps and are almost totally uncoordinated with the granite mouldings concealed behind. The details of the carved chlorite mouldings are extremely fine, and many of the elements and figurative and foliate friezes may be compared to sixteenth-century temple basements (see Figure 6.20). Throughout, there is considerable evidence of modern reconstruction; many stones are misplaced or altogether missing.

The bottom tier of chlorite mouldings projects away from the granite wall (phase one) in two stages. The mouldings include friezes of elephants and horses with attendants, warriors and battle scenes, dancing girls, female musicians, courtly couples, yalis, lions and bands of lotus ornament. More elaborate is the middle tier of mouldings which projects and returns either side of the steps; at the south end the mouldings wrap around the corner. Here are found rows of dancing women, musicians, and royal couples; bands of lotus ornament are carved on the various mouldings. Regularly spaced niches are also included, often damaged, with their own miniature basements, double pairs of pilasters, and capping roof forms. The top tier of mouldings is the most complex and also the most incomplete, particularly north of the steps. The vertical course of this tier has ornamental pilasters, some of which stand in ribbed pots flanked by flowing foliation and rearing lions. At the south end, these mouldings are interrupted by a "chamber" with basement, plastered walls, and cornice. Again, miniature niches and figurative friezes are incorporated.

The highly irregular granite steps — most probably later replacements — crudely abut the chlorite walls; at ground level these steps are flanked by chlorite fragments of striding elephants.

HUNDRED-COLUMNED HALL (IVa/1)
(Figures 6.4 and 6.15)

In his description of the capital, Abd ar-Razzaq mentions a large council room or audience hall, in the middle of which the chief eunuch or governor sits upon an elevated platform, presiding over the visitors and dispensing justice (Major 1857, p. 25). This audience hall of Abd ar-Razzaq is usually identified with the remains of an immense hundred-columned structure (Longhurst 1917, p. 69; Devakunjari 1970, p. 25). But there are also correspondences between what is preserved of this structure and the "House of Victory," which formed a significant part of the mahanavami festival. According to Domingo Paes, this "House of Victory" was "a great one-storeyed building [that] stands on pillars shaped like elephants [yalis?] and with other figures, and all open in front, and they go up to it by staircases of stone" (Sewell 1900, p. 263).

Located in the northwest corner of IV, this open columned hall faces northwards into IIIa; on the east and south it is surrounded by a gateway and other smaller features. A ruined elevated structure, incorporating a staircase, abuts the hall on the west; flights of steps provide access on the other three sides.

As preserved today, this monument consists of a vast floor area (more than 40m. square), with 10 by 10 regularly spaced stone column footings (six are obscured by buttress walls on the west). Each footing has an indented square (80-85cm. on a side) and a socket, indicating the ample proportions of the vanished timber columns. The floor — now covered with concrete, replacing the original plaster surfacing — is bounded on four sides by two tiers of finely finished mouldings (only partly visible on the west). The upper tier is set back almost 1m. from the lower one. Parts of the upper mouldings are missing on the north where much of the basement is badly damaged. As the ground level slopes down towards the north, an additional foundation course is introduced. On the north, two flights of steps ascend to the floor; between these steps is a later series of basement mouldings concealing the original foundation course. A small flight of steps flanked by chlorite balustrades is located in the middle of this later basement. On the east, the original basement is partly obscured by heaped granite blocks serving as steps; these do not appear to be part of the original scheme. A flight of steps on the south ascends to a vanished upper level. The granite walls supporting this south staircase crudely abut the moulded basement; clearly the staircase is a later addition. On the west, the partly collapsed structure is bounded on the south and west by high granite walls. (These walls may also be later additions, judging from the junction

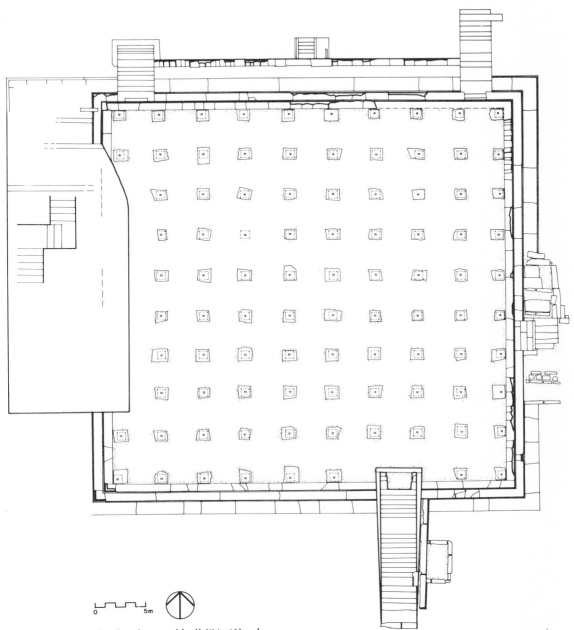

Figure 6.4   Hundred-columned hall (IVa/1), plan.

with the basement.) Within this structure, portions of an earthen ramp and several finely finished granite steps have been recently revealed. The steps make at least two turns before reaching the upper level, where traces of earth and rubble walls are found. Perhaps here a raised chamber looking down into the middle of the hall was located.

STRUCTURES OF IVa
(Figures 6.5, 6.6 and 6.7)

The dense arrangement of the various structures in the northwest quadrant of IV has already been noted. From the confusion of the different foundation courses, basement mouldings, and multiple layers of plaster flooring, it is evident that these

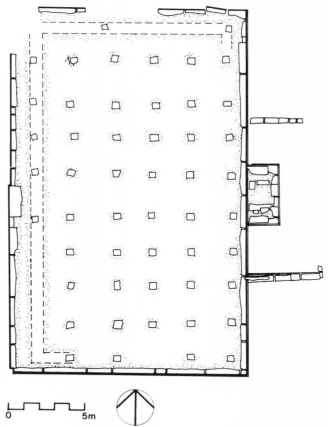

Figure 6.5   Structure IVa/10, plan.

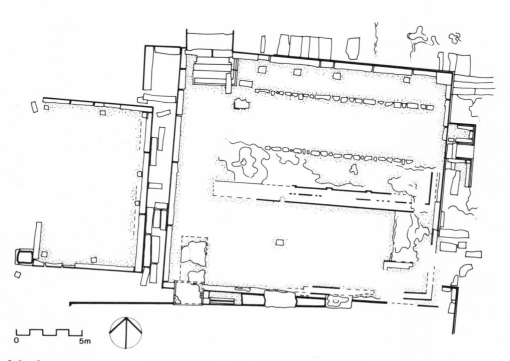

Figure 6.6   Structure IVa/12, plan.

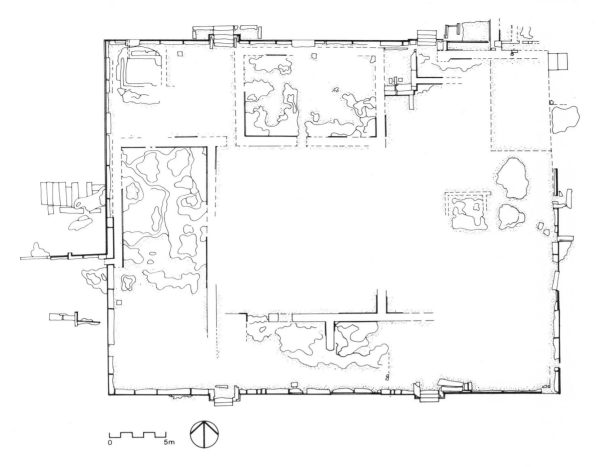

Figure 6.7   Structure IVa/26, plan.

structures were subject to many successive phases of rebuilding and renovation. We believe that this zone was in continuous use throughout the life of the capital.

Rectangular in shape, though of varying proportions, the multicolumned structures in IVa are mostly entered in the middle of their long sides, where stone steps are often found. Subfloor column footings indicate the different arrangements of the interiors, the larger structures having 6 by 7 columns (IVa/13) or 8 by 9 columns (IVa/25). Though some structures (IVa/6 and 8) have very few column footings still preserved in situ, it is likely that these were also divided by columns into regular bays. Traces of earth and rubble walls are seen on the peripheries of some multicolumned structures (north and west sides of IVa/10). The absence of walls in other multicolumned examples suggests that these were originally open halls.

Some of the other structures in this zone have portions of their walls still standing, demonstrating that these buildings were once partitioned into a number of separate chambers. Structure IVa/12 is divided by a wall (of several layers) into two almost equal parts; further subdivisions are suggested by other wall fragments. Built at a higher level than this example, and abutting it and overlapping it at an angle, is structure IVa/19, with two chambers at its west end and a columned area to the east (clearly this is later than IVa/12). The largest of all these structures (IVa/26) is approximately square and seems to have consisted of a central space (perhaps a courtyard?) with rooms on four sides. Two flights of steps provide access on each of the north and south sides; at the northeast corner stone steps apparently ascend to an upper level. An area of plaster-covered brickwork with a shallow channel within the northwest chamber may have been for ablutions.

6. PLATFORMS AND PALACES

Two other exceptional structures display neither column footings nor walls. The square example (IVa/17) is built at a higher level than its neighbours to the north and south, and has a complex series of basement mouldings. Fragments of balustrades fashioned as striding elephants are provided on the east, but the steps are missing. Structure IVa/27 may perhaps be associated with the series of palaces described below. Almost square in area, this example has a rectangular extension on the north provided with access steps flanked by chlorite elephants, now badly broken. Outlines in the middle of the concrete floor suggest a square chamber. The stone basement is remarkable for its finely carved friezes. Partly extended to the east, this basement demarcates another structure (IVa/28), now mostly collapsed.

UNDERGROUND CHAMBER (IVa/22)
(Figure 6.8)

Located in the middle of IVa, this subterranean structure is reached by a flight of steps to the northwest. These steps descend to a narrow corridor provided with engaged columns that surround a central chamber on four sides. Within this chamber are four free-standing columns (bases only preserved) with engaged columns against the walls and at the corners. Throughout, the floor, columns, brackets, walls, and ceilings are of chlorite. Clearly, the columns and brackets belong to the pre-Vijayanagara period, and appear to be clumsily reused (from a dismantled temple?). Column shafts have curved and angled motifs with lotus buds, behind which are recessed vertical bands; brackets are angled or gently curved. Cornicelike mouldings with angled uncut blocks, typical of the pre-Vijayanagara style, are found at the column bases in the central chamber, and also in the ceiling slabs over the entrance steps. Column shafts are composed of two or more pieces, not always matching; granite blocks sometimes replace missing chlorite brackets. The whole interior was probably once covered with plaster, concealing all the original carved decoration.

This underground chamber may have functioned as a storeroom or treasury, judging from the narrow (easily guarded) entrance and thick concrete roof (now mostly missing). We note, in this context, that Abd ar-Razzaq mentions a subterranean treasury within the palace where bullion was stored (Major 1857, p. 26). It is not certain if any other structure was erected over the chamber at an upper level, as there has been much restoration at the surface.

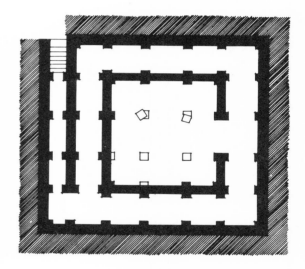

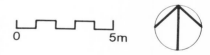

0   5m

Figure 6.8   Underground chamber (IVa/22), plan.

CHARACTERISTICS OF PALACE STRUCTURES

These monuments are closely related in plans, internal spatial divisions, and architectural details. The most common palace type is oriented to the east or north, and has a stepped outline, with one or more projections on three sides defined by stone basement mouldings. Steps are flanked by animal balustrades and provide access at one end only (east or north), either at the centre (single flight) or at either side (double flight). From here, a sequence of floor areas, each with its own basement mouldings and steps, ascends to the highest level at the back (west or south). Typical is the way in which these raised floor areas are arranged in a U-formation to define a court at the lower level. Thus, ascent is accompanied by a progression from open to closed spaces. The uppermost level is provided with a central chamber surrounded by a corridor, off which other rooms sometimes open.

Another palace type is exemplified by several structures in V (3, 6-8). Here, a rectangular outer court, flanked by platforms on three sides, leads into an inner square court at a higher level. Within this inner court, footings suggest a colonnade. Rooms on three sides open off this court; smaller chambers are located in the corners.

Unfortunately, all these structures are only incompletely preserved. Though the configuration of different levels is defined by clearly visible stone basements and steps, little of the original plaster flooring on packed earth is to be seen (often covered with modern concrete). Stone footings indicate the presence of columns, presumably in timber, regularly disposed in what appear to be open colonnades or verandahs. In those structures recently excavated (in V, XXV, and XXVI), earth and rubble walls with plaster coating have been revealed, indicating the internal spatial divisions, especially chambers with doorways and access corridors. These structures help us to interpret those less well preserved examples where the remains of earth and rubble walls were removed, and the original floor surface replaced with modern concrete. Several unexcavated structures of this type are indicated by mounds which display the characteristic U-formation of raised levels, in combination with traces of stone mouldings and plaster flooring.

The stone basement mouldings demarcating the changes in floor levels range from undecorated tripartite schemes to complex series with carved animal, figural, and foliate friezes. Where sufficiently well preserved, the walls are plaster-lined, with ornamental pilasters and niches. In at least one example (V/1), plaster fragments of three-dimensional figural sculpture (courtly portraits?) are found within deep niches (Srinivasan 1982, p. 78). As for the upper portions of these palaces, these have now vanished, though there are indications of fallen timbers, plasterwork and masonry.

PALACE COMPLEX (V/1)
(Figures 3.6 and 6.9)

This recently excavated complex in the north part of V is one of the most complete examples of a palace to be discovered in the royal centre (Thapar 1982, p. 45, pls. xii-xiii). Facing east, a central building is situated in the middle of a courtyard, surrounded on all sides by walls; at the northeast corner an entryway leads to another structure (V/2).

The characteristic stepped outline of the principal structure — with two projections on the north and south — is created by two series of basement mouldings which slightly overlap. At the extreme east end is a plastered floor at ground level bounded by a single stone course. A flight of steps ascending to the first level is flanked by yali balustrades, with clear evidence of painted ornamentation. At either side are short curved blocks carved with miniature figures (now broken) to support chlorite slabs (once seen lying in shattered pieces on the ground; now vanished). At the first level, a shallow step leads to a court with platforms on three sides defined by stone mouldings. In the middle of the west side, steps flanked by fragmentary yali balustrades ascend to the second level. This second level extends further westwards, and also to the north and south, where there are walls with niches. Another (central) flight of steps and a basement leads to the third and uppermost level. Steps on the north and south link this uppermost level to the walkway (at the second level) that proceeds around the building on three sides.

Further west again, three chambers with intermediate rectangular spaces are symmetrically disposed around a corridor on three sides. This corridor surrounds a central square chamber entered on the east. In the northwest corner, several steps ascend to a vanished upper level. Stone footings in the surrounding walkway indicate regularly spaced columns. At the east end of the court, stone footings are surrounded by bricks in a cruciform plan. Traces of plaster flooring are seen everywhere, even covering parts of the stone basements and steps. Surrounding the structure on all sides at ground level are traces of plaster on concrete.

Flanking the interior court on the north and south are walls of rubble and earth, with plaster-covered brickwork at the corners and niches. Of interest is the treatment of niches on both the exterior and interior. These niches are raised on a simple tripartite basement, and are defined by slender pilasters. In the niches facing into the court, brick and plaster circular pedestals support fragments of figural sculpture (feet and hands only surviving). On the exterior, miniature pilasters are provided with ornamental foliate arches. The chambers at the west are defined by rubble and earth walls covered with plaster, preserved in some places up to about 130cm. The interior surfaces of the rooms are plain, but the outer (corridor) surfaces have plaster skirtings with pilasters framing the doorways. On the exterior surfaces of the outer walls the plaster skirtings and corner pilasters have now mostly disappeared.

Surrounding this structure on three sides to create a large rectangular courtyard are parallel rubble walls. Notable is the uniform width (105-135cm.) and spacing of these walls, and the regular use of short cross walls running between the central and outer walls. At the east end of the south wall a number of stone footings define a rectangular structure (of 3 by 4 columns?); here also are exposed some stones of an earlier structure positioned at an angle beneath the courtyard walls. Portions of a stone basement line the courtyard face of the walls; a single flight of steps is preserved on the north. These walls are interpreted as the subfloor foundations of an upper structure, now completely lost. Many column footings are visible in this wall, suggesting a colonnade above. It is observed that as the ground level falls away to the north and west, buttressing is provided against the outer walls, occasionally in two layers. Running along the north side of the courtyard an additional subfloor wall is found; here also is a small square chamber with two steps on the east; in the southwest corner of this chamber a fragment of a subfloor drain is seen. Subfloor pipes also run northwards from near the northwest corner of the nearby entrance complex. At the south end of the west walls another subfloor drain is seen; this is covered with stone, emerging out of the west side of the walls. Steps are found at the north end of the west wall. To the east the courtyard is blocked off by a rubble wall (common with IXf).

The walls described above are interrupted by an entryway protruding into the northeast corner of the courtyard (see Figure 6.14). This entryway is entered on the south side, along a plaster-floored passageway flanked by rectangular platforms on a tripartite basement. Rubble and earth walls with plaster lining define small chambers at either side; to the east is another (later?) small chamber at courtyard level. The passageway leads northwards into a square court defined on all sides by basement mouldings. A small flight of steps in the southwest corner of this court ascends to a rectangular plaster-floored chamber. Around the court is a walkway bounded by walls. A doorway in the middle of the north wall provides access to one of the chambers of V/2. The

passageway then proceeds eastwards until it enters the large rectangular court of V/2. North and south of this east-west passageway are square chambers bounded by walls.

PALACE STRUCTURE (V/3)

This small rectangular structure is located at the extreme northeast corner of V. Laid out in a simple rectangle, the building has an entrance in the middle of the east side recessed between two platforms defined by simple basement mouldings; and separated from the interior courtyard by rubble and earth walls. The interior square courtyard is bounded on four sides by plaster-lined walls, with three (out of four?) stone column footings preserved in the middle. Plaster flooring on concrete is everywhere evident. An alley to the south has a plaster surface which passes beneath V/3, thus suggesting an earlier sequence in this area.

PALACE STRUCTURES (V/6-8)
(Figures 3.6 and 6.10)

South of the courtyard walls of V/1 are the remains of three small structures, facing each other from the west, south, and east, and partly enclosed by three parallel walls. All these features have been recently exposed by the excavators (Thapar 1982, p. 45, pl. xi; Nagaraja Rao 1983, pp. 11-14). The example to the west (V/6) is the best preserved, and appears to be more similar in layout and scale to that on the south (V/7), and to what can be made out of that on the east (V/8).

Facing east, structure V/6 has a simple rectangular plan, now missing most of its basement mouldings. A small court at the east end is bounded on three sides by platforms with basement mouldings. Steps in the middle of the west side lead up to the second level which has rectangular rooms to the north and south. A doorway in the west wall gives access to an inner square court, around which five rectangular chambers are symmetrically disposed on three sides. In the middle of the court is a depressed area (once open to the sky?). A small raised square, in plaster-covered brickwork, is found in the central south room.

PALACE STRUCTURE VI/1

Located in the middle of VI, this north-facing structure was possibly surrounded by a large courtyard (traces of enclosure walls are seen to the south and west).

Typical is the stepped outline of this structure defined by a stone basement (varying on the north). The first floor level at the front (north),

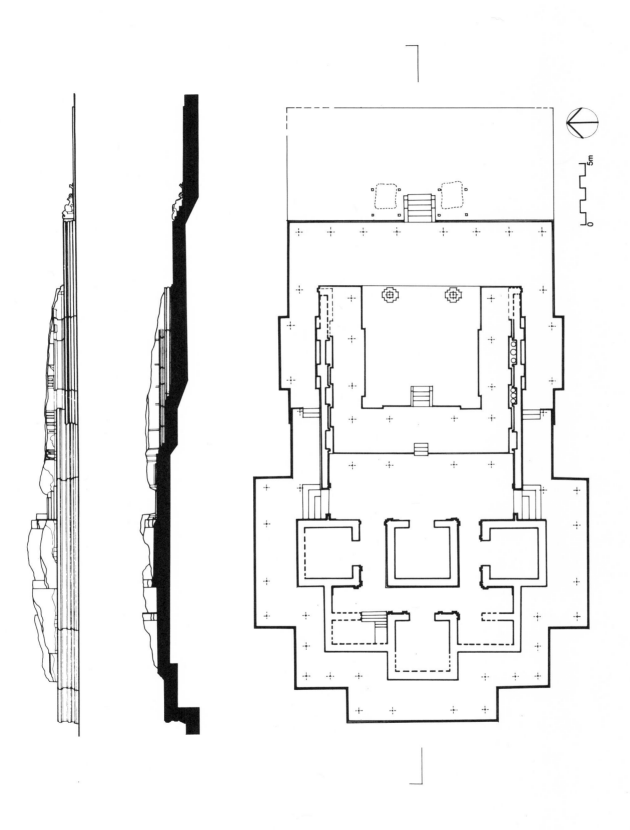

Figure 6.9   Palace complex (V/1), plan, section and elevation.

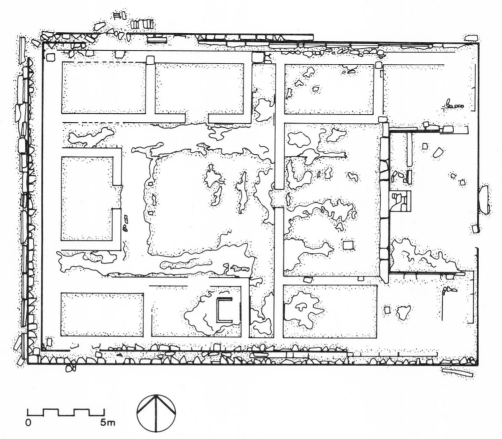

Figure 6.10   Palace structure (V/6), plan.

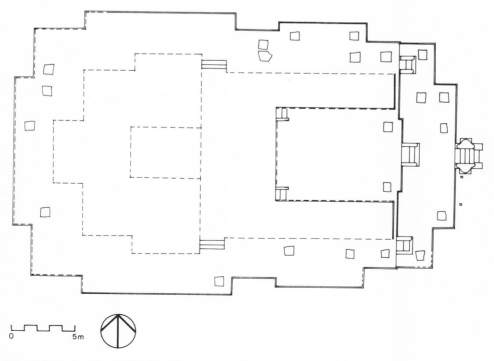

Figure 6.11   Palace structure (VIIIf/1), plan.

now missing its access steps, leads directly to a court. This court is bounded on three sides by platforms (second level) demarcated by basement mouldings, now badly smashed. This second level is reached by steps flanked by yali balustrades in the middle of the south side. Traces of walls are seen to the east and west. A further raised area (third level), reached by a single flight of steps, and demarcated by a basement moulding on the north only, is surrounded by a walkway; here there are projections on three sides. The outlines of a central square area and side rectangular areas (chambers?) are observed in the concrete floor.

Stone column footings with square depressions are found on the periphery of the structure (indicating an open colonnade?). At ground level, brickwork and plaster may be fragments of the original courtyard floor. At the north ends of the two raised areas flanking the first court are brick piers.

PALACE STRUCTURE (VIIIf/1)
(Figure 6.11)

Facing east, this structure is surrounded on four sides by earth and rubble walls. Though an elaborate entrance (VIII/d-e) is partly visible in the debris to the south, no communicating passage can be made out.

The characteristic stepped outline of this structure is created by a series of basement mouldings at different levels. At the east end, this basement (later addition?) is reduced in height but increased in complexity. Flanking the entrance steps in the middle of the east side leading to the first level are large striding elephants, now badly damaged. Three flights of steps with yali balustrades provide access to the second level; this level consists of an outer walkway on the north, west, and south, and a court in the middle of the east side. This court is flanked on three sides by platforms (third level) defined by moulded basements. The uppermost level is reached by two flights of steps with badly smashed balustrades on the west; to the north and south, steps descend to the walkway (at second level). Further west the floor level is raised slightly, revealing the outlines of several rectangular areas (chambers?). Several stone footings are seen on the outer walkway and court, some obviously misplaced. Throughout, concrete replaces the original floor surface; at ground level, however, traces of the original plaster floor of the courtyard are seen.

PALACE STRUCTURE (XIV/2)

This structure, one of the smaller of the group, is set within a rectangular tank at the southwest corner of XIV. The tank once had corner pavilions suspended over the water (partly preserved at the northeast and northwest). The central structure was originally reached by a bridge on the south. Supporting columns of these corner pavilions and bridge are still seen. Steps descend to the tank on the east and south, also from the east side of the central structure.

Oriented to the east, the central structure has projections in the middle of each side defined by basement mouldings. This basement was probably once partly submerged in the water; here are found carvings of fish and figures in boats. An upper series of mouldings (on the north and south only) define a raised area in the middle, with traces of plaster flooring. The sides of the tank are lined with a stone basement; this basement and also the floor of the tank are covered with multiple plaster layers.

PALACE STRUCTURE (XIV/3)
(Figure 6.12)

Located in the middle of XIV, this is the largest and most ornate example of a palace structure yet discovered in the royal centre. It has, however, been much rebuilt. The identification of this structure as a "queen's palace" (Devakunjari 1970, pp. 34-35) lacks archaeological and historical evidence.

Facing north, this structure has characteristic projections: double on the east and west, and single on the north and south, carried through three ascending levels. Each level is defined by a series of basement mouldings, now much damaged and restored, yet clearly displaying considerable ornamentation, including even (original?) traces of painted (coconut?) trees on the bottom series. A flight of steps at ground level is flanked by fragmentary striding elephants. These steps lead to the first level that continues around the building as a walkway. Another flight of steps flanked by damaged yali balustrades in the middle of the north side provides access to a court at the second level. Here, the outlines of L-shaped columns are seen. On the east and west, basements have projections on the outer faces; they are separated from another basement to the south. The second level also runs continuously around the building as a second walkway (wider than that below). Access to the third level is by two flights of steps, now badly smashed with fragmentary balustrades. Judging from the outlines in the concrete floor, four square areas (chambers?) were symmetrically arranged on this uppermost level.

STRUCTURE (XIV/8)

Little remains of the structure cut into and elevated upon boulders in the north part of XIV.

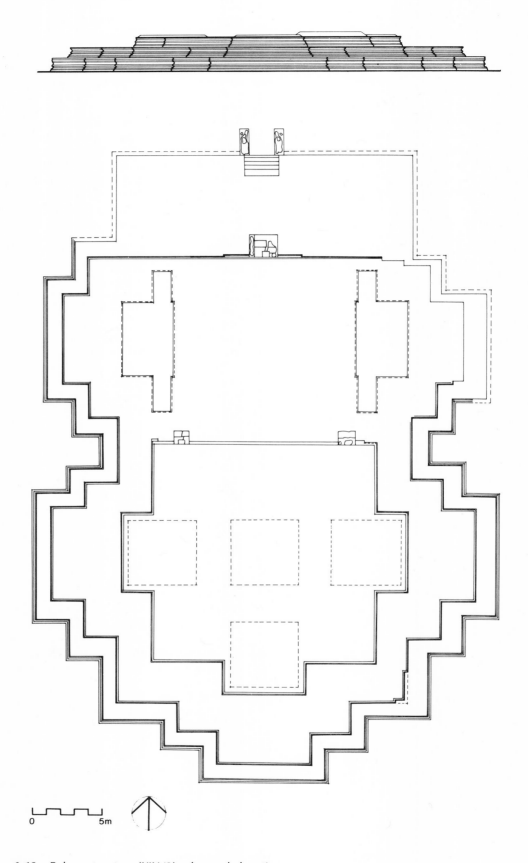

Figure 6.12   Palace structure (XIV/3), plan and elevation.

This structure appears to have been a long building, with a rectangular room at the higher (south) end and a court surrounded by platforms in the typical U-configuration at the lower (north) end. Traces of rubble foundations and stone footings are visible, also fragments of concrete and plaster floors, and brick and plaster walls. The only carved basement preserved in situ is seen at the north end of the west wall. At the south end, an outer wall (east and south sides) and fragments of plaster flooring appear to define an outer passageway. Broken areas of plaster flooring on the east side suggest the presence of further chambers at a lower level.

PALACE COMPLEX (XXV/2)

Northeast of the Virupaksha Temple (XXV/1), this complex has only recently been excavated (Nagaraja Rao 1983, pp. 28-29).

Here, a rectangular building is surrounded by subsidiary chambers and walls on three sides. The east-facing principal structure consists of a sequence of four ascending floor levels, each marked by a series of stone basement mouldings. Single flights of steps in the middle (bottom level) or two flights of steps at the corners (upper levels), are flanked by yali balustrades or striding elephants (damaged). These ascending levels are flanked by walls on the north and south, and are provided with plaster basement mouldings and also regularly spaced square holes (presumably for supporting timbers). The floors preserve their plaster coatings; stone column footings are seen at each level. The uppermost level (west end) has a single rectangular chamber open to the east, with an enclosed passageway on three sides. On its exterior, the palace preserves a high basement with carved stone mouldings covered with plaster.

The subsidiary chambers defining the courtyard on three sides have parallel rubble walls with short cross walls. Stone basement mouldings face into the courtyard, and flights of steps are positioned at regular intervals and at the corners. Doorways are flanked by plaster and brick pilasters. Some footings indicate regularly spaced columns, and there is abundant evidence of plaster flooring and wall surfacing. On the north and west, enclosure walls are found, angled to the main complex. The walls further to the west belong to a separate feature.

PALACE COMPLEX (XXVI/1)
(Figures 6.13, 6.18 and 6.21)

This complex has only been revealed recently by the excavators (Nagaraja Rao 1983, pp. 15-28). Facing north, the central building, together with its surrounding courtyard and subsidiary structures, is built upon sloping ground rising to the south. Located within a large courtyard, the principal building is entered by a flight of steps in the middle of the north side. The structure is defined by a series of basement mouldings. Here, a long court, bounded on the east and west by platforms, leads by way of a single raised step and two subfloor stone footings to a second court with platforms on three sides. All these raised areas are defined by basement mouldings. The second floor level is reached by a single flight of steps with plaster-covered stone yali balustrades in the middle of the north side. At this level, brick and plaster walls with recessed niches face into the court; from these walls two square areas (chambers?) extend outwards to the east and west. Two flights of steps, also with balustrades (with medallion designs), lead to the third and uppermost level; this is raised on a stone basement with figural friezes. Here, three rectangular rooms open off a corridor that surrounds a central rectangular chamber, which is entered from the north. Corner chambers are found at the southwest and southeast; the latter is divided into two compartments at different levels by stone slabs and has a shallow stone drain (for washing?). At its south end, the floor level of the structure is raised only slightly above that of the court. Throughout, plaster flooring and wall surfacing are preserved; square stone footings indicate regularly spaced columns.

The courtyard surrounding this structure is incompletely bounded by thick walls. The north wall (of perfectly jointed masonry) is interrupted by a long flight of steps with yali balustrades at the top. Large rectangular platforms defined by stone basements are located on the east and west; the former is provided with access steps. In the northwest corner the walls project westwards and there is a narrow bent passageway (now blocked up); the walls on the east also project outwards. A small square well with finely finished stonework is located near the northwest corner of the principal building; to the west are the subfloor remains of a small structure. In the southwest corner of the courtyard, part of a stone aqueduct leads into a deep narrow cistern. Beyond the enclosure walls on three sides is a second set of walls defining a passageway of irregular width. Here stone drains are seen projecting outwards from the inner walls; here, too, shallow vertical bands in plaster are seen. As the inner walls do not actually meet the outer north wall, this passageway eventually runs into the courtyard at either side.

Beyond the complex to the northeast, basement mouldings demarcate a rectangular court; passageways are found in the middle of the north and west sides. Excavations to the west have uncovered traces of earth and rubble foundations.

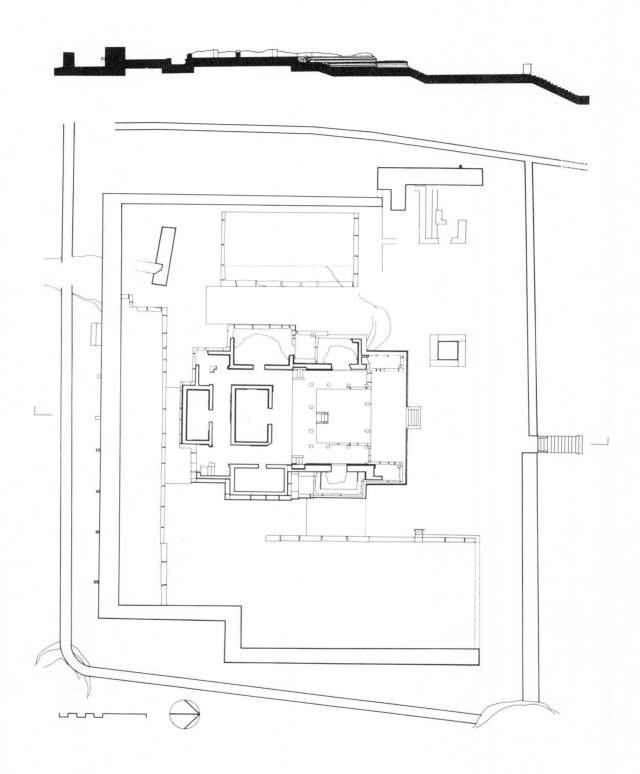

Figure 6.13   Palace complex (XXVI/1), plan and section.

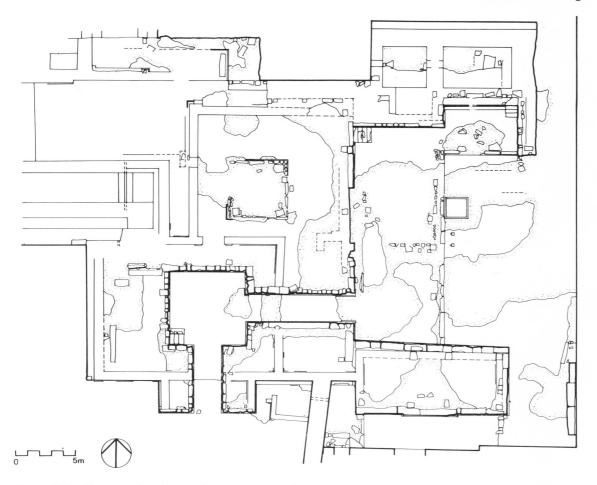

Figure 6.14   Entryway into V/1 and structure V/2, plan.

OTHER PALACE STRUCTURES

Unexcavated mounds in XXVI clearly display the characteristic stepped levels of typical palace structures; one example facing east is of the type with a single chamber at its highest level. Fragments of other similar buildings are found elsewhere within the enclosures of the royal centre, often closely associated with better preserved palaces. In VI, VIII, and XXX, for instance, fragments of stone mouldings and subfloor column footings indicate that here too are typical palace structures (VI/5, VIIIc/1, and XXX/3).

Zones east of the enclosures of the royal centre appear also to have contained extensive palace structures. The most obvious example is located beneath a large rocky outcrop on the south side of the east valley. Here are seen the remains of subfloor foundations, moulded stone basements, plaster floors, standing walls of earth or rubble, collapsed concrete roofing, and smashed earthenware tiling. In the middle is the characteristic stepped outline of a palace structure. Apparently facing east, this rises to the west in four ascending

levels; a rubble-walled chamber is located at the highest level. On four sides are courts, gateways, and subsidiary structures, perhaps even shrines, now mostly buried and overgrown. Elevated on the rocky boulders to the southwest of this complex is a small plaster-lined tank with an earthenware pipe descending into a small well.

Not far away to the south (northeast of the octagonal bath) another unexcavated palace structure is located. Now almost completely concealed by a mound with vegetation, traces of dressed stone mouldings indicate a square court open to the east, bounded on three sides by raised areas. To the west the mound rises gradually, and there is ample evidence of rubble stonework. Surrounding this mound on three sides are two sets of enclosure walls, one within the other.

STRUCTURE (V/2)
(Figure 6.14)

North of the large complex (V/1) already described, is a sequence of courts and chambers comprising a coherent building. Though utilizing

6. PLATFORMS AND PALACES

elements familiar in other typical palace structures, this example is quite different in layout.

Here a large rectangular court, open to the east, is divided into two levels. In the middle of the court is a square basin fashioned out of a single granite block, the sides of which are carved with geese and lotus medallions (Thapar 1982, pl. xiva). On three sides, the court is bounded by raised areas on basement mouldings. At the southwest corner an opening leads to the passageway that forms part of the entryway associated with V/1. The basement on the south side of the court is extended to the east; on the north, the basement makes two turns and eventually meets steps at the northeast corner. To the north are two chambers, the plastered floors exposed here do not relate to the walls, but to an earlier structure at a lower level.

Situated to the west is a large chamber reached by steps in the northwest corner of the court. On its east side this chamber has a line of stone footings set into rubble and earth walls; on the other three sides it is enclosed by walls. In the middle of this chamber fragments of chlorite and limestone mouldings define a central (unplastered) floor area. In the west wall is a doorway (later blocked up) with steps that descend to a narrow rectangular chamber beyond which is a large court. In the south wall another doorway leads into the entryway of V/1. North of the chamber, and at much lower levels, are the remains of a plastered floor and massive buttresses, and a finely finished basement moulding.

South of the principal court, the basement turns a corner and then abuts another (east-west) basement at a higher level defining a raised area. Where the east courtyard walls of V/1 meet this raised floor area there is a small irregular chamber with a plastered shelf (seat?) and a small outlet drain. Part of another basement is found southeast of this court, built up against the enclosure walls to the east. On the east and south the enclosure walls appear to cut off direct access to the court. Entry is only by a circuitous route from a small doorway in the west end of the enclosure walls to the south.

MISCELLANEOUS STRUCTURES IN ENCLOSURE V

Structure V/4 is located in the north part of the enclosure and is preserved only in its subfloor walls. Rectangular in layout, this building is divided into four irregular spaces by five north-south walls with additional buttressing on the west and south; there is only a single cross wall. Several stone column footings are embedded into the walls, suggesting a layout of 6 by 5 columns. To the east is a small square well.

V/5 is a small structure west of the courtyard of V/1; again, only the subfloor walls are preserved. Entered in the middle of the north side, where basement mouldings and foundations for steps are visible, this structure seems also to have consisted of 6 by 5 columns, according to the stone footings embedded into the subfloor walls; square extensions are to the west and south. Unusual is the plastered moulding on the exterior of the east and south subfloor walls; towards the south this plaster projection becomes a wide angled shelf.

More exceptional in layout is structure V/14 near the southeast corner of the courtyard of V/1. Here subfloor walls create a rectangle with a small extension at the west. A central row of column footings divides the building into two long bays. In the southwest corner of V, 7 by 4 columns (several missing) define a rectangular structure with a plastered floor and rubble walls (11).

BASEMENT MOULDINGS
(Figures 6.15, 6.16, 6.17, 6.18, 6.19 and 6.20)

Obviously, the various structures described in this chapter preserve few architectural features that can be analysed in terms of stylistic evolution. A study of the carved mouldings of the basements, however, does reveal a number of distinct styles that may also be chronologically determined. We divide these into four broad groups.

The characteristic feature of the first group of basement mouldings is a simple and undecorated tripartite scheme. Here, the top and bottom mouldings are inverted but otherwise identical; the intermediate course is vertical and plain. The top and bottom mouldings have angled or curved contours and are usually interrupted by undecorated semicircular medallions. Examples of this scheme are found in the structures of IVa (6, 10, 12, 13, 19, and 26) and IVd. In the basement of the hundred-columned "audience hall" (IVa/1) this series of mouldings is doubled; the upper series coincides with the scheme already described, while the lower series presents double-curved contours, a lack of medallions, and a projecting intermediate part-octagonal moulding. Here also there is a contrast between the carved details on the lower (finer) and upper (coarser) series, perhaps suggesting successive building phases. (Identical basement mouldings are also found on many of the gateways linking the enclosures of the royal centre; see Chapter 4).

The basement mouldings of the second group are more varied in form and decoration. Typical is the use of the double-curved plinth (upana) element with a potlike profile (kumuda), vertical course, and capping cornice (kapota), with regularly spaced medallions (kudus). Decoration is mostly confined to bands of petals and jewels,

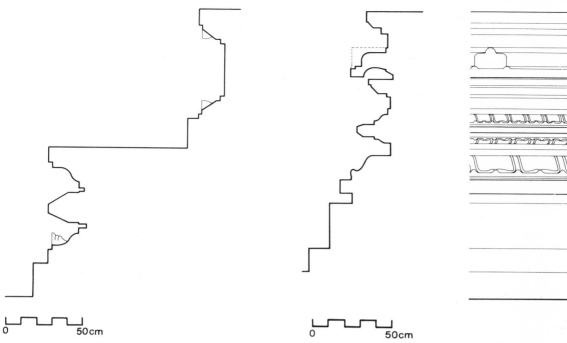

Figure 6.15   Basement detail, hundred-columned hall (IVa/1).

Figure 6.16   Basement detail, great platform (IVb/1), phase two.

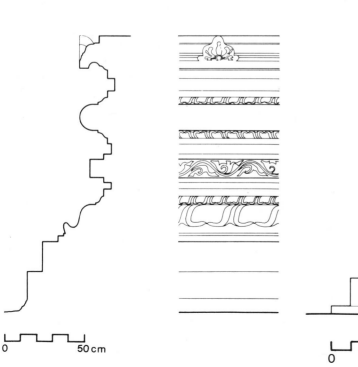

Figure 6.17   Basement detail, structure IVa/17.

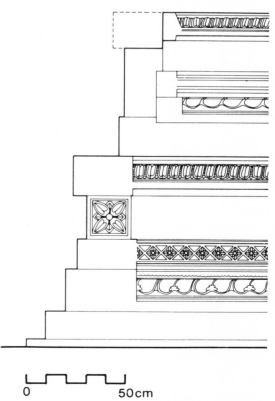

Figure 6.18   Basement detail, palace structure XXVI/1.

but friezes of elephants and geese also appear, anticipating the richly decorated schemes of group three. Perhaps the most elaborate version of this second group is the double series of mouldings constituting the second phase of the great platform (IVb/1). Here, the upana and kapota are ornamented with bands of wide petals, and the intermediate course has relief carvings (see p.100). An additional inverted upana carved with bands of petals is introduced above the kapota. In the upper series, a part-octagonal projecting band decorated with petals on its angled faces, and a plain moulding with an angled cut, are added. Other examples of this second group are found on several palace structures (V/1, VI/1, VIIIf/1, and XIV/2). Here, the basic scheme is an upana with a band of wide petals, a potlike element decorated with jewelled bands and miniature lotus buds, and a kapota with narrow petals and medallions.

The third group of basement mouldings presents yet more complex forms and a greater variety of decorative themes; furthermore, each individual moulding is more complicated, combining different profiles and ornamental treatments. Several varying schemes are presented here. For example, in structure IVa/17 there are five components: plain vertical course, upana with petalled bands, projecting band with undulating foliation, part-hemispherical element with petalled bands, and an overhanging kapota with medallions carved with foliate panels. Other similar five-part basements are found in two series of mouldings in palace structure XIV/3, and in the fragmentary mouldings beneath the Islamic-styled nine-domed structure (VI/3). The basic scheme in both of these examples consists of a plain vertical course, an upana decorated with petalled bands, a ribbed potlike element, a vertical course with projecting bands and foliate panels, and a kapota with petals and medallions having foliation and yali heads. Sometimes the vertical courses are carved with undulating lotus ornament and a frieze of horses and elephants; dancing women, musicians, and fighting warriors are also sometimes included (IVa/27, XXVI/1). The mouldings comprising the bottom series of the third phase of the great platform (IVb/1) are also of the same type, though here additional courses are included. In general, the carvings on this monument (in chlorite) are particularly fine and exuberant.

The middle and upper series of chlorite mouldings on this third phase of the great platform are delicately carved with profuse detail, and are described separately as our fourth group — the most elaborate category. The outstanding feature of these mouldings is the addition of projecting niches, each with its own miniature basement, pilasters, overhanging eaves, parapet, and surmounting roof forms. These niches incorporate

Figure 6.19   Basement detail, great platform (IVb/1), phase three. (height 2.32 m.).

tiny animals and birds and figural carving, particularly courtly scenes. Several unique decorative motifs are encountered here — square and diamond-shaped lotus medallions, hanging and looped garlands, wavy brackets, and clustered pilasters. Though these two series of mouldings appear to be a further elaboration of the bottom series (group three), it is not clear if these differences represent a significant lapse of time.

Figure 6.20   Basement detail, great platform (IVb/1), phase three (height 1.53 m.).

6. PLATFORMS AND PALACES

BALUSTRADES
(Figure 6.21)

Other relevant features of palace structures are the balustrades flanking the stone steps leading from one floor level to the next. Most common are stone slabs carved with walking yalis. The heads of these beasts are reversed, and out of their open jaws flow curved mouldings terminating in a roll and miniature lotus bud. Where preserved, the details of the beasts' manes and curling tails are delicately incised. As a further elaboration of this animal theme, a yali fights a lion, and an elephant lifts a foliated tree (south staircase of the great platform, IVb/1). (Some of these yali balustrades could be dated by a comparison with similar balustrades in temple architecture.)

Another balustrade design is found on the staircases on the north side of the hundred-columned hall (IVa/1) and on one of the recently excavated palace complexes (XXXVI/1). Here, the panels have finely carved full-lotus medallions accompanied by single pilasters with miniature curved brackets.

Some steps are flanked by free-standing, three-dimensional elephants. These beasts usually stride forward, picking up lotuses with their trunks (IVa/17 and 27, IVb/1 west side, VIIIf/1, XIV/3, and XXV/2).

Figure 6.21 Balustrade details: upper left and upper right, palace structure XXVI/1; centre left, palace structure V/1; centre right, northeast shrine of Ramachandra Temple complex; bottom left, structure IVa/17; bottom right, palace structure VIIIf/1.

ASSOCIATED ARTEFACTS
(Figure 6.22)

In the recent work accompanying the excavation of the various structures described in this chapter, the most common discovery has been large numbers of pottery sherds. These sherds are evidently of local production and contrast with the occasional fragments of Chinese wares also found here. Of course, such sherds are discovered all over the site, and certainly in most parts of the royal centre. The scientific study of this material can, however, provide information on Vijayanagara society, which is not available from any other sources.

A preliminary study (Sinopoli 1983) of the pottery associated with two palace structures (XXV/2, XXVI/1) reveals a wide range of production techniques, ware categories (plain, fine, and coarse), and colours (black and grey, brown or buff, and red). Vessel forms include low-necked open forms and high-necked, more restricted forms; fragments of neckless jars, bowls, and large shallow trays are also found. The variety of decorative techniques include stamped, incised, and applied motifs; a small number of examples with painted designs have been recovered.

Less common than these indigenous wares, but still found in abundance, are fragments of Chinese porcelain (Thapar 1982, pl. xivb; Nagaraja Rao 1983, pp. 24-27, pls. xxix-xxxi). The types identified here include celadon, blue and white (the greatest number), and polychrome wares. Foliate designs are the most popular decorative theme, but figurative motifs are also known. These imported sherds may all be dated to the late fifteenth and early sixteenth centuries.

Also found in recent excavations (XXV/2) is a miniature copper bowl, imitating basketry (Nagaraja Rao 1983, pls. xxxvi a-c). Copper coins, too, are discovered and, though mostly worn, are all of the Vijayanagara period. Other finds include stone, bronze, and terracotta figurines, presumably miniature votive objects. Fragments of plaster sculptures include decorative elements (roundels, foliate buds) and some miniature sculptured heads and animals (Thapar 1982, pls. xivc-d).

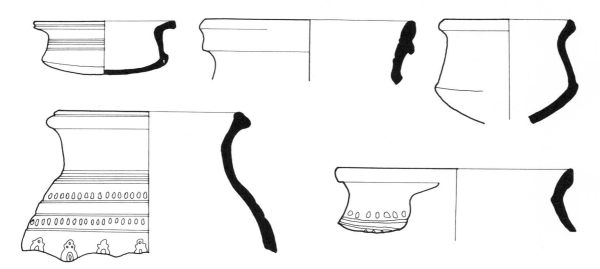

Figure 6.22   Pottery fragments found in palace complex XXVI/1 (Sinopoli 1983, fig. 26).

7. ISLAMIC-STYLED FORMS

Towers, Pavilions, and Stables

Concentrated in and around the royal centre at Vijayanagara is a group of secular monuments, distinguished by their overall Islamic appearance. No specific historical or epigraphical information can be definitely linked with any of these structures; as a result, these remain only tentatively identified and dated. Despite considerable typological variation — palaces, pavilions, towers, bathhouses, stables, etc. — these buildings clearly form a coherent group due to their common stylistic characteristics. However, these monuments should not be attributed to any direct Muslim patronage: on the contrary, they are closely associated with the remains of other secular and religious buildings within the royal centre, used by the Hindu rulers, court, and military. Though at least one scholar (Subrahmanyam 1974) has suggested that some of these monuments may belong to a post-1565 Muslim occupation of the site, no historical evidence is available to indicate any such building activity.

SOURCES OF ISLAMIC FORMS

By the middle of the fourteenth century, the Muslims were well established in the Deccan and had embarked upon various building projects at their capitals of Daulatabad and Gulbarga. During the next two centuries the region experienced an intensifying of Islamic artistic activity as more and more centres were established as Muslim headquarters: for example, Bidar and Firuzabad in the fifteenth century, and Bijapur and Golconda in the sixteenth and seventeenth centuries. At all of these provincial capitals numerous fortifications, gateways, palaces, mosques, and tombs were erected. Though modelled at first on Tughluq architectural schemes at Delhi, these Deccan structures rapidly evolved their own distinctive stylistic character.

In fifteenth-century Deccan Islamic architecture, columns are generally simple, supporting four-centred arches in one or two planes; walls sometimes slope slightly inwards and have arched niches; angled eaves are carried on corbelled brackets; parapets are created from rows of ornamental battlements with corner minarets; domes are mostly flattish; plaster decoration is applied in bands and roundels above the openings. The sixteenth century witnesses an overall elaboration of these schemes, including a marked increase in richly decorated plasterwork and even coloured tilework. Arches frequently become multilobed; domes and their supporting pendentives and squinches are profusely ornamented; parapets employ interlocking motifs; the corners of buildings and gateways occasionally utilize ornamental minarets; double-curved eaves are carried on carved stone brackets. Major monuments in this Islamic style were erected at the various Muslim cities in the Deccan, and from these centres the style was distributed all over the region.

Without doubt, the architects and craftsmen of Vijayanagara were well aware of this Deccan Islamic tradition. Despite the fact that the Hindu armies were almost continuously at war with their Muslim neighbours to the north, by the beginning of the fifteenth century the Vijayanagara militia had begun to employ large numbers of Muslim horsemen who introduced more advanced Islamic techniques of warfare. Soon there were influential Muslims at the capital who were able to act as building patrons. Evidence of this patronage is seen in the tombs erected in the various Muslim quarters of the city (northeast and west of the royal centre). The tombs are of a uniform type, consisting of a square domed chamber, with arched niches on the exterior, sloping walls, parapets of battlements, and flattish domes; no plaster coating is preserved (Michell 1984b). In all their features, these tombs resemble late fourteenth-century and early fifteenth-century Deccan Islamic models, such as the tombs at Gulbarga (Schotten-Merklinger 1981, pp. 11-16). As a confirmation of this date, one tomb at Vijayanagara is linked with a dharmashala — probably serving as a mosque — dated to 1439 (*South Indian Inscriptions* IX/II, no. 447; Nagaraja Rao 1983, pp. 64-65).

CREATION OF A NEW STYLE

Probably soon after these tombs were erected at Vijayanagara, other buildings at the capital began to imitate the Islamic style. Among those structures that appear to have closely copied Islamic forms are several gateways in the fortified walls. One example southeast of the royal centre displays a great dome of the fifteenth-century Deccan type carried high on four great arches with corner squinches. Though little of the original plaster decoration is preserved, this was probably also typically Islamic. Other gateways, too, incorporate Islamic arched forms, parapets, and decorative schemes, especially in the facades of upper chambers.

Before examining the various Islamic-styled structures within the royal centre, we must first point out that, though many of these buildings exhibit characteristic Deccan Islamic features, their overall appearance is unlike any known Islamic monument at Gulbarga, Firuzabad, Bidar, etc. We believe that these Vijayanagara structures should not be considered inaccurate or incompetent imitations of the Deccan Islamic style; rather, they represent something new. These buildings are the result of a consciously cultivated taste for Islamic forms in which a new artistic tradition was evolved incorporating "foreign" elements. Here, features derived from both Islamic and Hindu practice are combined together to produce a style that is neither "purely" Islamic nor Hindu. As for the inventors of this style, we acknowledge the creativity of the architects and craftsmen working at the capital under the direct encouragement of the Hindu court and military for whom these buildings were constructed. Instead of interpreting these monuments as products of an eclectic courtly indulgence, we recognize the variety of building forms and skill in manipulating the different architectural elements. Possibly "exotic" in the context of a Hindu capital, this Islamic-influenced style never lacked imagination and charm as the buildings themselves demonstrate.

That these monuments were closely linked with the king, court, and army, is suggested by their location within the royal centre and the various functions that can be tentatively assigned to them. There are also some revealing details in contemporary temple sculpture: here, standing royal donors, both male and female, are depicted in the lobed-arched entrances of their "typical" palaces. (Such Muslim-styled arches do not appear in comparable earlier depictions.) Thus is suggested the role of courtly taste in the evolution of this new architectural style. Nor did this Hindu preference for Islamic-styled civic buildings cease with the abandonment of Vijayanagara in 1565. Palaces at the later Vijayanagara capitals — Chandragiri and Penukonda, for instance — display a continuation of this tradition.

GENERAL FEATURES

In order for Deccan Islamic architecture to be adopted as an expression of the Vijayanagara courtly aesthetic, certain stylistic metamorphoses had to take place. Whether such a task was carried out by Muslim or Hindu architects and craftsmen is not the crucial question: what eventually came to be built at the capital was something new and characteristic of Vijayanagara. To examine the manner by which Islamic and Hindu traditions were fused together it is first necessary to isolate the different architectural and decorative elements.

To begin with, the Islamic-styled buildings at Vijayanagara reveal a fairly standardized repertory of construction techniques, plan types, elevational treatments, and ornamental schemes. Unlike the other structures at the capital, almost all parts of these monuments consist of stone blocks set in mortar. (This probably explains why these buildings have survived both war and weather better than other secular structures which utilized earth and rubble walls, and timber columns and roofs — see Chapter 6). Walls, piers, columns, arches, domes, roofs, and towers are all of stone blocks, sometimes quite crudely fashioned and jointed, even split into small bricklike pieces. Basically, the thick mortar secures the construction, especially the vaulted ceilings. Brickwork, too, is occasionally applied to complete the details of parapets and roofs. Nothing of this masonry was intended to be visible; all building surfaces, both internal and external, were originally covered with plaster. Today, only portions of this plaster coating are preserved.

The varied plans of these Islamic-styled monuments are easily reduced to symmetrical arrangements of square, rectangular, or octagonal bays, each provided with its own vaulted roof. Each bay is defined by walls, arched openings or piers, either free-standing or engaged to the walls. The bays are arranged in groups, opening off each other (nine-domed hall) or distributed around a square or octagonal chamber (fountain). Sometimes the bays proceed around an enlarged open space — square (water pavilion), rectangular, or octagonal (bath). More unusually, the bays are arranged in a low row (elephant stables).

Islamic-derived elements are obvious. Pointed arches are four-centred in one or more planes, or consist of three, five, and even nine lobes. Pendentives and squinches with angled and curved elements support the octagonal or circular drums of vaults and domes with different designs. Plaster decoration, in flat relief in bands and roundels, employs geometric strapwork, stylized arabesques, and friezes of merlons, trefoils, and palmettes.

Hindu-derived elements, however, are also found in abundance. The basements and cornices of Islamic-styled buildings frequently have mouldings derived from temple architecture, usually reproduced in plaster but sometimes also in stone (two-storeyed pavilion). Wall brackets are corbelled and support double-curved or angled eaves, familiar from the open porches of temples. Roof parapets, sometimes ornamentally applied to balconies or set within domes, are of brick and plaster, and are more or less identical to those above temple porches with miniature templelike roof forms arranged in rows. The roofs of these Islamic-styled buildings frequently derive their shapes from the tiered arrangements of temple superstructures, particularly the square-to-dome roof form culminating in a ribbed finial. Plaster decoration, too, draws on themes well known in temple art: lotus ornament in its many variations, yali heads with protruding eyes and open jaws, seated or rearing yalis, and parrots and geese.

All these features from both traditions are not only synthesized into startlingly original compositions — like the two-storeyed pavilion and elephant stables — they are in themselves subjected to transformation. Thus, moulded basements, templelike parapets, and sculptures are "Islamicized" by reducing the depth of carving to produce flat relief. In turn, Islamic features are "Hinduized" so that plaster decoration with geometric and arabesque motifs merges with lively animals and birds.

SQUARE WATER PAVILION (XX/1)
(Figures 7.1, 7.2, and 7.3)

Located southeast of IV, this water pavilion is generally identified as the "queens' bath" (Devakunjari 1970, p. 22), though it is not known on what occasions it was used or by whom. The square building is surrounded on four sides by a water channel (recently filled in at the northeast corner and south entrance). A spout on the east originally conducted water from this channel into the central basin constituting a square courtyard. Around this basin is a corridor of 24 vaulted bays defined by piers. Small windows are positioned in the outer walls of most bays, while the central bays on three sides are open; the central south bay is projected outwards over the water channel as a balcony. An entrance doorway is located east of this latter bay. The outer walls at the east end of the south side extend outwards to accommodate the staircase ascending to the roof. Facing into the open courtyard on each side are two raised seating areas projecting over the water basin as balconies. (On the east side these balconies have mostly fallen.) The four stone slabs with circular holes set into the (restored) plaster floor of the basin may have secured poles (carrying a canopy?).

No plaster mouldings and decoration are found on the exterior of the building (much restored). A multilobed arched doorway is seen on the south, together with a projecting balcony (which may have resembled those of the interior). Plain arches in simple rectangular frames are preserved in the middle of the three other sides. (The restored arched fragment on the west suggests that here, too, a balcony may have once projected

outwards.) Above, double stone corbels indicate the presence of an eave, now vanished. A fragment of the original parapet is seen on the south.

Throughout the interior corridor the arches are uniformly pointed in two planes, continuing the projections of the engaged and free-standing piers. Plaster-decorated domes and vaults above the bays display a remarkable variety in design. Where octagonal or circular drums and vaults appear, pendentives with angled tops in two planes and angled interiors are utilized. Octagonal or circular drums are ornamented with miniature arches, pilasters, and foliated brackets; also palmettes, lotus buds, and friezes of geese or crouching yalis. In two examples, the domes are supported on complex nets of intersecting angled bands. The domes are elaborately decorated, though the plasterwork has been much restored. Here are found concave and angled flutings, converging bands of foliate decoration, enlarged petals, trefoil palmettes sometimes incorporating parrots, foliate arabesques, and intersecting angled bands defining a central octagon. Pyramidal vaults employ ornamental strapwork and chains, or ascending and diminishing tiers of miniature curved ribs. At the centres of each dome and vault are enlarged lotus medallions, but few of these are preserved intact.

The small windows have pointed arches, also the doorway to the staircase; a miniature dome appears above the bottom landing. The inner facades of the projecting balconies only partly preserve their elaborate plaster ornamentation of geometric and foliate motifs. The openings are divided vertically into two, and are set in a rectangular frame. The ceilings within the balconies have miniature pyramidal vaults, domes, or nine-squared designs.

The sides of the water basin are fashioned out of masonry blocks, and steps once led down to the water, probably on three sides. The stone water chute is carved with flowing petal decoration at its spout. The principal interest on these walls is provided by the plaster-ornamented, projecting balconies supported on four brackets. Each bracket consists of three stone corbels. The lower part of each balcony is divided into a series of mouldings. The openings on the front and sides of each balcony have flat bands with foliate ornamentation. A projecting angled moulding separates the lower openings from those above. The latter are pointed, multilobed, or simple rectangles; on one example there are six smaller arched openings. Decorated bands and medallions ornament these upper windows, and projecting stones were probably once linked with brackets above by plaster rearing yalis (fragments of animal feet are clearly seen). An angled eave on three sides, and a parapet decorated with a

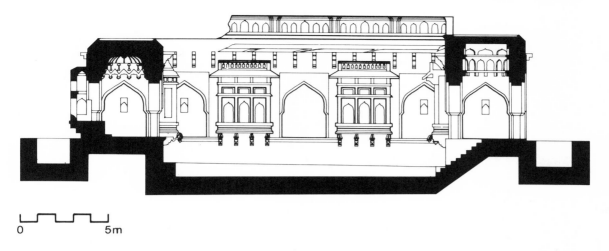

Figure 7.1   Square water pavilion (XX/1), section.

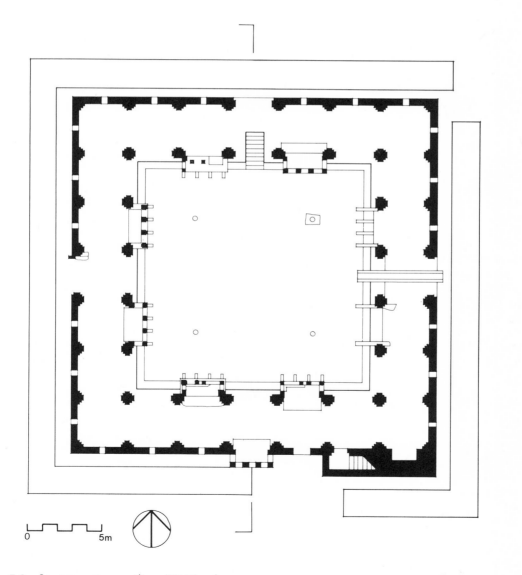

Figure 7.2   Square water pavilion (XX/1), plan.

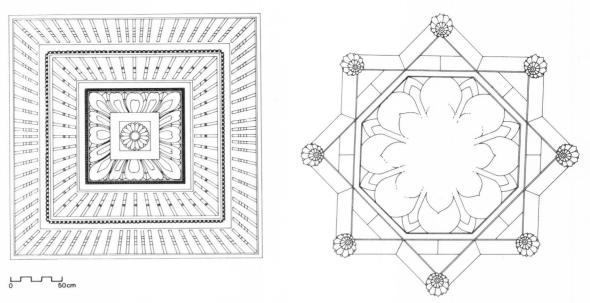

Figure 7.3   Square water pavilion (XX/1), examples of dome designs.

frieze of pointed arches and angled elements, complete the balcony scheme.

The principal walls facing onto the basin have arches in two planes set in recessed frames. Above, large brackets decorated with plaster once supported a beam and angled eave, now mostly collapsed. There is an elaborate parapet consisting of a series of pointed arched recesses, occasionally pierced as windows at rooftop level, with a frieze of merlons and angled squares above. Four intermediate pilasters in two tiers are positioned on each side, but only a few of these remain. The towers over the central north bay and the top of the staircase (southeast corner) are only known through the nineteenth-century photographs. Here are recorded two square chambers with a series of ascending and diminishing eaves capped by square-to-dome roof forms.

OCTAGONAL FOUNTAIN (XXII/1)
(Figure 7.4)

Near the southwest corner of the alley surrounding IV is this small fountain. East of the structure is abundant evidence of earthenware pipes thickly embedded in brick and mortar.

At the centre of this octagonal building is a small basin set into the plaster floor in several descending layers, one of which has twelve lobes. A separate rectangular stone basin is found nearby to the south. The central irregular octagonal chamber has openings in the cardinal directions, with smaller intermediate angled walls pierced by niches. Surrounding this chamber is a passageway created by eight piers between which

are arched entrances. (The angled buttresses against these piers are modern.)

The plain walls of the exterior (much restored) are pierced on each side by simple pointed arches in two planes. Traces of lobed bands rising from short horizontal mouldings appear above the arches over the four entrances on the cardinal directions. Small brackets support a short angled eave with an ornamental shallow beam on its underside (the latter mostly vanished). The short wall above is terminated by a frieze of pointed angled elements. Fragments of the parapet display angled and curved merlons with corner pilasters. The (regular) octagonal roof above the central chamber is basically pyramidal. Above is a double-curved contour and a surmounting dome with an upper capping piece; no finial is preserved.

Within the central chamber, pointed arched openings in two planes are found on four sides; the smaller intermediate walls have similarly arched niches above. The upper irregular octagon has a frieze of angled elements, pointed multilobed arches, and a band of interwoven loops forming the drum. Above rises the octagonal pyramidal vault, but the central medallion has now vanished. Pointed arches divide the surrounding passageway into eight bays with alternating octagons (cardinal directions) and irregular hexagons above, created by angled pendentives. Plain flattish domes rise upon the octagonal drums, while above the hexagons are pointed vaults. One dome (south bay) has sixteen concave flutings rising from trefoil palmettes converging on a central medallion.

TWO-STOREYED OCTAGONAL PAVILION (VI/2)
(Figures 7.5 and 7.6)

Located between the palace (1) and nine-domed structure (3) in VI, this is one of the better preserved Islamic-styled buildings in the royal centre. It is sometimes referred to as a "band tower" (Devakunjari 1970, p. 33). At the ground level the building consists of eight identical piers framing arched entrances leading into an octagonal chamber. Abutting the square stone basement at an angle on the northeast, but actually separated from the pavilion, is the staircase tower, clearly a later addition (or replacement?). The steps of this tower lead directly to the octagonal chamber at the upper level. Here, arched windows are provided on seven sides, while on the eighth (northeast) side an arched opening provides access to the upper staircase landing.

The square stone plinth on which the pavilion is erected displays a miniature tripartite moulding; a further stone course is provided on eight sides. The arched entrances of the lower storey are in two planes framed in simple rectangles. On the cardinal directions the arched entrances are more complex. Here an additional recessed arch is added within the other two, but not supported on any pier. Bands of decoration surround the outer arch, while roundels are positioned in the spandrels at the apexes; here a variety of geometric interlacing and knotlike designs is found. At each corner and at two intermediate points on each side, curved brackets support a horizontal beam and angled eave. These brackets have foliate ornamentation sometimes incorporating peacocks. The scheme of the upper storey is generally more elaborate. On four sides (intermediate directions) pointed arched windows are contained within larger arched frames. Both windows and frames employ ornamental half-pilasters at the sides, geese with foliate tails, and flamelike tufts of foliation around the openings. Medallions and roundels are found above the openings. On the cardinal directions four brackets with double pendant buds and a frieze of enlarged trefoil palmettes or foliate merlons are positioned beneath rectangular openings. Each wall here has an additional projection that tapers slightly as it rises. Three ornamental arches and four miniature brackets support a small eavelike moulding and an elaborate panel of foliate decoration above. Running around the building on eight sides is a sloping eave supported on brackets, now mostly vanished, and a cornice with angled elements. Above rises the octagonal tower consisting of a vertical course and two pyramidal sections separated by a small recess. The capping dome has a double curve with convex flutings; the lower rim and bulbous finial are now mostly missing. The exterior of the staircase tower is plain.

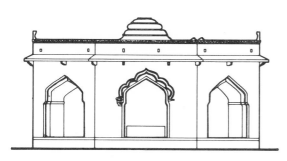

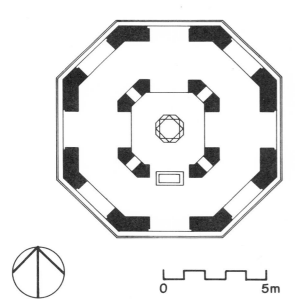

Figure 7.4 Octagonal fountain (XXII/1), plan, section and elevation.

0   5m

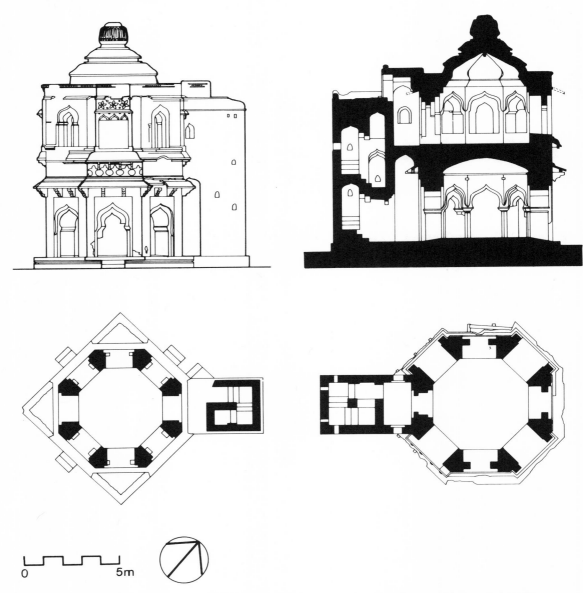

Figure 7.5   Two-storeyed octagonal pavilion (VI/2), ground and upper plans, section and elevation.

Within the lower octagonal chamber are pointed arches, in both two and three planes, rising out of simple roll mouldings on each pier. The circular projection at the base of the shallow dome is carried by angled blocks at the corners. The upper octagonal chamber is similarly plain. Here the recessed pointed arched windows are raised above the floor. The octagonal vault has both an angled and curved lower contour; the central (lotus?) medallion is not preserved. The entrance leading to the staircase and the staircase itself employ pointed arched vaults. However, a miniature dome with angled flutings is positioned over the upper landing. At the junction of the staircase tower and the upper chamber, part of the angled eave of the original exterior is seen.

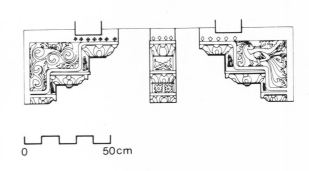

Figure 7.6   Two-storeyed octagonal pavilion (VI/2), plaster-decorated bracket.

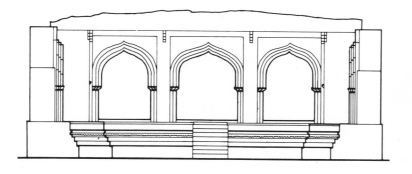

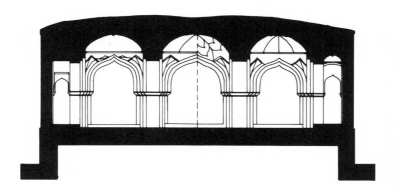

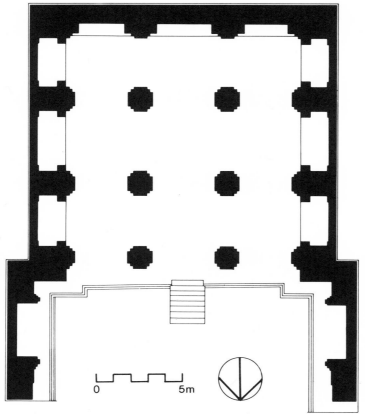

Figure 7.7   Nine-domed structure (VI/3), plan, section and elevation.

7. ISLAMIC-STYLED FORMS

NINE-DOMED STRUCTURE (VI/3)
(Figure 7.7)

Though sometimes tentatively identified as a mosque and idgah (Longhurst 1917, p. 87; Devakunjari 1970, pp. 31-32), this domed structure and its curious walled "appendix" to the northwest (VI/16) cannot have served as a place of prayer for Muslims. Oriented northwards (incorrectly for a mosque), this building may have functioned as some sort of reception hall. Furthermore, it appears to have been erected on the dismantled remains of a typical palace structure (see Chapter 6).

The hall consists of 3 by 3 domed bays laid out in a symmetrical manner, each defined by free-standing and/or engaged piers with projections on each side. The bays are open on the north, where a flight of steps is centrally positioned. Slightly raised above floor level on the east and west are three small rectangular chambers created by arched openings. Against the south wall similar arches frame shallow recesses. Projecting northwards from the northeast and northwest corners of the hall are two walls, each provided with a deeply recessed niche facing inwards. Both these walls, and also the arched openings on the north side of the hall, seem to be built upon the carved stone basement of an earlier (dismantled) palace structure. This palace must have had an open courtyard facing north, surrounded on three sides by raised areas defined by basements, the stone mouldings and friezes of which are still intact, though damaged. This typical palace configuration explains the unusual flanking side walls. Two large stones (column footings?) are set within the courtyard to the north.

On three sides the hall is perfectly plain except for the remains of corbelled brackets that once supported an eave, now vanished. These brackets are not found on the outer surfaces of the two projecting walls. The north facade of the hall is plastered with three arched openings set within rectangular frames. The arches are in three planes surrounded by flat bands, probably once decorated. Stone brackets between the arches and at either end consisted of three corbels (now mostly broken). The inward-facing surfaces of the two walls projecting northwards have deeply recessed arched niches covered in plaster (much restored). Each of these arches has five lobes framed by three recessed bands carried down to the floor. At their (north) ends these two walls have partly plastered projections.

Within the hall the piers are identical, with simple roll mouldings from which spring the pointed arches in two planes. Across the corners of the arches are pendentives with angled tops. The treatment of the domes varies. On the central (north-south) aisle the domes have eight ribs between which are enlarged petals converging on a lotus medallion. One example (northeast corner) has eight bands with interlacing strapwork, while two others (on the central east-west aisle) preserve traces of sixteen facets. The side chambers have pointed vaults.

Northwest of the domed hall is a detached wall (VI/16) running east-west. On its north face is a large arched niche identical to those just described in the domed hall. How this wall may have been coordinated with the hall is not clear.

STRUCTURE (VII/3)

Perhaps serving as some sort of small gateway (the two doorways face each other), this small structure is located in the south of VII, apparently unrelated to any other feature. Square in plan, the entrances on the east and west have arched openings in two planes. Above rises a brick vault, the upper portion of which partly preserves its pyramidal shape. Within the structure are pointed arched niches on the north and south. The square vault has a lower portion with a double curve; the upper part is now missing its plaster coating.

MULTIDOMED STRUCTURE (VII/1)
(Figure 7.8)

Apparently functioning as a watchtower (Devakunjari 1970, p. 32), this massive construction overlooks the approaches to the royal centre from the west and north.

The structure is built into and upon the walls forming the northwest corner of VII. Its mortared masonry clearly abuts the larger unmortared blocks of the enclosure walls and may, therefore, be a later addition. The domed chambers raised on the upper level are reached by a staircase at the south end of the east wall. The (vaulted?) chamber at ground level (noted by Subrahmanyam 1974, p. 329) is no longer accessible, though a blocked-up doorway is partly visible at the north end of the east wall.

The upper level consists of 3 by 2 bays. At the southeast corner is an open terrace bounded by a low wall. An arched entrance to the north leads to two square chambers. In the east wall defining these bays are small windows. The northeast chamber has a raised area projected outwards as a balcony, with a brick wall on either side. Three domed chambers at a higher level are positioned to the west. The northwest chamber is square with recessed windows and doorways flanked by small niches in the centre of each wall; on the west these niches become windows. The central chamber on the west is rectangular, with large arched openings on the east and west. The doorways in the north and south walls are flanked by niches partly concealed by (later?) arches. A raised area projects outwards beyond the arched

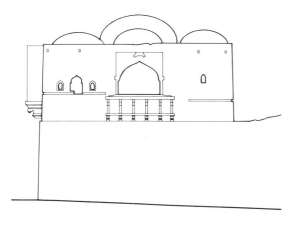

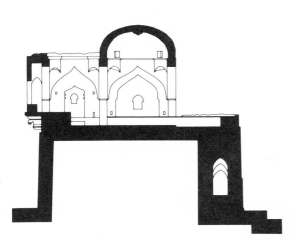

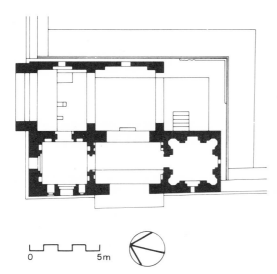

Figure 7.8 Multidomed structure (VII/1), plan, section and elevation.

opening as a balcony on the west. The square southwest chamber has stepped projections flanking the central windows and doorway; in the corners are part-octagonal recesses.

At the lower level the masonry walls are plain except for a horizontal indentation raised up over the staircase entrance to create a shallow rectangular frame. Another horizontal indentation marks the beginning of the upper level. The walls on the north and west noticeably taper as they rise above the enclosure walls. The projecting balcony on the north is supported on six brackets, each consisting of three corbels. The balcony was once filled with plaster-covered brickwork, but this only survives on the projecting sides and beneath the central arch. The projecting balcony on the west employs corbels of a different type, and these begin lower. Here six brackets, each consisting of two carved pendant buds, support a number of crudely fashioned (later?) horizontal and vertical elements. Over the arched opening is a recessed frame and masonry fragment, all that survives of a projecting vaulted bay. The northwest chamber is marked by three pointed arched windows on each side, the central opening being enlarged. Brickwork is seen in the smaller windows on the west. An empty recess, as if to take a horizontal projection, runs around the building on the north and west, and partly on the south. Above the walls the plaster-covered flattish brick domes are clearly visible.

Within the chambers of the upper level, pointed arches spring from plain masonry piers. The dome in the central east bay (fallen in the northeast bay) rises on an octagonal base supported on pendentives with angled tops. The dome in the central west chamber is similar, except that it has a circular base marked by a ring of angled masonry elements. The northwest and southwest chambers have domes rising out of octagons on corner arches. Small openings in the east wall and elsewhere may have been used for defensive purposes. The staircase is vaulted with a series of pointed arches.

RUINED STRUCTURE (VIIIa/1)

This ruined structure is built into the northeast corner of VIII. The raised square floor has rectangular balconies in the middle of the south and west sides. Stone piers of a cruciform plan are located at the corners and intermediate points. (Two piers are missing.) Access is by a flight of steps (mostly restored) at the southeast corner.

The basement walls of the structure are plain except for two horizontal projections. On the south and west sides, four brackets support the floor slabs of the balconies; the brackets are doubly curved and have flowing leaflike designs on their undersides. Preserved for only three or

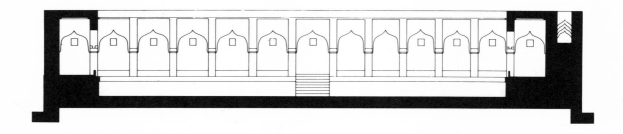

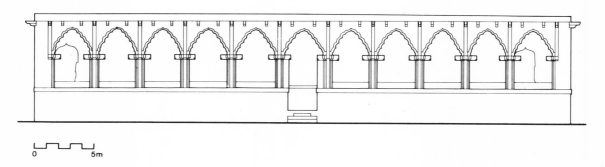

Figure 7.9   Rectangular structure (XXX/2), elevation and section.

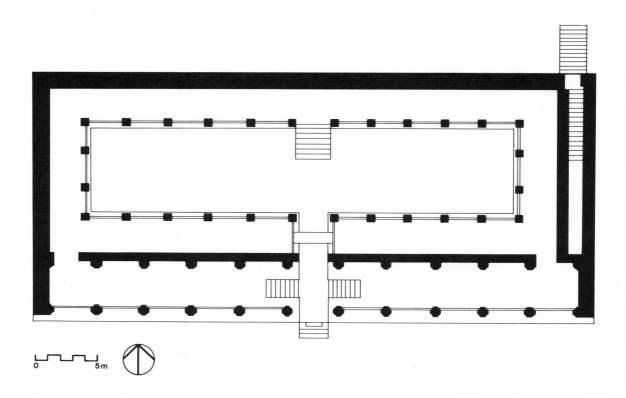

Figure 7.10   Rectangular structure (XXX/2), plan.

four courses, the piers are plain, lacking their original plaster coating. No doubt, these piers would have supported pointed or lobed masonry arches, but these and the vaulted roof have now completely disappeared.

RECTANGULAR STRUCTURE (XXX/2)
(Figures 7.9 and 7.10)

Together with the elephant stables to the east and a ruined structure to the west, this building defines a rectangular open area possibly used for military displays. It is, therefore, likely that this monument had some martial purpose. Today it is usually identified as the "guards' quarters" (Longhurst 1917, p. 86; Devakunjari 1970, p. 39), though it has also been refered to as a "concert hall" and even a "treasury" (Havell 1927, p. 190).

This rectangular building contains within its interior an open courtyard surrounded on four sides by a raised colonnade. This colonnade is discontinuous in the middle of the south side where a walkway at courtward level leads to the principal entrance. An additional colonnaded verandah is found to the south, facing onto the open area. Breaks in the wall at either end of the verandah link the two colonnades. A long staircase built into the thickness of the east wall ascends to the roof.

Except for the arched entrance to the staircase at the east end of the north wall, a slight indentation indicating the floor level of the interior, and some small square holes, the walls on three sides are plain. The south facade consists of a colonnade raised up on a high wall with a plain projection at floor level; the latter is broken by a walkway reached by a flight of steps. The stone piers supporting the arches have brackets with simple roll mouldings; these once supported stone frames (according to the nineteenth-century photographs). Above rise the nino-lobed pointed arches in two planes, fasioned of angled stones set in mortar; the plaster covering has now disappeared. Each arch is set within a recessed frame. On three sides of the building, pairs of projecting corbels with rounded ends indicate the presence of an eave, now vanished.

Within the interior courtyard the colonnade consists of plain columns with roll mouldings supporting pointed arches. Transverse arches spring from brackes in the wall. The recesses in the arches may have once housed (timber?) frames. The ceilings are horizontal and lack their original plaster covering. In the south colonnade the arched recesses against the walls and transverse arches are pointed in two planes. The ceiling here is higher and is provided with ribs dividing each bay into nine squares. Stepped arched vaults roof the staircase.

ELEPHANT STABLES (XXX/1)
(Figure 7.11)

Certainly the most monumental of all the Islamic-styled structures at the capital, this colossal building is generally acknowledged as the royal stables, despite the occasional effort to recognise in these chambers the remains of a vast mosque (Havell 1927, pp. 190-191).

Open to the west (not to the east as a mosque in India requires) onto the rectangular space of XXX, eleven square chambers are arranged in a north-south row more than 85m. long. The plan of each chamber is identical, with recessed niches on three sides and an arched entrance on the west. Small communicating doorways are found between four of the chambers, while eight chambers have doorways in the east wall. In the thick walls either side of the central chamber, two corridors lead to staircases that ascend to an upper chamber.

Except for several small arched entrances on the east, the building is plain on three sides. The front (west) facade has eleven enlarged arched entrances leading to the chambers. These arches are created in two planes, and are framed within a rectangular recess. Fragments of plaster decoration are seen in the bands around the arches and in the roundels over the arches and in the spandrels. Above the frame are two corbels with roll mouldings. Either side of each arched entrance is a smaller arched niche in a rectangular frame; above this are three similar niches, the central one having three or five lobes, and three miniature recesses with angled tops. Four brackets with curved corbels separate these recesses. This line of double corbels continues around four sides of the building. The deep recess above the brackets indicates the position of the angled eave, now completely vanished. The parapet is a modern reconstruction.

Rising above all but the central chamber are domes of varying designs, symmetrically arranged: hemispherical with rows of merlons on the circular drums (end domes on each side), hemispherical with convex flutings that diminish as they ascend (central domes on each side), and twelve-sided vaults rising in three tiers with curved profiles (intermediate domes). The hemispherical domes culminate in projecting circular capping pieces while the twelve-sided domes have tripartite fluted capping pieces. In general, much of the original plaster detail has been lost in the restoration.

Within the building the lower parts of the chambers are identical, with recessed pointed arches on three sides and enlarged corner arches creating an octangonal drum. The varied vaults and domes are symmetrically organised. From the

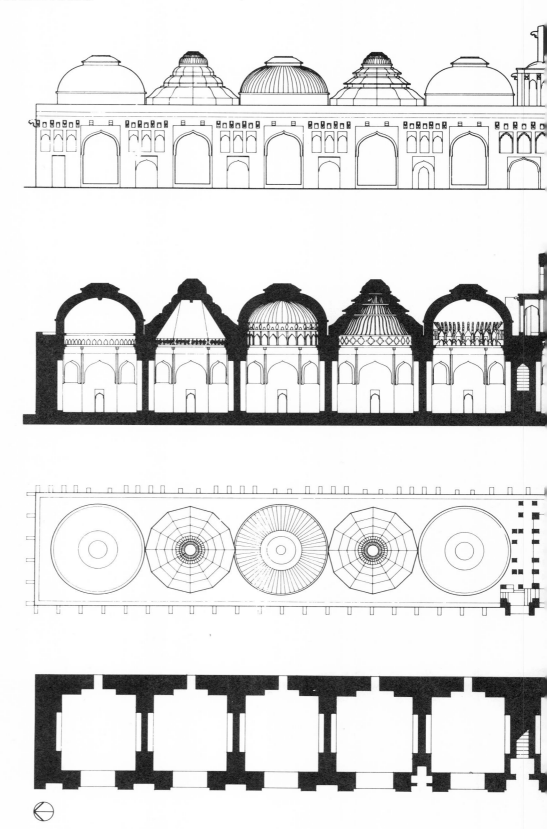

Figure 7.11   Elephant stables (XXX/1), ground and roof plans, section and elevation.

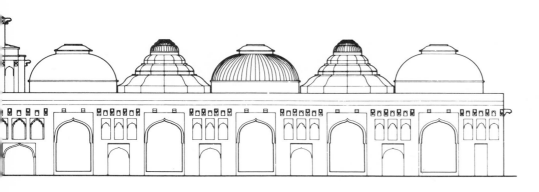

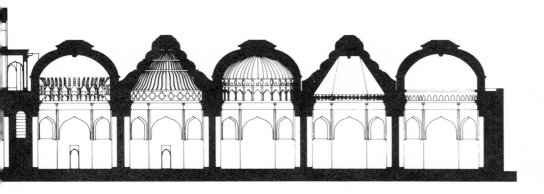

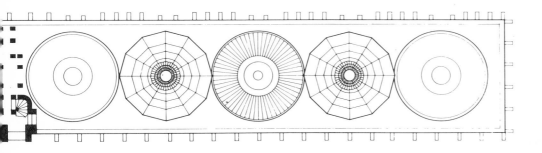

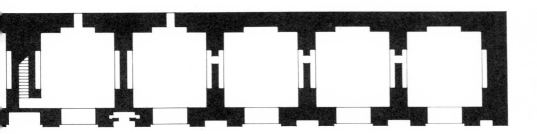

end chambers towards the middle these consist of: plain domes with rows of alternating large and small merlons; pyramidal vaults with friezes of palmettes and medallions; domes with convex or concave flutings above a frieze of small pointed arches and merlons; vaults consisting of three sets of converging ribs meeting at a central medallion; and, domes rising out of an almost free-standing frieze of lobed arches on projecting brackets supporting templelike roof forms in brick and plaster. The ceiling of the central chamber is flat with brackets and angled niches. Throughout, the plaster decoration is elaborate, but is now only partly preserved. Still, looped stalks and flowers, arabesques of strapwork, palmettes and medallions can be seen. Few of the central lotus medallions, however, are intact. The circular staircase and approach corridors are roofed by arched vaults.

In the middle of the roof is a ruined two-storeyed structure, open on all sides at the lower storey. In plan the structure consists of a central square chamber, slightly raised above the roof. Piers create a surrounding narrow passageway on four sides, extending outwards in triple bays in the middle of each side. This passageway is roofed with horizontal slabs and a similar roof probably once covered the central chamber; now, only the corbelled brackets are seen. The upper storey is enclosed by four walls with windows in the middle of each side. Above are brackets that once supported a ceiling, now vanished. The exterior of this two-storeyed structure is poorly preserved. Alternating five-lobed and pointed arched openings with traces of plaster decoration are found at the lower storey. The corbels above once supported an overhanging eave and there was also a parapet of miniature templelike roof elements. (Both eave and parapet are partly visible in the nineteenth-century photographs.) The upper storey has projections in the middle of each side with pointed arched windows. Corbels once supported another overhanging eave, and there was probably also a second smaller parapet of miniature roof forms. Unfortunately, nothing of the (square-to-dome?) capping roof has survived.

TWO-STOREYED PAVILION ("LOTUS MAHAL") (XIV/1)
(Figures 7.12, 7.13 and 7.14)

This celebrated monument in the middle of XIV is now popularly known as the "Lotus Mahal," though it has been previously labelled "sleeping apartments of the king" (Mackenzie 1800) and "council room" (Madras Survey 1880).

The two-storeyed structure is symmetrically laid out in a series of projecting squares to create thirteen bays with an additional bay (fourteenth) for the staircase tower at the northeast corner.

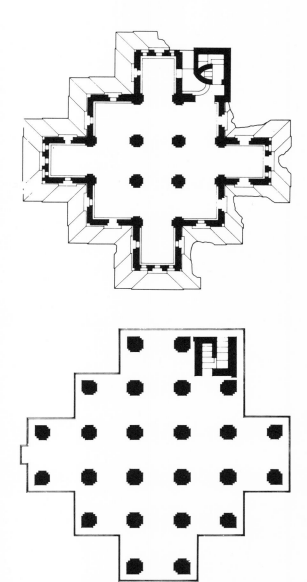

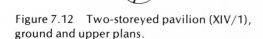

Figure 7.12   Two-storeyed pavilion (XIV/1), ground and upper plans.

136

(The continuity of plinth mouldings indicates that this staircase is part of the original conception; however, the present tower containing the staircase is clearly a later addition or replacement.) At the lower level the pavilion is open, each bay defined by piers with projections. The staircase tower is an enclosed square with steps leading from the ground to the lower level of the pavilion which it enters through a doorway. Thereafter, the steps ascend to the upper level which is laid out in the same manner as that below, except that the space is completely enclosed by walls with openings. A narrow low shelf lines the inside of the walls; outside is the projecting eave. Four free-standing piers are in the middle of the chamber, with eight engaged piers at the various corners. The junction between the staircase tower and the upper level of the building is crudely achieved through an arched entrance, and there is a curious raised (seating?) niche at the uppermost landing.

The pavilion stands on a stone plinth, the top and bottom mouldings of which are identical but inverted, with a central part-octagonal element. At the furthest projections on three sides decorative motifs are found — ribbed potlike mouldings and bands of foliation and geometric ornament. In the middle of the west side there is an additional basement projection supported on a pointed arch flanked by miniature pilasters. The walls above taper slightly, and at the lower level are pierced by open arches. The supporting piers bulge slightly at the springing points of the arches where horizontal plaster mouldings are located. Stone brackets also appear here, projecting in three or four directions. (These brackets once supported stone frames according to the nineteenth-century photographs.) The arches have five lobes in three planes, the central lobe being enlarged and flattened. All the lobes are thickly encrusted with plasterwork (not always preserved) in which a variety of foliate motifs is found, including meandering and looped stalks, tufts of foliage, and even parrots and geese. Yali heads appear at the apexes of the arches. Medallions with foliate and geometric designs are positioned above at either side, with enlarged medallions above the apexes. Three or four brackets with plaster decoration support a beam decorated on its underside, and an overhanging double-curved eave. This eave has slight extensions on each side to produce a more complex outline. Beneath the corner brackets, plaster yalis and riders were positioned; fragments of these can still be observed (east side).

Above the eave are the walls of the upper storey with a series of mouldings at the base, and also at an intermediate point coinciding with the springing of the arched windows. These mouldings continue across the openings dividing them into upper arched windows and lower rectangular windows. The multilobed arches of the upper windows are created in three planes with thick plaster decoration, including flamelike tufts of foliation. The windows are flanked by plain pilasters; on the furthermost projecting walls on the north, west, and south, the windows are tripled. The arches over the central windows on these walls, and also over the single windows on the intermediate walls, are extended outwards. Brackets with simple roll mouldings carry a horizontal beam and a double-curved eave, projecting slightly over the windows.

The superstructure of the pavilion actually consists of nine separate towers. Those over the extended bays on the cardinal directions have three diminishing and ascending tiers on a rectangular plan with slight extensions in the middle of each side. Each tier has a curved eavelike moulding with quarter medallions at the corners (not always preserved); the capping roof form is rectangular-to-dome. The square tower over the central bay is raised high above the others, and repeats the basic scheme of those on the cardinal directions. The lower walls of this central tower have a marked projection on each side with a multilobed arched window in three planes. Curved brackets support the lowest of the tiered eavelike mouldings. The capping roof form is square-to-dome with a central projection; the surmounting square pinnacle is only partly preserved. The corner towers are different in design and lower. Part-octagonal in plan, these have a simple eavelike moulding on a vertical course; above is a circular capping piece with ribbed convex fluting and a lower rim with medallions. The circular finials are incomplete.

Contrasting with this complex facade are the blank and slightly tapering walls of the staircase tower, broken only by the arched entrance and small windows. A parapet of merlons is partly preserved above. The staircase walls crudely abut the projecting eaves above the lower storey of the pavilion. At the upper level there is a change of construction with the use of brick.

The principal interest of the interior of the lower storey is provided by the piers and arches which repeat the basic scheme of those on the exterior, but without any decoration. Between the arches in the peripheral eight bays pendentives with multilobed arched tops reduce the square to an octagon; above rise low domes (mostly restored). The central bay has a flat ceiling divided into nine smaller squares while the remaining bays are roofed with square pyramidal vaults. The piers and arches of the upper storey are also of the same basic design, though here the roll moulding on the piers is continued around the walls and projected on either side of the openings. The windows are multilobed, and are flanked by

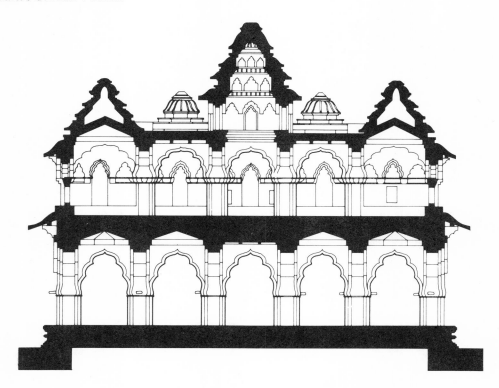

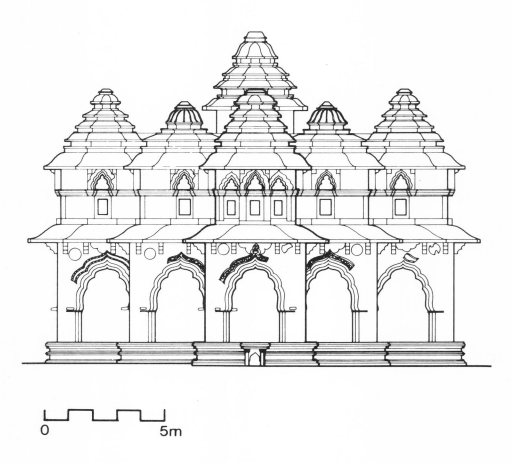

Figure 7.13   Two-storeyed pavilion (XIV/1), section and elevation.

0   5m

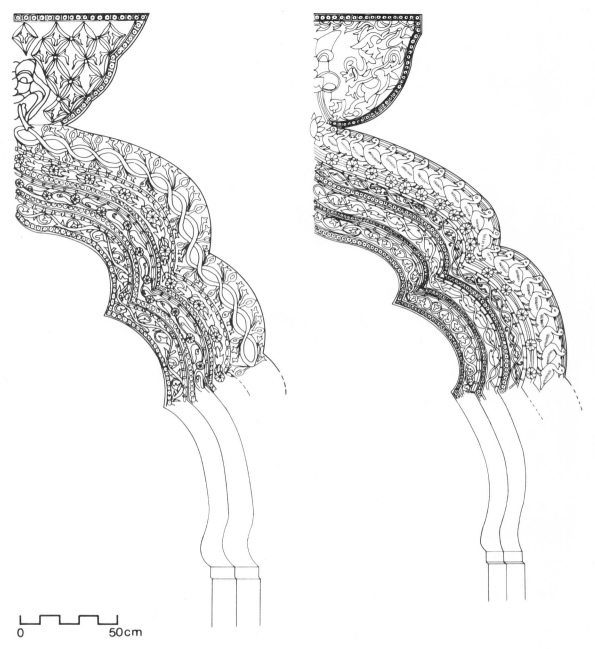

Figure 7.14   Two-storeyed pavilion (XIV/1), plaster decoration on arches.

similarly shaped niches, pierced as openings on the north, west, and south. The vaulting scheme is varied: the furthermost projecting bays on the cardinal points have square pyramidal vaults; the corner bays employ pendentives with multilobed tops to support shallow octagonal vaults; and the intermediate bays have flat ceilings divided into nine squares. The central bay is roofed by a square tapering tower. Within this tower are three tiers of multilobed niches, tripled on each side

with a window in the centre of the lower storey. Miniature foliated brackets and projecting corbels with pendant buds separate these tiers. Plaster fragments of seated figures, too damaged to be identified, are found in the upper niches. The domelike vault within the tower has sixteen ribs converging on a central lotus medallion. The staircase is roofed with a series of pointed vaults with a miniature pyramidal vault over the uppermost landing.

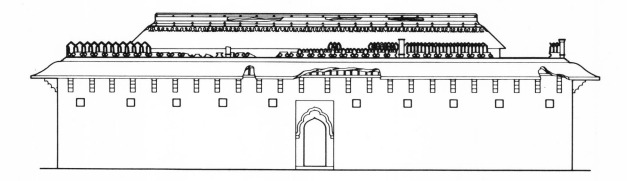

Figure 7.15   Rectangular structure (XIV/4), elevation.

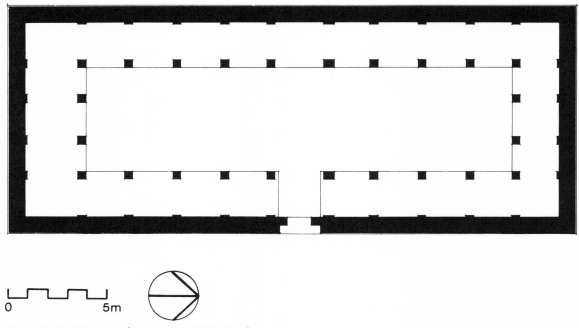

0   5m

Figure 7.16   Rectangular structure (XIV/4), plan.

RECTANGULAR STRUCTURE (XIV/4)
(Figures 7.15 and 7.16)

This well preserved building in the northwest corner of XIV is variously identified as a "hall of exercise" (Mackenzie 1800) or "guards' quarters" (Devakunjari 1970, p. 34). Its complete masonry construction and lack of openings, other than a small doorway and a series of ventilation holes, however, suggest some sort of storeroom or treasury.

Rectangular in layout, the building is entered through a small doorway in the middle of the long east side. Within, a raised colonnade surrounds a rectangular area at ground level. The colonnade consists of 24 columns. The bays in the middle of the long sides and at the ends are larger; those at the corners are smaller. A small brick infill wall is preserved at the northwest corner.

On the outside the plain walls of the building taper inwards slightly. A multilobed arch in two planes is positioned over the pointed arched doorway set within a rectangular recess. Running around the building is a row of small square openings. Above, plaster-covered curved corbels support a horizontal beam, a number of angled rafterlike elements decorated on their undersides with plaster snake hoods, and a double-curved eave. The pierced brick and plaster parapet is best preserved on the east and consists of interlocking pointed arches on stepped bases and diagonal lotuses. The scheme changes slightly in the central section of the parapet which is demarcated by two short pilasters. Here the pointed arches become a complex pattern of interlacing. The masonry roof is gabled at the short ends, and is raised on a vertical course with small openings partly concealed beneath the overhanging roof. Beneath the ridge a frieze of enlarged petals is incised into the plaster coating. The vertical projection rising upon the long ridge is provided with a series of mouldings.

The principal interest of the interior is seen in the arches of the colonnade and the unusual vaulting system. The colonnade consists of alternative multilobed arches and pointed arches in shallow frames. Secondary pointed arches link the colonnade to the exterior walls. Four bays on the long side employ pointed pendentives with angled tops to create an octagonal drum from which rise shallow domes; all other bays, on square or rectangular plans, have pyramidal vaults. The central vault is raised high on eight arches springing from roll mouldings; the arches have nine lobes, the central lobe being enlarged and flattened. At the north and south ends the vault is angled, three triangular planes meeting at a single point.

SQUARE TOWER (XIV/5)
(Figures 7.17 and 7.18)

Positioned in one of the north angles of the enclosure wall of XIV, this square tower dominates the area, overlooking the approaches to the royal centre from the north and west. The junction of the enclosure walls with the north and east sides of the tower demonstrate that the walls are later constructions.

The tower has a hollow square shaft at its centre around which a staircase proceeds upwards. Large windows at the lower level, and small windows higher up, look outwards; an occasional window even faces inwards into the shaft. At the upper level a square chamber has arches in the middle of each side leading to raised areas projecting outwards as balconies. Each balcony has three arched openings at the front and an arched opening at either side. (The balconies on the east and west are no longer completely preserved.) In each of the four corners

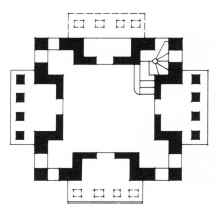

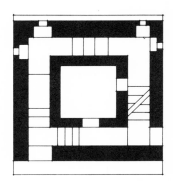

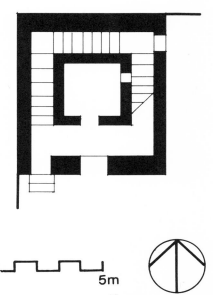

Figure 7.17 Square tower (XIV/5), ground and upper plans.

of the central chamber is a small recess with two arched openings.

The plain tapering shaft of the tower is broken only by the multilobed arched entrance on the west (now partly buried) and the ascending arched windows and small square openings. (At the northwest corner, part of a vertical earthenware pipe is preserved, embedded into the brickwork.) At the level of the upper chamber the wall projects outward slightly. The balconies, as preserved on the north and south sides, are supported on four multicurved brackets and elaborately decorated with foliate ornamentation. Just beneath the arched tops of the openings are stone brackets. Each opening has plaster bands over the arches with ornamental finials at the apexes; roundels appear above at either side. The tower is sheltered by an angled eave supported on a beam and multicurved brackets, not all of which are in position. Above are the fragments of a ruined brick superstructure.

Except for the arched windows and ascending pointed vaults, the square shaft and staircase are perfectly plain. Small pyramidal vaults, however, are located above the lower landings. The upper chamber is missing its (octagonal?) vault, the only interest being the pointed arched windows. Pyramidal vaults are found within the balconies, while similar vaults on irregular hexagons appear above the corner recesses.

RUINED TOWER (XIV/6)

Continuous with the enclosure walls, this square tower is positioned in the extreme northeast corner of XIV. It is only preserved in its lowest two storeys, the upper portions having fallen. At ground level three out of four bays are open, the northeast bay being reserved for the staircase. On the first upper level the staircase shifts to the centre of the tower, with a small corridor at the rear and two bays on both the south and west. The same scheme seems to be repeated at the second upper level, now ruined.

On the exterior, the ground level presents two openings with pointed arches in two planes on both the south and west. At the corners the arches spring directly from the enclosure walls. The brackets with roll mouldings have now lost their overhanging eave. The first upper storey repeats the pointed arches beneath, but here the bays are mostly filled in, except for small pointed arched openings. The intermediate vertical pilasters in plaster-covered brickwork are only partly preserved, while the overhanging eave has completely disappeared. An octagonal dome is found above the southwest bay at ground level, while simpler vaults are utilized over the other bays. The staircase is roofed with stepped pointed arches.

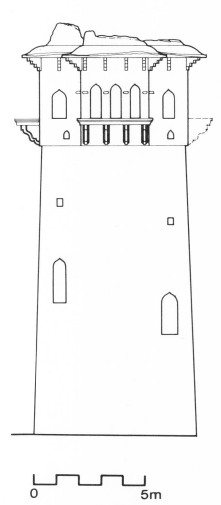

Figure 7.18   Square tower (XIV/5), elevation.

OCTAGONAL TOWER (XIV/7)
(Figures 7.19 and 7.20)

Positioned in the southeast corner of XIV, this tower overlooks the approaches to the royal centre from the east and south. Clearly, the tower is earlier than the enclosure walls which wrap around its base, blocking several openings.

At ground level the entrance to the tower is on the northeast, where the original square platform (with plastered sides) is now concealed within a later and larger extension to the north and west. At the first and second upper levels, the circular staircase is surrounded by an octagonal corridor divided by transverse arches into eight bays. Each bay is lit by a small window; those on the south and east being partly blocked by the enclosure walls. At the third and uppermost level the staircase is contained within four columns. The surrounding sixteen-sided space has eight raised areas (seats?). Full-height arched windows and smaller projecting windows alternate on the exterior.

Octagonal throughout, the exterior of the tower at the ground level is plain except for the arched doorway leading to the staircase. Five small projections provide the transition to the first upper level, which has slightly tapering walls and small square openings. The second upper level rises above a flat band, and displays on each side pointed arches in two planes. These arches are partly filled in with brickwork. On the southwest, three smaller arched openings are created in the brickwork. The uppermost level has eight pointed arched openings positioned across the corners. In the middle of each side are arched windows in two planes, projected slightly outwards as small balconies and supported on curved brackets. A double-curved eave runs continuously around the building and is also extended outwards over the balconies. Above are eight separate parapet elements, each consisting of a small rectangular brick construction with an eavelike moulding and a capping templelike roof form. The roof of the tower itself is octagonal and has three diminishing and ascending tiers of angled eavelike mouldings. The capping roof form is hemispherical with convex flutings; little of the surmounting pinnacle is preserved.

Within the tower, pointed arches are utilized throughout, and above the staircase the vaults are stepped and pointed. At the third upper level the pointed vault runs around a complete circle. The square columns at this level have octagonal central sections. Over the staircase the dome is plain and curiously recessed behind the circular drum (restored?). No original plasterwork is preserved.

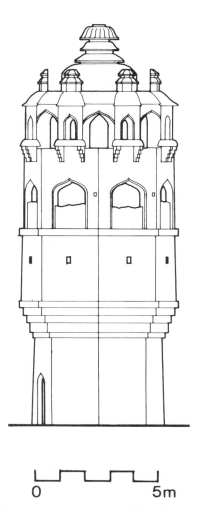

0   5m

Figure 7.19   Octagonal tower (XIV/7), elevation.

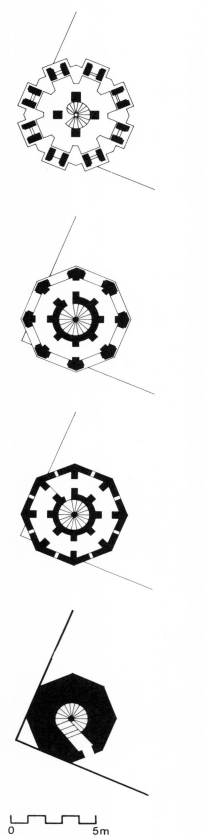

Figure 7.20 Octagonal tower (XIV/7), ground and upper plans.

RUINED STRUCTURE (XXIX/4)

Located directly to the north of one of the openings in the northern enclosure wall of XIV is a small ruined structure. This seems to have consisted of a square chamber with doorways on the north and south, flanked by small rectangular chambers. Only the east side chamber and a portion of the central chamber are standing. The central chamber is roofed with a flat dome on corner pendentives; the side chamber has a flat ceiling. The arches are pointed and rise from a simple angled projection. A small arched window is seen on the north, above which is a portion of a short plaster parapet. Lying everywhere around are fragments of stone rubble embedded in thick mortar.

OCTAGONAL BATH
(Figure 7.21)

Located some distance to the east of the enclosures of the royal centre is this octagonal structure. Here an open colonnade, consisting of two rows of 24 columns, surrounds an open octagonal water basin. In the middle of the basin is a raised octagonal platform. The sides of both the basin and the central platform are finished in finely cut stone mouldings.

Little of the exterior decoration is present, but within the colonnade are fragments of plaster friezes of petals. A stone channel with small circular openings in each corner fed water into the basin (there is no evidence of how the water was conducted into the channel). Both the floor of the basin and top of the central platform are covered with plaster.

Built up against one of the columns of the outer colonnade to the west is a ruined rectangular structure, crudely reconstructed. This is open to the north and was apparently divided into three bays, now missing their vaulted roofs. The exterior of the building appears to have been plain; nothing of the original interior is preserved.

OTHER ISLAMIC-STYLED MONUMENTS

It has already been observed that almost all the Islamic-styled buildings at Vijayanagara are located in and around the royal centre. There are, however, several exceptions. The tombs in the various Muslim quarters of the capital have already been noted. Fortified gateways with domes or Islamic-styled facades are found southeast of the royal centre, on the road leading northeast towards the river crossing to Anegondi, and in at least one partly collapsed example to the east. The ruined arched gateway flanked by niches within the royal centre (Ic-XVb) has been described elsewhere (see Chapter 4).

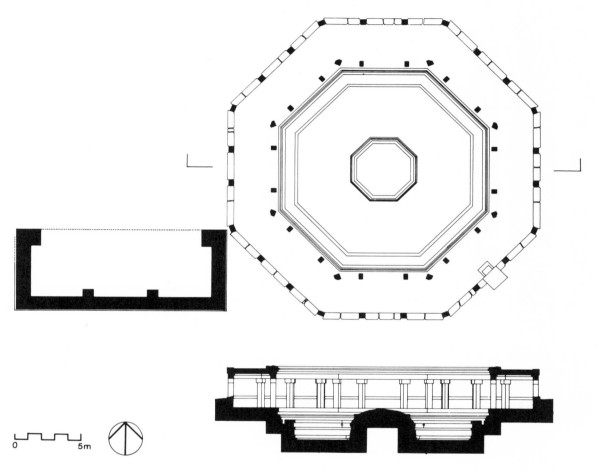

Figure 7.21 Octagonal bath, plan and section.

In the irrigated valley north of the royal centre, a fairly well preserved U-shaped pavilion is found, almost concealed in the fields of sugar cane. This open structure has pointed arches in several planes, a variety of domes, and finely executed plasterwork. Possibly this was some sort of garden palace. More unusual, though, is the six-domed structure within one of the courtyards of the Krishna Temple complex. This probably functioned as a storehouse, maybe even a granary, according to the external staircase leading up to the roof where holes are discovered in the domes; as well, there is an overall lack of large openings in the walls. Beyond the urban core, beside the road leading to Hospet near the village of Malpannagudi, is an Islamic-styled well. Reached by a long flight of steps leading down to the water, this well is surrounded by an octagonal corridor with arched openings. Apparently, this well is mentioned in an inscription dated to 1412 lying in front of the nearby Mallikarjuna Temple (*South Indian Inscriptions* IX/II, no. 436).

8. THEMES OF INTERPRETATION

The Meeting of King and God

In our introduction (Chapter 1) we suggested that the central theme of our investigation was the relation of king and god at Vijayanagara. We recognize that this theme is complex and multi-faceted. On the one hand, there are questions of relevant historical and archaeological "fact" — the activities of the king, concepts of godliness, the forms and functions of the different urban elements, etc. On the other hand, there are questions of interpretation — in what ways did kings embody divinity? how was royal power based on a perceived relation of king and god? how was this relation embodied in different symbolic media?

Having completed our description of the archaeological and architectural features of the royal centre, we now attempt to link these "facts" to some preliminary interpretations concerning the relation of king and god at the capital. At this stage in our research, however, we do not claim any finality for our conclusions. Rather, we are exploring a number of questions in the hope that these will contribute to an overall understanding of our theme.

We first suggest a framework in which urban form may be seen to communicate basic meanings of social life. Then we briefly examine the character of medieval Hindu kingship, concentrating on the relation of royal power to divine order. The sacred associations of the site is the next topic to be considered; here we stress the mythical geography of the environs of the capital. We then discuss several spatial definitions for the city with the royal centre as the nucleus. Here we stress the "structuring" functions of axial and circumambulatory routes of movement, and postulate the locations of the various activities of the court and army. Thus we establish the domain of the king within the city. Next we discuss the temples of Virupaksha and Ramachandra, two deities who were of paramount importance for the Vijayanagara rulers. In conclusion, we propose the symbolic systems embodied in the layout of the royal centre that convey the meeting of king and god.

MEDIEVAL HINDU KINGSHIP

As the capital of one of the most powerful dynasties of Hindu rulers, Vijayanagara was much more than a mere "setting" for courtly life. We believe that the layout of the city, together with its monumental architecture and sculpture, affirm a particular "argument" for royal power. Since Vijayanagara was, above all, an imperial capital — defined in many of its significant aspects by the activities of the king and those in his service — its spatial organization may be considered to be directly related to concepts of kingship as evolved in medieval Hindu society. In this respect, we agree with various "architectural anthropologists" who have elicited social meaning from urban form (see, for example, Gutschow 1977; Pieper 1980, etc.).

Recent historians of south India have discussed medieval kingship from two perspectives. One point of view — exemplified by the later work of Nilakanta Sastri (1964) — emphasizes the "feudal" character of state institutions. While in earlier periods, kings had feudal relationships with brahminical communities, during the Vijayanagara era, military governors (nayakas) appointed by the king became the chief feudatories. Rulers had well defined administrative roles, and an attendant bureaucracy of ministers, officers and priests.

A quite different perspective derives from the work of Hocart (1970). Here is stressed the essentially ritual and ceremonial roles of kings, as distinguished from those of brahmins. Stein (1980) — the most prominent exponent of this view — argues that there is no evidence for an administrative apparatus in medieval states. While kings exercized little direct control over the affairs of the empire, except in the region immediately surrounding the capital, they were able to unify disparate elements through their sacral and incorporative roles. Together with their ministers, generals, and governors, rulers participated in highly charged political "dramas" in which a complex hierarchy of status was affirmed or disputed.

Here we have chosen to interpret particular royal activities as symbolic expressions which constituted regal power. As for the possible administrative role of the Vijayanagara kings, we consider this still to be an open question.

ROYAL POWER AND DIVINE ORDER

Studies of Vijayanagara history (Krishnaswami Aiyangar 1919; Saletore, B.A. 1934; Nilakanta

Sastri and Venkataramanayya 1946; Mahalingam 1975; etc.) have compiled vast amounts of epigraphical and literary sources on the activities of kings. We make no attempt to survey the various roles of the Vijayanagara rulers; rather, we are concerned to outline the relationship of the rulers to divine order.

The Vijayanagara kings appear to have been influenced by texts (shastras) that provided clearly articulated models for royal behaviour that would result in the maintenance of moral values (dharma), and the increase of power and influence (artha). In their inscriptions and literary works, these rulers express themselves in a rhetoric of cosmo-moral conceptions familiar in shastric literature. They evidently saw themselves as upholders of traditional law, and agents of moral well-being and material prosperity (Mahalingam 1955). In these theoretical texts — dharmashastras and arthashastras — the roles of rulers are related to fundamental systems of order that regulate the activities of kings and gods. Embodied in such systems are cycles of good and evil which encompass both the human and divine spheres.

According to Inden (1978), this cyclical rhythm is reflected in the annual pattern of the ruler's life. At Vijayanagara, periods of rest alternated with periods of movement. For part of each year, the king, court, and army resided at the capital; the other part of the year was set aside for pilgrimage and war. Accompanied by his courtly and martial retinues, the king would leave the capital and travel around the empire (and even beyond) on peaceful missions, or on aggressive campaigns of conquest and plunder.

For the Vijayanagara kings, the moment of transition from "passive" to "active" periods was marked by a great festival — the mahanavami. As the annual climax in the life of the capital, the mahanavami affirmed the central role of the king in the state and empire. Religious in atmosphere, this festival was undeniably political in significance (Saletore, B.A. 1934, II, p.372) since it commemorated the day on which Rama propitiated Durga before marching against Ravana. As such, this occasion was a celebration of anticipated victory, the principal theme being the infusion of the royal throne and weapons with cosmic energy (Appadurai-Breckenridge 1978).

Stein (1980 and 1983) stresses the sacral and incorporative character of this event. He argues that the rites of the mahanavami constituted the "centralized and hierarchic" phase of the state during which all the components were incorporated into the king's realm and, even more importantly, into the partnership of ruler and deity. From what we learn about the mahanavami from the foreign travellers — who were encouraged by the king to visit the capital to witness this event — the king appeared at this festival in his multiple roles as ritual celebrant, warrior, giver and receiver of honours, and host of lavish entertainment. The chronicles of these visitors provide vivid descriptions of the spectacular rituals, ceremonies, processions, contests, and feasts of the mahanavami.

The display of military strength was an obvious expression of royal force and might (danda). At the capital there were many reasons — invasion, usurpation, assassination, etc. — for keeping a formidable concentration of infantry, cavalry, elephants, artillery, and a special palace guard. The structures related to this military force — fortifications, defensive gateways, stables, guards' quarters, stores, treasuries, etc. — were also indicators of royal might. (Significantly, the city was never taken by siege.) In their inscriptions, too, the kings styled themselves as "angry punishers of rival kings ... fierce in war ... victorious at the head of battle" .. etc. (*Epigraphia Indica I*, no.42).

The king's household was another important symbol of his power since it was a microcosm of the kingdom. The royal queens represented important dynastic alliances, both within and outside the empire. The presence of these queens and their retinues at the capital signified the incorporation of regional, linguistic, and even religious differences. The size and wealth of the household — shown publicly at the mahanavami festival — expressed the well-being of the kingdom.

There were also daily displays of royal power. All the sources of information about the daily routine of the Vijayanagara court insist upon the great splendour and pomp which accompanied the king. Elaborate rituals of reception were evidently the rule, and here insignias and other signs of regal status were visible. On these occasions, the king acted as host, and often bestowed favours and gifts. At the capital the king enjoyed various entertainments and sports; hunting expeditions, incorporating elements of the army, conveyed the prowess of the ruler.

Certainly the most enduring testimony of the power of the Vijayanagara rulers are their ambitious building projects. Large-scale structures, both sacred and secular, were often directly commissioned by the king, and these were erected at the capital and at other important centres. City building was also a royal activity, and kings certainly constructed forts and citadels. While we do not know to what extent the king participated in the planning of the capital, the strength and wealth of Vijayanagara were easily identified with that of the king.

Since the effective worship of temple divinities assured the king of prosperity, health, and success in all his endeavours, peaceful or otherwise, kings were usually devout worshippers. Empowered by divinities, kings promoted particular cults by providing for regular worship and festivals, and by renovating and rebuilding sanctuaries. (Numerous temple inscriptions record the substantial royal investment in brahminical cults.) The early kings were orthodox Shaivas, with Virupaksha as their tutelary deity. However, during the two hundred years and more of their rule at Vijayanagara, there was a shift of cult preference; the later kings became staunch Vaishnavas, particularly worshipping Venkateshvara (= Tiruvengalanatha) at Tirumala. Though the kings patronized other sects, and even supported non-Hindu groups within the empire, they never relinquished their connection with Virupaksha who was their protective divinity.

SACRED SETTING OF THE CAPITAL

The sacred associations of the landscape in which the capital is set partly explain the dependence of the Vijayanagara kings on Virupaksha. In the *Ramayana,* Pampa is the ancient name of the Tungabhadra River. According to the *Pampamahatmya* — a Sanskrit mythological text — Pampa is also the name of an indigenous goddess who seduced Virupaksha (who is locally known as Pampapati, the lord of Pampa). The identification of the river and the settlement on the south bank with the presence of the goddess is indicated by an equivalence of names (Pampa = Hampi). The site of the bethrothal and marriage of Pampa and Shiva is marked by the Virupaksha Temple. Elsewhere (Chapter 5), we noted that this sanctuary, as well as several others nearby, date back to a period well before the Vijayanagara era. Thus the capital incorporates an earlier tirtha, or place of local sacrality. Not only was the site sacred before the foundation of the empire, even today, more than four hundred years after the abandonment of the city, it is still a holy place.

But the Tungabhadra River and its rocky environs are also connected with the events of the *Ramayana.* Local legend identifies the site with the mythical Kishkindha, the realm of the monkey chiefs, Vali and Sugriva. Here, Rama encountered Sugriva and Hanuman; here, too, Sugriva was crowned by Rama. Several natural features of the landscape are linked with particular episodes in the *Ramayana* (Longhurst 1917, pp. 7, 9). For example, Matanga hill is where the sage Matanga lived who gave protection to Sugriva and Hanuman; Rama waited on Malyavanta hill while Hanuman searched for Sita, his abducted wife. Reinforcing such mythic associations of the site are several temples and shrines endowed with a specific *Ramayana* iconography. We have already noted the Ramachandra Temple (Chapter 5); the Raghunatha Temple complex on Malyavanta hill, for instance, has within its principal sanctuary a

natural boulder carved with seated Rama and Sita, standing Lakshmana, and kneeling Hanuman. Other similar sculptures are found on boulders near to the river. Most numerous by far are images of Hanuman sculptured on both loose slabs and natural rocks. In addition, one epigraph designates part of the site as the "bastion of Hanuman" (Nagaraja Rao 1983, p.39).

SPATIAL DEFINITIONS OF THE CITY

Before we take a closer look at the characteristics of Vijayanagara's morphology, especially the principles by which individual elements within the different zones are "structured", we must first determine what the urban limits were conceived to be. From the perspective of one period, it is the royal centre within its ring of fortifications that constitutes the city of Vijayanagara. This interpretation is supported by a recently discovered fourteenth-century inscription which identifies the gate on the northeast road as the main entrance to Vijayanagara (Nagaraja Rao 1984). (At this time, the walls of the urban core may not have been built). From the perspective of another period, the urban core (containing the royal centre) within a complete circuit of massive fortifications was viewed as the furthest extent of the city; all the zones beyond being "extra mural." The chronicle of the early sixteenth-century visitor, Domingo Paes, supports this definition; he describes only the urban core as "Bisnaga" (Vijayanagara); "Crisnapor" (the area around the Krishna Temple complex) to the northwest, for example, he considers another city (Sewell 1900, p.290). From yet a third point of view, the capital may be considered to embrace the whole site, of which the urban core represents the most important zone for the ruler. Accordingly, all the urban elements — sacred centre, urban core, sub-urban centres — comprise "metropolitan" Vijayanagara.

Though the royal centre is undeniably the nucleus of each of these three definitions for Vijayanagara, there are some significant differences. In the first two schemes (covering smaller areas), we have a galactic system with Vijayanagara as the focal element; other "centres" (sacred and otherwise) are spread over a considerable distance. All elements in this galactic network are interconnected by a radial road system converging on the royal centre. In our third scheme (covering a larger area), we distinguish a sequence of zones, with the royal centre in the middle. Here, too, the urban elements are linked by convergent routes of movement. (Though there is no evidence that this third system was an indigenous concept, it has proved useful for our documentation and description of the site).

SACRED CENTRE AND ROYAL CENTRE

Perhaps the most outstanding single characteristic of Vijayanagara's layout is the contrast between sacred centre and royal centre. The distinction between these two zones is emphasized by the intervening irrigated valley, as well as by the many differences in planning and architecture. By labelling these two parts of the capital as "sacred" and "royal" we do not intend to suggest a simple sacred/profane duality, in which residential zones exclusively for gods and priests are opposed to those for king and court. On the contrary, kings played a significant role in the temple rituals and festivals of the sacred centre; the royal centre incorporated numerous temples and shrines, and priests were important advisors to the king.

As we have observed, the sacred centre is provided with several large-scale, geometrically organized temples, long straight streets with colonnades, tanks, irrigated lands, and waterworks (including also the valley to the south). If we accept the suggestions of Appadurai (1978) and Stein (1980) that temple institutions were the most significant agrarian managers during the Vijayanagara period, then we may interpret the sacred centre as a zone where material resources (water, food, wealth) were produced and stored. The many inscriptions on the monuments in this part of the site testify to substantial investment — by kings and other influential individuals — in temple institutions. The management of such investment (land, produce, money, and goods) was a continuous activity for these temples and, by extension, of the sacred centre.

In contrast, the royal centre exhibits a different sort of order. Streets, enclosures, and temples are geometrically interrelated in a more complex way, with many smaller structures crowding together within the enclosures. Here we find very few donative inscriptions, presumably because the king does not usually record gifts within his own domain. Following the suggestion of Appadurai-Breckenridge (personal communication), we propose that this is the zone where resources are consumed rather than invested; expenditure is mostly directed towards royal display — in large luxurious households and retinues, in monumental architecture and sculpture, and, in urban rituals and festivals.

SPATIAL STRUCTURE OF THE ROYAL CENTRE

We may now examine those formal attributes of the royal centre which are essential for a functional and symbolic interpretation. Here we are especially concerned with axial systems and circumambulatory routes; these emphasize the importance of the Ramachandra Temple as the nucleus of the royal centre. Around this complex are arranged all the enclosures and architectural elements of this zone. The temple helps to define an axial scheme that divides the royal centre into two parts; it also acts as a pivot for concentric circumambulatory routes. We have already noted that the temple is the focus for the radial road system of the city.

To begin with, a north-south axis passes through the sanctuary of the principal shrine of the Ramachandra Temple (see Figure 8.1). This axis is clearly marked by walls bounding the alley south of the complex, and is extended to the north by a road (N1). Other less obvious axial relationships are also detected. West of the Ramachandra Temple is the shrine dedicated to Virupaksha; the two complexes are probably aligned on an east-west axis. To the east of the Ramachandra Temple, a small shrine and a monolithic column are also aligned on an east-west axis. Both these axes are extended well beyond the royal centre. To the north, one axis passes through Matanga hill; north of east, another axis meets Malyavanta hill. Each hill is visually linked with the Ramachandra Temple (as observed from the columned hall adjoining the sanctuary). Significantly, these prominent natural features are associated with episodes from the *Ramayana* epic; that is, the story of the god to whom the temple is dedicated.

This sacred complex is also related to systems of circumambulatory movement within and around the royal centre (see Figure 8.2). The sculptures on the principal shrine (recounting the episodes of the *Ramayana*), and the friezes of the enclosure walls, too, proceed in a clockwise direction. Movement from the enclosures in the southwest to those in the southeast also proceeds in a clockwise motion about the temple. Another important clockwise route circumambulates enclosure IV. Beginning at the great platform, this path follows the alley (surrounding IV on three sides); its final destination is the small doorway in the south enclosure wall of the Ramachandra Temple. Thus are linked two of the most important monuments of the royal centre.

We have already suggested that the Ramachandra Temple in the middle of the royal enclosures functioned as the state chapel. The outstanding quality of its architecture, and the royal themes of its sculptured imagery have been noted (Chapter 5). The limited space within the principal shrine suggests a restricted use (for the king, his priests, and, perhaps, also his ministers and high officials?). The temple is located between the zones of royal performance and royal residence (see below). It opens onto public spaces to the north and east, but permits discrete entry (for the ruler?) from the south.

Also of importance for this temple is the long road that leads away from the complex in a northeasterly direction. Throughout its length, temples and shrines along this route create a "sacred way", with the Ramachandra Temple as the ultimate destination. These temples — together with their associated images and attendant priests — were probably patronized by subordinate leaders or prominent members of the court and army. These influential individuals and groups may have attempted to associate their own cults — Hindu or Jaina — with that of the king.

ROYAL PERFORMANCE AND ROYAL RESIDENCE

We have already established that a north-south axis separates features within the royal centre into two groups. We designate the east half as the zone of royal performance. Here we suggest that the public roles of the kings and those in his services were enacted. The physical remains of the enclosures east of this axis indicate structures connected with the outward expression of the ruler's power: thus, holding audience, receiving guests, giving gifts, making administrative decisions, bestowing justice, directing the military, participating in the mahanavami rites, etc. The hundred-columned hall, the great (mahanavami) platform and tank, and the elephant stables are the most monumental expressions of this public aspect of the king's behaviour; other smaller and less well-preserved structures, too, possibly housed related functions. The largest enclosure (IV) may have served a number of different purposes — administrative and ceremonial. Sculptures on the great platform depict public activities that convey royal power — audience, reception of supplicants, and hunting — as well as other symbols of royal wealth and might — military processions; horses, camels and elephants; and, athletes and entertainers. (The similarity in style of these sculptures to memorial stones suggests that these depictions were essentially commemorative and heroic in nature.) To the north (enclosures XIV and XXX), activities connected with the military seem to have taken place. The watchtowers here overlook the junction of the city's principal routes.

The features in the west half of the royal centre belong to an area that we designate as the zone of royal residence. Significantly, the Virupaksha Temple — the shrine of the king's household — is located here. We have already noted (Chapter 4) the complexity of access routes leading into enclosures V — IX, many of which are dominated by one or more palace structures with subsidiary features. We believe that within these enclosures were enacted the private roles of the royal household, particularly those involving the women of the court (as mentioned by the European visitors). We interpret this area in terms of

the taking in of food, entertainment, instruction, rest, etc. Judging from the numerous pavilions, towers, fountains, baths, etc., this may also have been a site of recreation and pleasure. The layouts of individual palace complexes suggest that important personages, (queens and royal children?) were surrounded by various attendants (maidens, servants, eunuchs, guards, etc.). The entrance courts, passageways, gateways, and doors provided both protection and privacy; the succession of spaces and barriers probably also conveyed the status of those residing within. (It is in this part of the royal centre that new palaces are currently being revealed by the excavators.)

We note that the carved panels that encircle the Ramachandra Temple complex lead from the zone of residence to the zone of performance. Not only do these panels communicate the wealth and power of the ruler, they also symbolize the unification of the different aspects of the king's world. The military celebrations depicted here involve large numbers of dancing women and entertainers — perhaps drawn from the king's household — in addition to foot soldiers, cavalry, and horses and elephants. The diverse styles of clothing and head-dress worn by the members of the army may indicate the variety of regions from which military support was obtained.

CONCLUSION

Throughout our description and analysis of the sacred centre and the royal centre we have stressed the worship of Virupaksha and Ramachandra, both of whom were of paramount significance for the Vijayanagara ruler. A consideration of these divinities, and the temples dedicated to their cults within the city, provides insights into the development of symbolic systems that, we believe, are embodied in the layout of the capital, particularly the royal centre. While Vijayanagara, like other imperial capitals, incorporated a wide range of peoples and purposes, much of the city's life was dictated by the activities of the king. One of the most important of these regal activities was to enact the partnership of ruler and deity.

We propose three phases in the process by which the Vijayanagara kings attempted to define their relation with the sacred. Here we follow the model proposed by Kulke (1980) for Orissa. First, as purely local rulers, the Vijayanagara kings obtained the support of the sacred power (shakti) of Pampa, the indigenous goddess linked with the sacred centre on the south bank of the Tungabhadra River (see above). The first seat of royal power may have been established nearby on Hemakuta hill (Filliozat 1978b, p.54). The second stage in this process was the incorporation of the shakti into an orthodox male deity, Virupaksha. This divinity was adopted by the Vijayanagara kings for their dynastic signatures on copper-plate grants. In order to be supported by the power of Virupaksha, the kings erected a temple dedicated to this god in a newly laid out royal zone (the royal centre, see above). The third stage of this process involved the reorganization of Vijayanagara into a capital of supra-regional significance. The city became a manifestation of a cosmic scheme, with Ramachandra, the divine hero-king, at its core. By an ever-expanding process, the cults of Virupaksha and other deities were incorporated into the king's realm. Over two centuries, this empowered the Vijayanagara rulers as they continually enlarged their capital and empire.

Characteristic of this third phase is the emphasis on the hero of the *Ramayana*. The god Rama has long been a paradigm for south Indian rulers; since he descended to earth to right all wrongs, this divinity embodied all the virtues of the ideal king. He ruled from Ayodhya, the urban symbol of the ideal moral world, housing the perfectly organized society, protected from all danger and pollution (Ramanujan 1970, pp.232-235). In fact, the Vijayanagara kings often compared themselves with Rama, and equated their capital with that of the divine hero-king. Thus, in an inscription of 1379, we read that: "in the same city [Vijaya-nagara] did [King] Harihara dwell, as in former times Rama dwelt in the city of Ayodhya" (quoted in Saletore, B.A. 1934, I, p.221). Even contemporary literary portraits of Vijayanagara (Sridhara Babu 1975, pp.131-141) employ the same language as that found in epic descriptions of Ayodhya. Such historical sources identify the kings realm — particularly his terrestrial capital, Vijayanagara — with the domain of Rama. We interpret the overall purpose of such equivalences as asserting that the king manifests the heroic and regal qualities of the god. The morphology of the city, and in particular the layout of the royal centre, also convey this relationship. Specific urban elements reinforce the role of Ramachandra as the focus of the royal centre, the expanded "palace" of the king. In our proposed divisions of the royal centre into zones of royal performance and royal residence, we noted that the sanctuary of the Ramachandra Temple — that is, the seat of the god — is located precisely on the dividing line. Here Ramachandra is both an agent of separation and a means of cohesion since we view these zones as incorporating a number of dualities: performance/residence, activity/rest, public/private, male/female, giving out/taking in, etc., Ramachandra, of course, is above and beyond such "human" dualities; yet, his position on the axis separating these zones suggests that he contains these contrasts within his divine and unified being. As it is in the power of the god to create the realm of distinctions, so too is it in his

power to transcend and resolve these distinctions.

Beyond the royal centre, in the landscape in which the city is set, the significance of Rama is asserted. We have already pointed out that certain natural features are associated with the mythology of the god, and that axial alignments link these features with the temple. Such an emphasis on Rama as the nucleus of the city plan suggests the outstanding significance of this deity for the Vijayanagara rulers. Here, the morphology of the city and the mythic landscape established a homology between the domain of the king and that of the god. The rituals that took place in and around the Ramachandra Temple affirmed this connection between king and god.

Such a correspondence between earthly order and cosmic order is, in fact, the very basis for Indian theories on town planning. Numerous mythological compendia (puranas) and technical manuals (shastras) from different periods discuss the layout of royal cities. The texts reiterate a pattern in which the royal capital embodies the organizational principles of the universe, affirming the link between a terrestrial scheme and a cosmic archetype. Though the range of urban forms described in these Indian texts is beyond our present discussion (but see, for example, Pfeil 1935; Dutt 1925), we note what is perhaps the most outstanding feature of these ideal plans. Dominated by a regulating diagram — usually a grid of squares — all these urban models stress the centre where the creator-god is located; nearby is the throne of the ruler. From the centre, power enters the world and engenders the life of the kingdom.

While Vijayanagara does not appear to incorporate a regular grid layout as portrayed in these theoretical texts on town planning, the city plan clearly embodies the principles of centrality and axiality. By focusing the urban elements on the royal centre — and within this, the Ramachandra Temple — Vijayanagara reveals its underlying symbolic meaning. Not only is the attention of the city and empire directed towards the ruler, but the power of the king — with that of Rama at his core — diffuses outward creating form and ensuring order. Vijayanagara is a cosmic city where king and god meet, not only for the affirmation of royal power, but also for the protection and welfare of the empire.

DIRECTIONS

Interpretations of the Vijayanagara capital are tentative; the present architectural/archaeological statement is no exception. It seems, therefore, appropriate to consider some of the directions which appear promising within our approach, assuming that our full understanding of the site will ultimately depend upon the work of others

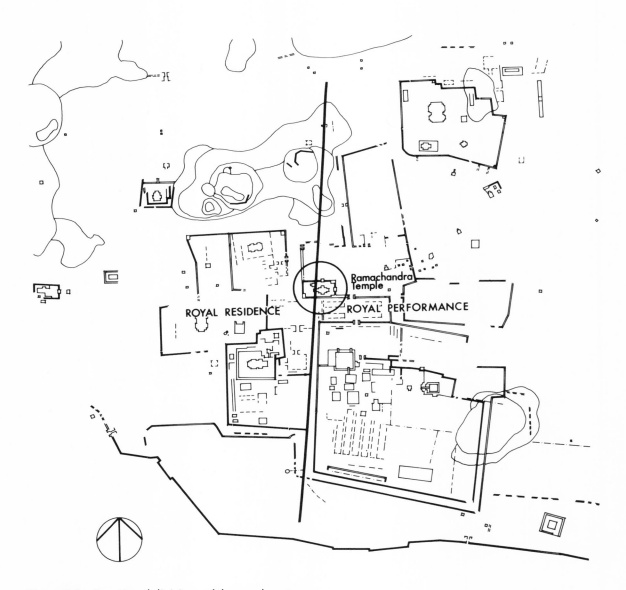

Figure 8.1   Functional divisions of the royal centre.

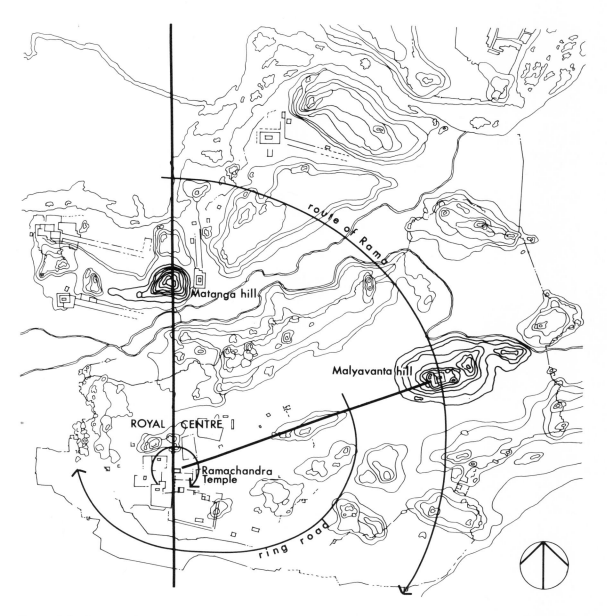

Figure 8.2 Routes of circumambulatory movement around the royal centre; axial alignments with the Ramachandra Temple.

as well, in particular, historians and epigraphists. The present analysis suggests the validity of the technique which has been pursued, while supposing that other lines of research at the site will, in their way and time, also enlarge our final comprehension of Vijayanagara.

Of the several important problems that await investigation, that of the internal chronology of the site is perhaps first. To determine the temporal sequence of the principal monuments and features of the site, and the stages by which the earlier settlement beside the Tungabhadra River grew into an imperial capital, detailed analysis of stratigraphy and changes in stylistic expression will be required. Along with the temporal sequence, there is also the spatial delineation of the site. We have yet to estimate the full extent of what we call the "metropolitan" region of Vijayanagara; we note sub-urban centres as distant from the site as 25 km. Such a clarification of the temporal and spatial co-ordinates of Vijayanagara will be necessary if we are to understand the interplay of cosmologic and mundane elements of order at the capital.

Having decided at the outset of our work at Vijayanagara to be guided by a consideration of the connection between king and god, we have sought to illuminate how royal and sacred forces were integrated or opposed. In the beginning we face many questions: What meaning did the cluster of great temples beside the river have for the Vijayanagara rulers and their subjects? In what manner was this riverine zone of sacred complexes, each identified as a separate place by the designation "pura", conceptually linked to the zone to the south where we have documented an unusual density of what appear to be courtly and military structures? In what ways were the worship of Virupaksha (Shiva) and Ramachandra (Vishnu), in what we call the "royal centre", related to temples in the "sacred centre"? What is the temporal relationship of the *Ramayana* associations of Vijayanagara with those of Pampa and Virupaksha? How are we to explain the connection between the two Virupaksha sanctuaries at the site, and that of the Ramachandra Temple to either or both?

These and similar questions raise yet others which are significant: In addition to its antiquity as a sacred Shaiva place, was the Vijayanagara site also one of ancient and continuous settlement, agriculture and trade? Inscriptions and literary sources will tell us much here, but so also will historically sensitive archaeology. In the same way, we should also seek clearer answers to questions about royal authority; in particular, how cosmic and moral dimensions of kingship were realised in the layout of the capital. The mahanavami festival, for which detailed descriptions exist, provides a promising and tantalising clue;

it points to a rich potential for literary-archaeological investigation into the elaborate display of royal, courtly and military forces at the capital, and the underlying, pre-Vijayanagara, history of the site.

The possible managerial roles of kings, and the nature of an attendant bureaucracy, are very much open questions. Archaeologists trained in interpretive perspectives which emphasize the evolution of systems rooted in their adaptation to a complex natural and social ecology, will be predisposed to seek for residues of a central organ of decision-making among the palaces, platforms and temples of the capital. To confirm the existence such an organ, careful analysis of the artefactual and stratigraphic record of the royal centre will have to be carried out. If a centralized bureaucracy is not confirmed — as some historians believe — then the nature of management in preindustrial states may have to be reassessed.

Vijayanagara also offers a promising test of extant theories about medieval Indian kingship, including Kulke's suggestion of a sequential model for royal empowerment (1980). It is even possible that Kulke's phases may have coexisted at Vijayanagara at one time. Such questions elaborate the central orienting theme with which we began our investigation — the partnership of king and god.

How will we proceed with these various lines of research? To begin with, we realise that we need a better command of the inscriptional and literary sources of the Vijayanagara period. The epigraphs at the site are now being studied, and soon we hope to have at our disposal critical texts and English translations. Sanskrit, Teugu and Kannada literary works, too, may shed light on practices at the capital. Only recently, a manuscript of the *Pampamahatmya* has been discovered in London; this contains information about the mythological associations of the site, especially the area around Hemakuta hill.

Meanwhile, documentation continues at the site, and new data accumulates at an alarming rate. Detailed description, analysis and publication of the forms and spatial relationships of the artefactual record will answer some questions about function and temporal sequence; new interpretive problems will also be raised. But it is the interaction of scholars working with different kinds of historical sources that gives Vijayanagara research its special and exciting dynamic. As each discipline makes its particular contribution, challenging or supporting the understanding developed by others, a closer approximation to Vijayanagara kingship and state should be realised. At the same time, the productive cooperation of Indian and foreign students of this most dramatic of south Indian capitals, continues to be a source of inspiration.

BIBLIOGRAPHIC REFERENCES

Acharya, P.K.
  1978   *Encyclopaedia of Hindu Architecture*, Bhopal.

Appadurai, A.
  1978   "Kings, Sects and Temples in South India 1350-1700 A.D.", *South Indian Temples, An Analytical Reconsideration*, edited by B. Stein, New Delhi, pp. 47-73.

Appadurai-Breckenridge, C.
  1978   "From Protector to Litigant: Changing Relations Between Hindu Temples and the Rajas of Ramnad", *South Indian Temples, An Analytical Reconsideration*, edited by B. Stein, New Delhi, pp. 75-106.

Basava Raja, K.R., editor
  1978   *The Vijayanagara Urbanity*, Hospet.

Begde, P.V.
  1978   *Ancient and Mediaeval Town-Planning in India*, New Delhi.

Briggs, J., translator
  1829   *History of the Rise of the Mohamedan Power of India till the Year A.D. 1612, Translated from the Original Persian of Mahomed Kasim Ferishta*, London.

Champakalakshmi, R.
  1979   'Growth of Urban Centres in South India: Kudamukku-Palaiyarai, the Twin City of the Colas," *Studies in History*, I/1, pp. 1-29.

Dallapiccola, A., and S. Zingel-Ave Lallemant, editors
  1985   *Vijayanagara: City and Empire*, South Asia Institute, Heidelberg, forthcoming.

Dames, M.L., translator
  1918   *The Book of Duarte Barbosa*, London.

Devakunjari, D.
  1970   *Hampi*, Archaeological Survey of India, New Delhi.

Dowsen, J., compiler
  1872   *The History of India as Told by its own Historians*, IV, London.

Dumont, L.
  1970   *Homo Hierarchicus*, Chicago.

Dutt, B.B.
  1925   *Town Planning in Ancient India*, Calcutta and Simla.

Fergusson, J.
  1876   *History of Indian and Eastern Architecture*, London.

Fergusson, J., and P. Meadows Taylor
  1866   *Architecture in Dharwar and Mysore*, London.

Filliozat, V.
  1973   *L'epigraphie de Vijayanagar du debut a 1377*, Paris.

  1977   "Les quartiers et marches de Hampi", *Bulletin de l'Ecole Francaise d'Extreme-Orient*, LXIV, pp. 39-42.

  1978a   "Nouvelles Identifications de Monuments a Hampi", *Journal Asiatique*, CCLXVI, pp. 125-132.

  1978b   "The Town Planning of Vijayanagara", *Art and Archaeology Research Papers*, XIV, pp. 54-64.

  1983   *Le Ramayana a Vijayanagar*, Paris.

  n.d.   "Inscriptions of the Vitthala Temple at Vitthalapura," manuscript.

Fritz, J.M.
  1983   "The Roads of Vijayanagara", *Vijayanagara: Progress of Research 1979-1983*, edited by M.S. Nagaraja Rao, Mysore, pp. 51-60.

  1985a   "Features and Layout of Vijayanagara: The Royal Centre," *Vijayanagara: City and Empire*, edited by A. Dallapiccola and S. Zingel-Ave Lallemant, South Asia Institute, Heidelberg, forthcoming.

  1985b   "Was Vijayanagara a Cosmic City?" *Vijayanagara: City and Empire*, edited by A. Dallapiccola and S. Zingel-Ave Lallemant, South Asia Institute, Heidelberg, forthcoming.

Fritz, J.M., and G. Michell
  1981   "The Grand Ruins of the Ancient City of Vijayanagara", *Inside Outside*, XXI, pp. 40-43.

  1984a   "The Vijayanagara Documentation and Research Project," *South Asian Archaeology 1981*, edited by B. Allchin, Cambridge, pp. 295-304.

  1984b   "The Meeting of Kings and Gods: The Royal Centre at Vijayanagara," *Journal of the Islamic Environmental Design Research Centre*, pp. 39-45.

BIBLIOGRAPHIC REFERENCES

Fritz, J.M., and G. Michell (continued)

1985 "Interpreting the Plan of a Medieval Hindu Capital: Vijayanagara," *Medieval Archaeology*, edited by C. Redman, New York, forthcoming.

Geertz, C.

1980 *Negara: The Theatre State in Nineteenth Century Bali*, Princeton.

Goetz, H.

1966 "Muslims in Vijayanagara: The Record of the Monuments", *Studies in Indian Culture: Dr. Ghulam Yazdani Commemoration Volume*, Hyderabad, pp. 66-70.

Gutschow, N., editor

1977 *Stadt und Ritual*, Technische Hochschule, Darmstadt.

Havell, E.B.

1927 *Indian Architecture*, London, pp. 187-191.

Heras, H.

1926 "Historical Carvings at Vijayanagara", *Quarterly Journal of the Mythic Society*, XXVII/2, pp. 85-88.

1927 *The Aravidu Dynasty of Vijayanagara*, 2 volumes, Madras.

1931 "Seven Days at Vijayanagara," *Journal of Indian History*, IX, pp. 103-118.

Hocart, A.M.

1970 *Kings and Councillors*, edited by R. Needham (reprint of 1936 edition), Chicago.

Inden, R.

1978 "Ritual Authority and Cyclical Time in Hindu Kingship", *Kingship and Authority in South Asia*, edited by J.F. Richards, Madison, pp. 28-73.

Jones, J.W., translator

1863 *The Travels of Ludovico di Varthema*, London.

Kelsall, J.

1872 *Manual of the Bellary District*, Madras, pp. 290-295.

Kotecha, D.

1982 *Hindu Ritual Movement: Study of Sri Virupaksha Temple, Hampi*, unpublished thesis, School of Architecture, Ahmedabad.

Kotraiah, C.T.M.

1983 "Hampi Before Founding of Vijayanagara," *Sriniddhi: Perspectives in Indian Archaeology, Art and Culture*, Madras, pp. 381-387.

Krishnaswami Aiyangar, S.

1919 *Sources of Vijayanagara History*, Madras.

Krishnaswami Aiyangar, S. (continued)

1936 "The Character and Significance of the Empire of Vijayanagara in Indian History", *Vijayanagara Sexcentenary Commemoration Volume*, Dharwar, pp. 1-28.

Kulke, H.

1980 "Legitimation and Town-Planning in the Feudatory States of Central Orissa," *Ritual Space in India: Studies in Architectural Anthropology (Art and Archaeology Research Papers XVII)*, edited by J. Pieper, pp. 30-40.

Lakshminarayan Rao, N.

1971 "Portrait Sculpture of the Vijayanagara King Mallikarjuna", *Studies in Indian History and Culture*, edited by S. Ritti and B.R. Gopal, Dharwar, pp. 181-182.

Longhurst, A.H.

1917 *Hampi Ruins, Described and Illustrated*, Calcutta.

Mackenzie, C.

1800 Map of Vijayanagara, India Office Library and Records, London.

Madras Survey

1880 Map of Hampi Ruins.

Mahalingam, T.V.

1955 *South Indian Polity*, Madras.

1975 *Administration and Social Life under Vijayanagara*, 2 volumes, Madras.

Major, R.H.

1857 *India in the Fifteenth Century*, London.

Mate, M.S.

1983 "Daulatabad: Road to Islamic Archaeology in India", *World Archaeology*, XIV/2, pp. 335-341.

Mehta, R.N.

1979 *Medieval Archaeology*, Bombay.

1981 "Champaner: An Experiment in Medieval Archaeology", *Madhu: Recent Researches in Indian Archaeology and Art History*, edited by M.S. Nagaraja Rao, New Delhi, pp. 119-128.

Meyer, J.F.

1976 *Peking as a Sacred City*, Taipei.

Michell, G.

1981 "Australians at Vijayanagara: A Field Report", *Hemisphere*, XXVI/1, pp. 2-7.

1982a "Vijayanagara: City of Victory", *History Today*, XXXII, pp. 38-42.

1982b "The Royal Centre and the Great Platform at Vijayanagara", *Rupa Pratirupa: Alice Boner Commemoration Volume*, edited by B. Baumer, New Delhi, pp. 109-118.

Michell, G. (continued)
1983 "A Small Dated Temple at Vijaya-nagara", *Vijayanagara: Progress of Research 1979-1983,* edited by M.S. Nagaraja Rao, Mysore, pp. 45-49.
1984a "Two Temples from the Early Vijayanagara Period: Studies in Monumental Archaism", *Sivaramamurti Commemoration Volume,* edited by M.S. Nagaraja Rao, New Delhi, forthcoming.
1984b "Architecture of the Muslim Quarters at Vijayanagara," *Vijayanagara: Progress of Research 1983-84,* edited by M.S. Nagaraja Rao, Mysore, forthcoming.
1984c "The Royal Centre at Vijayanagara," *Transactions,* II/2, Royal Institute of British Architects, pp. 92-99.
1985a "A Never Forgotten City," *Vijayanagara: City and Empire,* edited by A. Dallapiccola and S. Zingel-Ave Lallemant, South Asia Institute, Heidelberg, forthcoming.
1985b "Architecture of Vijayanagara: I Temple Styles; II Islamic Styles," *Vijayanagara: City and Empire,* edited by A. Dallapiccola and S. Zingel-Ave Lallemant, South Asia Institute, Heidelberg, forthcoming.
Michell, G., and V. Filliozat, editors
1981 *Splendours of the Vijayanagara Empire: Hampi,* Marg Publications, Bombay.
Mitra, D., editor
1983 *Indian Archaeology 1980-81: A Review,* Archaeological Survey of India, Calcutta, pp. 26-28, pls. xiv-xvii.
Nagaraja Rao, M.S., editor
1983 *Vijayanagara: Progress of Research 1979-1983,* Directorate of Archaeology and Museums, Mysore.
1984 *Vijayanagara: Progress of Research 1983-1984,* Directorate of Archaeology and Museums, Mysore, forthcoming.
Nilakanata Sastri, K.A.
1964 *Sources of Indian History,* Madras.
Nilakanata Sastri, K.A., and N. Venkataramanayya
1946 *Further Sources of Vijayanagara History,* 3 volumes, Madras.
Panchamukhi, R.S., editor
1953 *Virupaksha Vasantotsava Champu,* Dharwar.
Pfeil, K.
1935 *Die Indische Stadt,* Leipzig.

Pieper, J., editor
1980 *Ritual Space in India: Studies in Architectural Anthropology, Art and Archaeology Research Papers,* XVII.
Rajasekhara, S.
1983 *Masterpieces of Vijayanagara Art,* Bombay.
1984 *Inscriptions at Vijayanagara,* Sujata Publications, Dharwad, forthcoming.
Rama Sharma, M.H.
1978 *The History of the Vijayanagara Empire, Beginnings and Expansion (1308-1569),* edited by M.H. Gopal, Bombay.
Ramanujan, A.D.
1970 "Towards an Anthology of City Images", *Urban India: Society, Space and Image,* edited by R. Fox, Duke University, pp. 224-244.
Rangasvami Sarasvati, A., translator
1926 "Political Maxims of the Emperor-Poet Krishnadeva Raya," *Journal of Indian History,* IV, pp. 62-88.
Rao, Bahadur
1910 *A guide to the Ruins of Ancient Vijayanagar,* Mysore.
Ravenshaw, E.C.
1836 "Translations of Various Inscriptions found among the Ruins of Vijayanagara," *Asiatic Researches,* XX, pp. 1-40.
Rea, A.
1886/7 "Vijayanagara", *Christian College Magazine,* Madras, pp. 428-436, 502-509.
Saletore, B.A.
1934 *Social and Political Life in the Vijayanagara Empire,* 2 volumes, Madras.
1940 "Vaisnavism in Vijayanagara," *D.R. Bhandakar Volume,* edited by B.C. Law, Calcutta, pp. 181-195.
Saletore, R.N.
1936 "Some Aspects of Art during the Reign of Krishnadevaraya the Great", *Vijayanagara Sexcentenary Volume,* Dharwar, pp. 197-206.
1937 "Town Planning in the Vijayanagara Empire", *Karnataka Historical Review,* IV 1/2, pp. 43-50.
1982 *Vijayanagara Art,* New Delhi.
Sandananda, S.
1964-5 "Islamic Influence in Vijayanagara Capital", *Journal of the Andhra Historical Research Society,* XXX, pp. 85-88.
Schotten-Merklinger, E.
1981 *Indian Islamic Architecture: The Deccan 1347-1686,* Warminster.

BIBLIOGRAPHIC REFERENCES

Sewell, R.
1900   *A Forgotten Empire,* London.
Sherwani, H.K., editor
1974   *History of Medieval Deccan,* 2 volumes, Hyderabad.
Sinopoli, C.
1983   "Earthenware Pottery of Vijayanagara: Some Observations", *Vijayanagara: Progress of Research 1979-1983,* edited by M.S. Nagaraja Rao, Mysore, pp. 68-74.
Sitaramiah, M.V., and V.S.S. Acharya, editors
1983   *Shri Krishnadevaraya Dinachari,* Bangalore.
Slater, A.R.
1911   "The Ruins of Vijayanagar", *Quarterly Journal of the Mythic Society,* II/2, pp. 49-55.
Spink, W.
1973   "Vijayanagara - City of Victory", *Journal of Indian History,* LI/I, pp. 123-140.
South Indian Inscriptions
I   nos. 152-153
IV   nos. 250-253
IX/II   nos. 436, 447, and 491
Spodek, H.
1980   "Studying the History of Urbanization in India", *Journal of Urban History,* VI/3, pp. 251-296.
Sridhara Babu, D.
1975   *Kingship, State and Religion in South India According to Historical Biographies of Kings,* dissertation, Georg August University, Gottingen.
Srinivasan, L.K.
1982   "The Hindu Heritage", *Homage to Karnataka,* Marg Publications, edited by S. Doshi, Bombay, pp. 51-82.

Stein, B.
1978   "All the Kings' Mana: Perspectives in Kingship in Medieval South India", *Kingship and Authority in South Asia,* edited by J.F. Richards, Madison, pp. 115-167.
1980   *Peasant State and Society in Medieval South India,* New Delhi.
1983   "Mahanavami: Medieval and Modern Kingly Ritual in South India", *The Gupta Age,* edited by B.L. Smith and E. Zelliot, New Delhi.
Subrahmanyam, R.
1974   "Architecture: Vijayanagara", *History of Medieval Deccan,* edited by H.K. Sherwani, Hyderabad, II, pp. 315-344.
Suranarain Row, B.
1909   *A Short Description of the City of Vijayanagara,* Madras.
Thapar, B.K., editor
1982   *Indian Archaeology 1978-1979: A Review,* Archaeological Survey of India, Calcutta, pp. 43-45.
Vasudeva Sastri, K., editor
1958   *Visvakarma Vastusastram,* Tanjore.
Venkataramanayya, N.
1933   *Origin of Vijayanagara: The City and the Empire,* Madras.
1945   "The Date of Construction of the Temples of Hazara-Ramasvami and Vitthala at Vijayanagara," *Journal of Oriental Research,* Madras, XV, pp. 84-90.
Venket Rao, G.
1944   "Status of Muslims in the Vijayanagara Empire", *The Proceedings of the Indian History Congress: Seventh Session,* Allahabad, pp. 251-256.

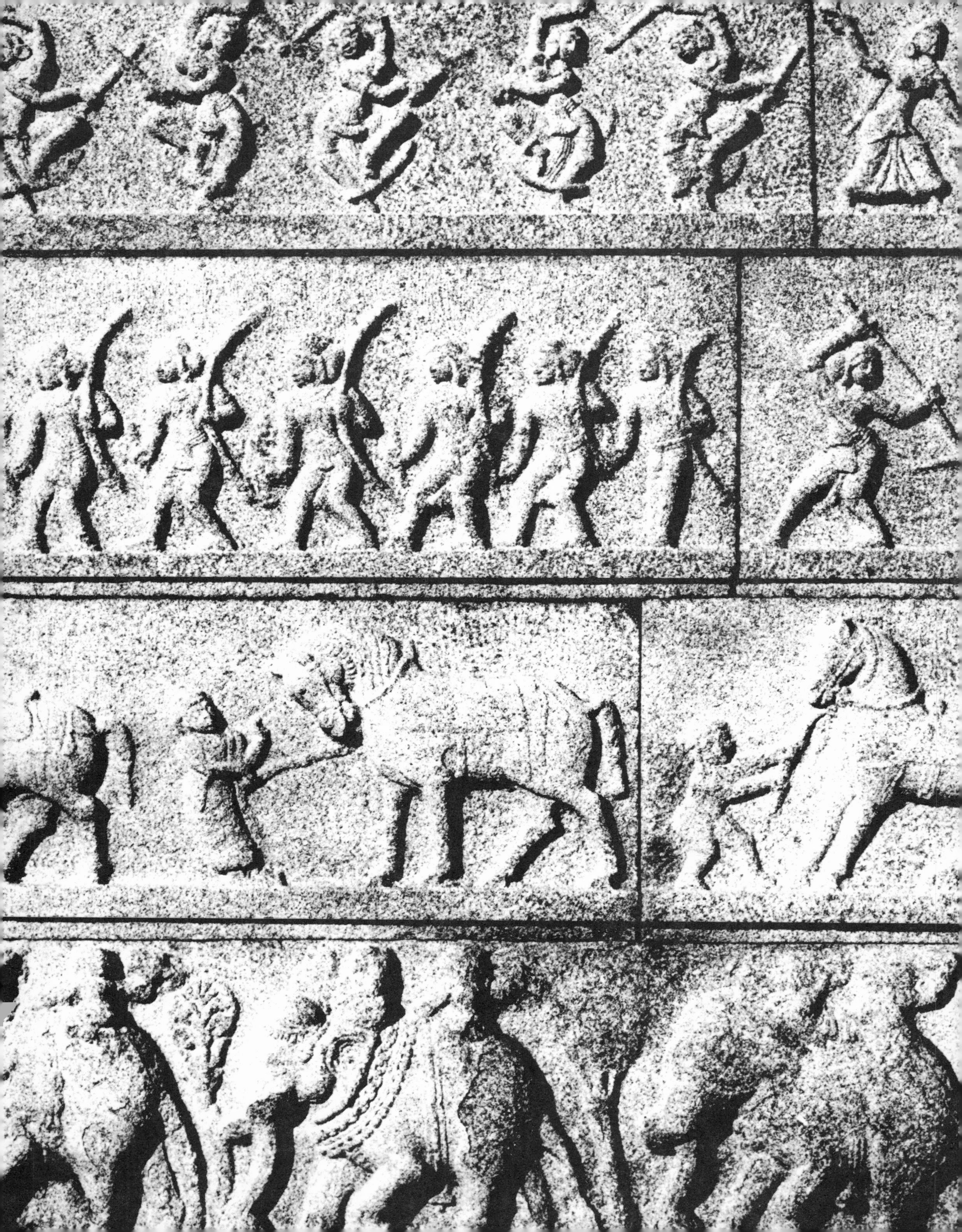